BEST OF THE BEST

Fast & Fabulous

Party Foods
and
Appetizers

BEST OF THE BEST

Fast & Fabulous

Party Foods

and

Appetizers

Gwen McKee
and
Barbara Moseley

Illustrated by Tupper England

QUAIL RIDGE PRESS
Preserving America's Food Heritage

Library of Congress Cataloging-in-Publication Data

Best of the best fast and fabulous party foods and appetizers / edited by Gwen
    McKee and Barbara Moseley ; illustrated by Tupper England.
    p. cm.
        Includes index.
        ISBN-13: 978-1-934193-10-5
        ISBN-10: 1-934193-10-0
    1. Appetizers. 2. Entertaining. I. McKee, Gwen. II. Moseley, Barbara.
    TX740.B49287 2008
    641.8'12--dc22   2008000734

On the cover: Chipper Chocks 240, Veggie Ranch Pinwheels 136, Olé Chicken Stars 206,
Coconut Shrimp Caribe 146, Party Martinis 34, Ring Around the Berries 89

Cover photos by Greg Campbell
Illustrations by Tupper England • Design by Cynthia Clark
Printed in Canada

First printing, September 2008 • Second, September 2010

QUAIL RIDGE PRESS
P. O. Box 123 • Brandon, MS 39043
info@quailridge.com • www.quailridge.com

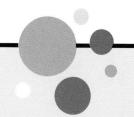

Contents

Preface 7

Parties and Menus 9

   Alphabetical Listing of Parties 10

   Quick Fixes 23

   Fun Foods 24

Wet Your Whistle 25

Crunchy Munchies 41

Big Dippers..53

Some Like It Hot 67

Cheese, Please 85

Garden Goodies 105

Just a Bite...129

Heavy Hors D'Oeuvres 147

Embellished Breads...175

Spread It On..193

Savory Pastries 205

Sweet Pick-Ups...213

Have Your Cake and Eat It, Too! 243

Delightful Desserts 261

Index 275

Authors Gwen McKee and Barbara Moseley

It's Party Time!

Preface

Who doesn't perk up when they hear "appetizers and party foods"? Those words say fun and happy times are coming your way, along with delicious food. Whether you're having a party or going to one, whether it's a huge open house or a casual get-together with a few friends, everybody loves parties and appetizers. No doubt about it, there's joy in parties and party foods . . . in the planning, in the making, in the presenting, in the bringing, and best of all, in the tasting!

Today's cook has precious little time, especially around holidays. So with that in mind, we have gathered together a year-round assortment of fabulous recipes that are quick and easy to prepare, using few ingredients, and that don't require a whole lot of time or a degree in chef-ology.

In our thirty years of searching for and bringing you the best recipes, we have found that people want uncomplicated recipes that taste great. Barbara and I are thrilled to share our little secrets that could make a big difference for you, our wonderful friends.

Check out our Party Menus. We devised a list of prospective parties you could be hosting throughout the year—two for each month. We suggested recipes that would fit the occasion, including more dishes than you will probably need, leaving room for you to choose what appeals to your taste. What often happens is that you bring a dish that is so popular, you are asked to bring it every time!

Because all 424 recipes selected for this book are mostly appetizers—usually the first chapter in most cookbooks—grouping them into different chapters was a bit of a challenge. And so we collected recipes together that were most related to the type of dish they are: for instance, if you can pick it up with your fingers, it will most likely be in the chapter titled, "Just a Bite." But all recipes can easily be found by using our cross-referenced index, where you will be able to find any recipe by title, category, and/or main ingredients.

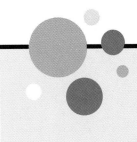

Because we know many of you read cookbooks like novels, we provided in our sidebars information that will inform and hopefully entertain you with ideas and interesting stories pertaining to parties and appetizers.

As with our popular *500 Fast & Fabulous Five-Star 5-Ingredient Recipes Cookbook*, we have again kept the idea of "simple, and simply delicious," uppermost in our thoughts. Our three-part criteria for including a recipe remains the same . . . taste, taste, and taste.

Have a party! Have a ball!
Gwen McKee & Barbara Moseley

It's Party Time!

Parties and Menus

"Let's have a party!"

Who doesn't love to hear these happy words?
Having a party says you want to get together
with friends to celebrate . . . whatever! And, of
course, the first thing you think about is . . .
what are we going to serve?

Need some help? We have tried to make this easier for you by
presenting twenty-four party themes—two for every month—with
suggested menus using recipes in this book. Each menu has recipe
suggestions for particular types of occasions. Use them merely
as guides to give you ideas for what kinds of foods might be
appropriate. You may want to make only a few for a small party,
or all if you're having lots of guests. Or better yet, hand out recipes
to guests for a bring-a-dish party. Whatever you do, whatever you
serve, have fun!

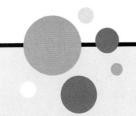

Alphabetical Listing of Parties

After the Holidays Get-Together 11

Birthday Pajama Party 18

Bridal Luncheon 16

Bunko or Bridge Party 11

Christmas Open House 22

Deck or Pool Party 18

Family Reunion 17

Father's Day Cookout 16

Fourth of July Picnic 17

Friday Night Bored Meeting 21

Graduation Party 15

Halloween Spooktacular 20

Homeroom Party 19

Housewarming Party 20

It's a Baby Shower 14

It's Your Turn to Have the Meeting 13

Mardi Gras Madness 12

Mexican Fiesta 14

Mother's Day Brunch 15

New Year's Eve Party 22

St. Patty's Day Shindig 13

Super Bowl Party 12

A Terrific Tailgate 19

Wine-Tasting Party 21

It's Party Time!

January

After the Holidays Get-Together

Shed the winter doldrums and warm up with friends.

Warming Winter Wassail.....................39

Hot Tamale Dip 77

It's a Snowman Cheese Ball..............92

Porto Mushroom Fries 116

Cheesy Italian Garlic Bread 177

Crocked Cheese Fingers 191

Pecan Momoons............................219

Chocolate Cappuccino Mousse.....271

Bunko or Bridge Party

Let the games begin!

Iced Coffee Coolers 33

Buttery Sweet Toasted Pecans.........47

You-Won't-Believe-How-Good-It-Is
    Mustard Dip 54

Awesome Artichoke Dip...................69

Coconut Chicken Bites 130

Impressive Peanut Butter Cream Cheese
    Chocolate Swirl Pie 265

Impromptu parties can be the most fun! "Let's get together at my house tonight" is usually responded to with, "What can I bring?" You know right away who can come and what they will bring. (And guests don't expect your house to be spotless since they know it wasn't a "planned" party.) Just do it!

Let's Celebrate!

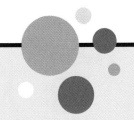

February

Mardi Gras Madness

Get out the mask and Mardi Gras beads, and let the good times roll.

Category 5 Hurricanes 35

Cajun-Style Packet Potatoes 114

N'Awlins Party Pull Bread 178

Quick and Tasty Shrimp Wedges..................200

Bayou Crawfish Spread....................................202

Mardi Gras Microwave Pralines.....................234

Big Easy Praline Cake 246

Super Bowl Party

Nibble while you quibble over who's going to win.

Party Martinis 34

Wonderful White Trash 52

Irene's Shrimp Dip 55

Ring Around the Berries 89

Super Nachos 98

Veggie Ponies..120

Sweety Meat Bites...141

Chipper Cookies..216

Touchdown Football Cake.............................252

Show your colors! If you're having a TV game party, don't be afraid to wear your team's colors. Encourage your guests to wear theirs. But show your "game-ness" by decorating for both teams.

It's Party Time!

March

St. Patty's Day Shindig

It's a day for the wearin' o' the green.

Luck-Of-The-Irish Cream 38

Greener Pastures Dip..54

Waldorf Spinach Dip in a Bread Bowl 56

Potato Salad Boats...112

Pimento on Rye Snackwiches.........................196

Yummy Chocolate Bourbon Balls 241

Fat-Free Key Lime Pie.....................................265

It's Your Turn to Have the Meeting

Garden club, bible study, sorority . . . whatever you volunteered to host.

Company Tea...30

Crescent-Wrapped Pepper Jelly Brie..............90

Zucchini Stix Dippers 106

Mama Mia Mushrooms 117

Cool Garden Pizza Rounds.............................119

BLT Bites..134

Black-Bottom Toffee-Top Cheesecake
     Bars 226

Orange Pecan Balls..241

You can create a lively environment with simple decorations. Use solid tablecloths—even black—to make colorful tableware and accent pieces pop. Use scented candles and play appropriate music. The room is already in a party mood before the first guest arrives.

Let's Celebrate!

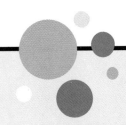

Do people still enjoy playing word games at showers? Sometimes they do. Playing games at showers has been part of the occasion a very long time. It brings mingling guests together in one area before the honoree opens her gifts. And guests get a chance to win a prize. The choice is yours.

April

It's a Baby Shower

An occasion to welcome the new bundle of joy.

Mama's Spiced Tea...29

Pretty Cranberry Cream Cheese Spread.........66

Zucchini Stix Dippers 106

BLT Bites..134

Veggie Ranch Pinwheels..................................136

Fast and Fabulous Sugar Cookies 219

Pineapple Paradise..245

Mexican Fiesta

Get out your maracas and huaraches for a south of the border party. This is also a good menu for a Cinco de Mayo party on May 5th.

Killer Margaritas..35

Sombrero Dip 59

Avocado Salsa 61

Mexican Mix-Up 121

Can-Can Taco Soup 162

Mexicali Shotgun Bread...................................180

Olé Chicken Stars...206

Margarita Pie in a Glass 262

May

Mother's Day Brunch

Treat your mother . . . and don't let her cook!

Mellow Mallow Fruit Dip 64

Bundles of Sweet Beans 109

King Crab Louie...125

Tiny Quiche Bites 135

Simply Sensational Skewers 166

Pecan Muffinettes...188

Easy Bisquiks...190

Hidden Kiss Meringues.....................................234

Fruit Bowl Trifle...268

Graduation Party

Congratulations are in order . . . serve with pride.

Simply Refreshing Punch 31

Good-To-The-Last-Drop Cheeseburger
   Dip 82

Crispy Onion Chicken Nuggets 131

Dogs in Coats 142

Sloppy Joe Bunners 198

Chocolate Pretzels 238

Honeycomb Cake...245

Strawberry Brownie Pizza.................................270

Let's Celebrate!

June

Bridal Luncheon

It's a girl thing.

Pink Mimosas 34

Creamy Amaretto Dip.......................................65

Elegant Crabmeat Imperial 165

Open & Closed Cucumber
    Sandwiches 196

Granny's Old-Fashioned Teacakes.................218

Voted-Most-Popular Pink Meringues 235

Heavenly Almond Candy..................................237

Chocolate Cappuccino Mousse.....................271

Father's Day Cookout

No matter who cooks, it's fun to eat outdoors.

A Jolly Good Bloody Mary 37

Pepper Canoes..121

Zesty Beefy Cheese Log.................................103

Spicy Grilled Corn Cobbies............................106

'Bello Beef Bites 135

Tangy Grilled Chicken Kabobs.......................167

Extra Special Chocolate Chip Cookies 214

Streaked-With-Strawberries
    Cheesecake Bars 227

It's Party Time!

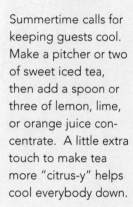

July

Family Reunion

Looking forward to Aunt Suzie's chess pie bars is almost as exciting as getting to see all your relatives! Promise them family-famous food and they will come.

Aunt Mamie's Mint Tea 29

Chocolate Peanut Butter Chow 52

Perfected Baked Beans 109

Potluck Potato Salad.....................................112

Colorful Corn Salad.......................................124

Easy-Do Crocked Barbecue 160

Lemony Garlic Bread 179

Simply Divine Chess Pie Bars 225

Super Easy Dump Cake 251

Fourth of July Picnic

Take-along goodies for serving on a blanket, a bench, or the beach.

Berry Mint Iced Tea 30

Roll-Out-The-Barrel Crackers 42

Miracle Red Grape Broccoli Salad.................124

Mango-Stuffed Celery Bites 128

Cracker Crusted Drummettes 156

Easy Egg Salad Sandwiches...........................194

Peanut Butter S'mores Bars 228

Summertime calls for keeping guests cool. Make a pitcher or two of sweet iced tea, then add a spoon or three of lemon, lime, or orange juice concentrate. A little extra touch to make tea more "citrus-y" helps cool everybody down.

Let's Celebrate!

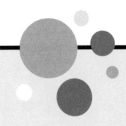

When giving a party for your child, encourage them to help with invitations and preparations. Have them greet each guest, and thank them for their gift. Sometimes children enjoy sending thank-you notes, which teaches politeness and responsibility. People are always impressed to receive a handwritten thank-you note.

August

Birthday Pajama Party

Kids love to have a sleepover for their birthday.

Old-Fashioned Root Beer Float 26

Party in a Bag 172

Crispy Pizza Dip Sticks 186

Funny Face Muffins 188

Peanut Butter Quickie Cookies 217

Chocolate Dessert Pancakes 271

Classic Chocolate Trifle 267

Deck or Pool Party

A splash or dip . . . on the table or in the pool.

Island Splendor Punch 31

Chocolate Peanut Butter Chow 52

Cocktail Garden Platter 107

Bacon and Tamale Bites 141

Dare Deviled Eggs 146

Gingered Shrimp Kabobs 170

Buttery Bacon and Cheese Bread 178

Brownie Cheesecake 259

It's Party Time!

September

Homeroom Party

Kids love things that look fun to eat.

Fun-To-Munch Oyster Crackers 42

Crispy Cheese Wafers..45

Pearly Whites 128

Hoppy Chocolate Frogs 215

Cornflake Creatures 218

Cookie Pops...230

Frosted Cone Cakes 254

A Terrific Tailgate

Take-along goodies . . . so welcome before and after the game.

Climb-A-Mountain Mix 50

Bread Boat Sausage Dip 78

Game-Time Nachos...98

Easy Corn and Tomato Salad.........................123

Ham and Cheese Pinwheels............................138

Dog Bites Everybody Likes.............................141

Some-Like-It-Hot Crockpot Tailgate
  Chili..163

None Better Pecan Squares............................231

October

Halloween Spooktacular

A ghostly excuse to throw a party . . . .

Circus Citrus Slush 28

Pigs in a Cheese Trough 83

Banana Pepper-Ronies 120

Betsy's Tomato Crackers 134

Brownie Popsicles 224

Halloween Spider-Web Cake 250

Halloween Pumpkin Muffins 258

Housewarming Party

Come see our new house!

Welcome Wine 36

Cheesy Salsa Spinach Dip 79

A Sweet Bite of Brie 91

Savory Stuffed 'Shrooms 115

Pepperoni Tomato Pops 121

Smokey Red Wingers 155

Cheesecake Bonbons 242

Pineapple Orange Squares 248

Here's a fun game: Pin index cards with spooky characters on back of guests as they enter (like Frankenstein, Darth Vadar, Dracula, Lord Voldemort, and Wicked Witch of the West). Make sure they don't see it. Now they have to go to other guests, asking only one question—yes or no—to try to find out who they are. First person to guess wins—but let the game go on. Great way for guests to mingle.

November

Wine-Tasting Party

Everybody brings their favorite wine.

Tropical Fruit Dip...65

5-Minute Boursin Cheese 101

Pop-In-Your-Mouth Chicken Nuggets 132

Deli-Licious Party Wheels 137

Favorite Scallops Appetizer 144

Cheesy Vidalia Fingers....................................191

Fast and Fabulous Sugar Cookies 219

Baklava Diamonds...263

Friday Night Bored Meeting

What better way to end the work week?

MJ's Flavored Water Cooler.............................34

Crispy Pita Wedges 44

Easy Breezy Broccoli Dip 80

Haystack of Onion Rings 118

Crockpot BBQ Balls 151

Buttery Boursin Spread..................................204

Olé Chicken Stars...206

Toasted Butter Pecan Cookies......................220

Moose-On-The Loose Brownie Dessert........272

Leftover wine? Make wine jelly! Cook 2 cups wine with 3 cups sugar till boiling; stir in a 3-ounce pouch of liquid pectin till well dissolved. Pour into 4 or 5 half-pint jars. (Works best with pink champagnes and wines . . . it's prettier.)

Let's Celebrate!

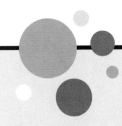

For a pleasing menu, combine foods with contrasting colors, textures, and temperatures. Avoid dishes that are all the same color or are all creamy or all crunchy. Plan a pleasing mix of hot and cold foods. Variety is indeed the spice of life.

December

Christmas Open House

Share the Christmas spirit by opening your home or office to friends. Deck the halls and let's be jolly!

Holiday Party Punch 30

   or Holiday Wassail 39

Delectable Crabmeat Mornay.........................70

A Pine Cone Made of Cheese 102

Meatball Penguins...149

Pita Christmas Trees...183

Deli Ham Salad Finger Sandwiches..............197

Gnome Hats...221

Cranberry Candy Crunch 236

Tiny Pecan Pies...263

World's Best Turtles...239

New Year's Eve Party

Should auld acquaintance be forgot? Never!
Serve with a cup of kindness.

Sangria Serenade 36

Crazy Craisin Party Mix 50

Sweet Georgia Onion Dip 68

Almond Chip Cheese Ball 95

Gwen's Baked Sausage Meatballs.................148

Grilled Mozza-Roma Bites 181

Burst-Of-Flavor Chicken Sandwiches 195

Margarita Cookie Bars 223

Zebra Pecan Clusters 237

It's Party Time!

Quick Fixes

All the recipes in this book are fast and fabulous, but here's a list of appetizers that are super quick!

Old Fashioned Root Beer Float......................26

Summertime Peach Smoothie 27

Company Tea..30

Roll-Out-The-Barrel Crackers 42

Toasted Parmesan Triangles...........................44

Buttery Sweet Toasted Pecans.......................47

Kicked-Up-A-Notch Peanuts 49

Cowboy Popcorn..49

Quicker-Than-Quick Shrimp Dip......................55

Easy Breezy Veggie Dip 57

Fiesta Dip 57

Rainbow Corn Dip 58

Creamy Amaretto Dip....................................65

Sweet Georgia Onion Dip 68

Quick Hot Crab Dip 70

Speedy Gonzales Chili Dip.............................76

One-Ingredient Crispies 88

Sweet Bacon-y Brie 90

Quick Mozzarella Tortillas...............................97

5-Minute Boursin Cheese 101

Veggie Ponies...120

Mexican Mix-Up 121

Crispy Onion Chicken Nuggets.....................131

Pop-In-Your-Mouth Chicken Nuggets...........132

Betsy's Tomato Crackers 134

Bacon and Tamale Bites 141

Peanut Butter Quickies.................................217

Cranberry Candy Crunch...............................236

Let's Celebrate!

Quick Fixes (continued)

Zebra Pecan Clusters 237

Nutty Peanut Butter Balls 240

Fudge in Minutes 242

Honeycomb Cake...245

Bing-Bing-Bing Cherry Pie 264

Fat-Free Key Lime Pie......................................265

Chocolate Dessert Pancakes........................271

Cheery Cherry Parfait.....................................274

Fun Foods

Some recipes are more than just tasty . . . they are fun to make, shape, and delight your guests.

Deep-Fried Banana Logs..............................128

Pearly Whites 128

Dog Bites Everybody Likes............................141

Dogs in Coats 142

Meatball Penguins...149

Drummette Lollipops 159

Funny Face Muffins 188

Reindeer Sandwiches.....................................199

Hoppy Chocolate Frogs 215

Gnome Hats..221

Brownie Popsicles 224

Cookie Pops..230

Boogie Bars 231

Halloween Spider-Web Cake 250

Frosted Cone Cakes 254

Always Fun Dirt Cake Trifle............................257

Wet Your Whistle

Shakes

Floats

Smoothies

Slushes

Teas

Punches

Coolers

Wines

Wassails

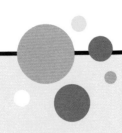

Shakes and floats are popular with kids and teenagers. Great for a late-night snack for sleepovers. It could also get kids started in the morning. You, too!

It's Party Time!

Sherri's Frosted Chocolate Shake

Delicious! Use a blender, shaker, or just a jar.

2–3 tablespoons Hershey's chocolate syrup
¾ cup chilled milk
½ teaspoon vanilla
1 (6-ounce) container vanilla or chocolate yogurt
½ cup vanilla ice cream

Combine everything except ice cream in a shaker. Shake vigorously. Add ice cream and shake again. Serve immediately by pouring into tall glass. Can garnish with cherry, if desired. Serves 1.

Old-Fashioned Root Beer Float

Kids, teenagers . . . everybody loves them. What could be simpler or more delicious?

1 gallon vanilla ice cream
2 (1-liter) bottles root beer

Scoop 2 scoops ice cream into glass mugs or other tall glasses and pour root beer over. Serve with a spoon-straw (or an iced tea spoon and a straw). Makes 8–10.

This is also fun to chunk the ice cream into a punch bowl and pour root beer on top, then serve in punch cups. This will serve 12–16.

Editor's Extra: Use other flavors of ice cream and carbonated drinks. A Purple Cow is grape juice with ice cream. Or try chocolate ice cream with Coke. And Sprite goes well over lime sherbet for a refreshing summer drink.

Summertime Peach Smoothie

Your tummy loves to see this coming.

2 peaches, peeled, cut
1½ cups apple juice
1 cup milk
1 (8-ounce) container peach yogurt

Place all ingredients in blender for 40 seconds or until smooth. Pretty served in tall glasses or stemware. Serves 4.

If your party involves overnight guests, have them wake up to a delightful morning drink that will enhance a simple toast-and-jelly send off.

27

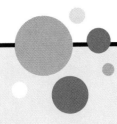

Freeze lemon and lime slices to put in water for guests who just want water. Lay slices on parchment paper on pan to freeze; then put in zipper bag for easy individual use.

Cut some in half for short cocktails or to push into the neck of a bottled drink.

Lovely to have on hand for garnishes, and to cool down a cup of hot tea.

Circus Citrus Slush

Ready in the freezer—nice.

1½ cups sugar
6 cups water, divided
½ cup fresh mint leaves
1 (6-ounce) can frozen orange juice concentrate, thawed
1 (6-ounce) can frozen lemonade concentrate, thawed
3 (10-ounce) bottles club soda, chilled

In a very large pot, heat sugar, half the water, and the mint leaves to boiling (save a few for garnishing glasses). Reduce heat; simmer a few minutes. Cool to let flavors blend. Strain, then add juice concentrate and remaining water, stirring to mix well. Freeze in non-metal container.

When ready to serve, spoon ⅔ cup slush into each glass; pour ⅓ cup club soda over each. Top with a mint leaf. Serves 12–16.

Kicky Lemon Tea Slush

5 cups water, divided
2 green tea bags
1 cup sugar
1 (12-ounce) can lemonade concentrate, thawed
1 cup vodka
1 (1-liter) bottle tonic water

Pour 1 cup boiling water over tea bags; let steep 10 minutes. Remove tea bags; cool. Boil remaining 4 cups water. Stir in sugar until dissolved. Remove from heat; cool.

Mix all except tonic in 3-quart plastic container. Cover and freeze at least 10 hours. To serve, place ⅔ cup in each glass and fill with ⅓ cup tonic water; stir. Garnish with lemon slices, if desired. Serves 10–15.

Aunt Mamie's Mint Tea

A refreshing beverage that serves a crowd deliciously, yet inexpensively.

8 cups water, divided
1½–2 cups sugar
2 family-size tea bags
7–8 sprigs fresh mint
½ cup lemon juice

In saucepan, boil 4 cups water with sugar for 5 minutes. Remove from heat and steep tea bags and mint for 5–10 minutes. Add lemon juice. Strain. Add remaining 4 cups cold water. Serve over ice. Serves 10–15.

Mama's Spiced Tea

Nice to package and give as gifts.

1 cup instant tea
2 cups Tang
3 cups sugar
2 packages lemon Kool-Aid
1 teaspoon ground cinnamon
½ teaspoon ground cloves
½ teaspoon ground allspice

Mix all ingredients together and store in an airtight container. Mix 3 tablespoons of mix into mug of hot water. Can adjust strength of mix according to personal taste. Makes about 2 quarts of dry mix.

Have a tea party! Here's what to use:

- Cups with saucers
- Milk, not cream
- Sugar cubes with tongs
- Lacy napkins
- Classical or vintage music
- Flowers and candles
- Tea sandwiches and sweets on a tiered plate

It's okay to eat with your fingers . . . but not necessary to hold your pinky out when you drink your tea!?!

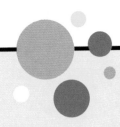

Serving tea or punch is sometimes a better option than having to have a large assortment of drink choices. Serve in a glass pitcher, or pour directly over ice into tall glasses. Or carry in a thermos . . . to a picnic, on a car trip, to the beach . . . .

It's Party Time!

Berry Mint Iced Tea

Pretty . . . and so refreshing.

5 cups cranberry juice cocktail
3 tablespoons sugar
3 tea bags
7 mint leaves

Heat cranberry juice cocktail in saucepan; stir in sugar. Pour boiling juice over tea bags and mint into heat-proof pitcher. Let stand 5 minutes to steep; remove tea bags. Serve over ice. Makes 6 servings.

Company Tea

So simple . . . so special . . . .

1 cup Lipton lemon iced tea granules
1 (2-liter) bottle ginger ale
Ice

Mix tea and ginger ale in pitcher; stir to dissolve. Pour over lots of ice in tall glasses. Serves 6–10.

Holiday Party Punch

1 (12-ounce) can frozen orange juice concentrate
1 (12-ounce) can frozen lemonade concentrate
1 (46-ounce) can pineapple juice
1 cup sugar
Water
1 (2-liter) bottle Sprite, chilled

In a 1-gallon plastic container, stir together orange juice, lemonade, pineapple juice, and sugar. Fill rest of container with water. Freeze.

Several hours before serving, remove from freezer. Punch should be mushy. At serving time, pour into punch bowl and add Sprite. Serves 40.

Simply Refreshing Punch

1 (½-gallon) container orange, lemon-lime, or any
  flavor sherbet
1 (2-liter) bottle Sprite, chilled
Lemon or lime slices (optional)

Spoon sherbet into punch bowl in chunks; pour soda over; give it a swirl. Garnish with lemon or lime slices, if desired. Serves 10–16.

Island Splendor Punch

To spike or not to spike . . . that is the question.

½ cup water
⅓ cup sugar
2 (¼-inch) slices fresh ginger
2 (6-inch) sticks cinnamon
½ teaspoon whole cloves
1 (64-ounce) carton pineapple-orange-banana juice
1 (6-ounce) can frozen lemonade concentrate,
  thawed
½ (2-liter) bottle Sprite, chilled
3 cups light-colored rum (optional)

Bring water, sugar, ginger, cinnamon, and cloves to a boil; reduce heat. Cover and simmer 10 minutes. Remove from heat. Transfer to a small bowl. Cover and refrigerate 2 hours.

Strain spices from sugar syrup. Mix sugar syrup, pineapple-orange-banana juice, and lemonade concentrate in punch bowl. Slowly pour Sprite and rum, if desired, down the side of punch bowl; stir to mix. Serve over crushed ice. Makes 16 (8-ounce) servings.

For a large party, spread the food around. Separate drinks from food so guests do not congregate in one place. Be aware of having open table space for people to put their drinks.

Let's Celebrate!

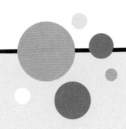

My nephew, Raymond McKee, has been making this for so many years that he has perfected it . . . and is expected to bring it to many occasions. It is ideal for tailgates, as these frozen cartons travel well. Game-goers love to shake the jug and pour punch into team cups. Not just for tailgates, you'll find many party occasions to make this ahead and handily pull it out of the freezer.

—Gwen

It's Party Time

Raymond's Milk Punch

Okay, we're abusing the word fast, but this is so fabulous that you won't mind the fast-each-day prep time.

3 cups white sugar
1 cup brown sugar
1½ cups water
6 cinnamon sticks, broken
½ gallon milk in 1-gallon jug
1 fifth dark rum or bourbon
1 (2-ounce) bottle vanilla
1 tablespoon almond extract

Two days before the party, stir and boil sugars and water, then simmer with cinnamon sticks for ½ hour to make flavored simple syrup; let cool, preferably overnight.

Next day, using ½ gallon of milk in a full-gallon jug, pour rum or bourbon into milk; put cap on and shake well. Now pour in 1½ cups strained simple syrup (you may not use it all) and extracts; shake hard, then freeze overnight.

On party or game day, thaw out 1–1½ hours till partially thawed. Shake occasionally while thawing; an icy middle assures serving nice icy milk punch.

Editor's Extra: Color granulated sugar red or green, then dip dampened stemware rims for fun Christmas drinks. Add a tiny candy cane and a sprig of mint!

Hello Punch

You tweak the flavor.

10 cups water
4 cups sugar
1 (3-ounce) package Jell-O (any flavor)
1 (7.5-ounce) bottle Minute Maid Lemon Juice*,
  thawed
1 (46-ounce) can pineapple juice
1 teaspoon almond extract

In a large pot, bring water and sugar to a boil; add Jell-O to dissolve. Add lemon juice, pineapple juice, and almond extract. Add enough water to make 2 gallons. Serves 36.

Editor's Extra: Not to be confused with frozen lemonade, *this is found in the freezer section of your grocery store near the frozen orange juice.

Iced Coffee Coolers

This is make-ahead, put-in-the-blender delicious!

½ cup instant coffee
½ cup favorite flavor liquid creamer
¾ cup sugar
¾ cup hot water
⅛ teaspoon ground cinnamon
6 cups milk, divided
40 water ice cubes, divided

Stir first 5 ingredients together in bowl until coffee dissolves. Pour into 2 ice-cube trays. Freeze to harden. Transfer frozen coffee cubes to zipper freezer bag.

  For 2–3 servings, place 4 coffee cubes, 1⅓ cups milk, and 8 water ice cubes in blender. Blend on high 20 seconds or till slightly slushy. Pour into glass. Top with a dollop of whipped cream and a dash of ground cinnamon, if desired. Makes about 10 servings.

Keeping canned and bottled drinks iced down for a party can be solved by using your top-loading washing machine—if it's near the kitchen. Fill it ⅔ full of ice, and put drinks in. After the party, remove drinks, let ice melt, and run the last rinse cycle.

Let's Celebrate!

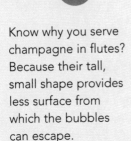

Know why you serve champagne in flutes? Because their tall, small shape provides less surface from which the bubbles can escape.

Save a few wine bottles before your party. Clean well, then funnel punches and drink mixes into them if you run out of pitchers. Fun to make your own label for the bottle.

For a festive New Year's Eve toast, drop washed fresh cranberries into champagne flutes, pour champagne over, then watch berries rise and float as the bubbles rise, then subside.

MJ's Flavored Water Cooler

Enjoyably refreshing.

1½ ounces vodka
¼ cup cranberry juice
½ cup flavored water of choice (strawberry-kiwi is great)
Sprig of mint (optional)

Fill a (10-ounce) glass ¾ full with coarsely crushed ice. Mix vodka, cranberry juice, and flavored water together. Pour over ice; give a stir; top with mint. Serves 1.

Party Martinis

So colorful in different flavors.

Martini mixer of choice (sour apple, orange, mango, raspberry, lemon)
Vodka
Shaker
Ice

Mix a jigger each of mixer and vodka in a shaker with ice. Strain into martini glasses. Decorate with a fruit slice on a fancy toothpick.

Pink Mimosas

Always pretty and welcome.

2 cups chilled orange juice
2 cups chilled cranberry juice cocktail
1 (1-liter) bottle dry champagne or sparkling wine, chilled

Mix juices in 1½-quart pitcher. Pour champagne into glasses until half full; fill with juice mixture. Serves 10–15.

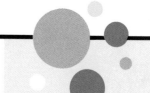

Killer Margaritas

. . . at your own risk.

3 cups plus 2 tablespoons Triple Sec
5 cups tequila
1¾ cups plus 2 tablespoons fresh lime juice
Coarse salt

Combine all ingredients except salt in a large pitcher; add ice, and stir vigorously about 30 seconds. Spoon out the ice cubes. Store pitcher in refrigerator until party time. Serve in glasses with salted rims. Makes about 20 drinks.

Category 5 Hurricanes

Not really all that strong, this is a snap to mix, and so fun to serve.

1 cup sugar
1 cup water
1 (12-ounce) can frozen pineapple/orange juice
2½ cups light rum
1 (12-ounce) bottle grenadine
½ cup lemon juice
½ cup lime juice
½ cup Triple Sec or Grand Marnier liqueur
1 teaspoon almond extract
1 (2-liter) bottle ginger ale
Orange slices and cherries for garnish

Mix all ingredients except garnish; adjust to taste. Serve over shaved ice and garnish with orange slices and cherries, if desired. Serves 16–20.

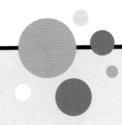

For a party of wine drinkers, plan on stocking ½ (fifth) bottle per person. You should get roughly 5–6 servings per bottle.

Don't throw away left-over wine. Freeze it in ice cube trays to use in casseroles and sauces.

It's Party Time!

Welcome Wine

Such a nice way to say hello.

1 (6-ounce) can frozen lemonade concentrate
1 (6-ounce) can frozen orange juice concentrate
2 cups water
1 fifth white wine
1 cup orange liqueur
1 (1-liter) bottle carbonated water
Orange and lemon slices

Pour juices in punch bowl or large pitcher. Stir in water. Add wine and liqueur, then carbonated water. Stir to blend. Add ice and float orange and lemon slices on top. Serves 20–24.

Sangria Serenade

This is so pretty and festive, it makes you want to sing! Ladies particularly love it.

1 each: lemon, lime, orange
1½ cups rum
½ cup sugar
1 (750-ml) bottle merlot
1 cup orange juice

Slice fruit into thin rounds and place in a large glass pitcher. Stir in rum and sugar. Chill.

When ready to serve, stir in wine and juice. Serve in festive glasses with fruit slices on rim or on fancy toothpicks. Serves 6–10.

Blender Bloody Mary Mix

This is delicious all by itself . . . or spiked.

5 cups tomato juice
1 tablespoon Worcestershire
1 tablespoon horseradish
1 tablespoon lemon juice
1 tablespoon black pepper
1 tablespoon celery salt
1 cup vodka (optional)

Blend all ingredients in blender. Add vodka, if desired. Serve over ice. Serves 4–8.

A Jolly Good Bloody Mary

1 (1-quart) bottle Bloody Mary mix
1¼ cups vodka
2 tablespoons lime juice
1 teaspoon Tabasco
½ teaspoon freshly ground black pepper
5 stalks celery

Mix all but celery in big pitcher. Serve over ice in tall glasses with a celery stick. Serves 8–10.

When making Bloody Marys, it's good to rub a lemon or lime wedge around the glass rim and dip in Old Bay Seasoning before filling with ice. You get a taste kick in advance of the spicy liquid. Wow!

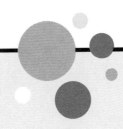

It's Party Time!

Wonderful Rita, innkeeper at The Inn at Montpelier, treated us to her coveted stash of limoncello on their beautiful porch on a delightful late summer night. She graciously shared her Italian recipe which is now a staple in my freezer. Thanks, Rita.
—Gwen

Sweet Sippin' Limoncello

2 pounds very fresh lemons (6 huge)
1 quart grain alcohol (750ml) (Everclear 190-proof)
6 cups water
2½ cups sugar

Wash and dry lemons well; peel in strips (do not zest, and do not include any white pith). Put peel in a jar or crock; add alcohol, cover, and let stand in the dark for 3 days; stir or swish once a day.

When lemons are pale (this will be 3–5 days), all the oil has been extracted. Strain liquid; discard peel. Heat water with sugar over medium heat until well dissolved and clear. Let come to room temperature; mix with infused alcohol. Strain again in a fine strainer (or coffee filter). Bottle and keep in freezer. Always ready to serve chilled. Makes about 3 bottles.

Luck-Of-The-Irish Cream

Super to sip . . . delicious on ice cream . . . beautiful gift.

1 heaping teaspoon coffee crystals
¼ cup boiling water
1¾ cups half-and-half
1 (14-ounce) can sweetened condensed milk
1 teaspoon vanilla
¾ cup brandy or bourbon

Dissolve coffee crystals in boiling water in blender. Add remaining ingredients and blend well. Bottle and chill. Keeps for several weeks. Makes 1 quart.

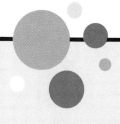

Holiday Wassail

Makes your whole house smell good.

6 cups apple cider
2½ cups apricot nectar
2 cups unsweetened pineapple juice
1 cup orange juice
1 teaspoon whole cloves
4 whole allspice
3 (3-inch) sticks cinnamon

Combine all ingredients in a Dutch oven. Bring to a boil. Reduce heat and simmer 15 minutes. Strain and discard spices. Serve hot. Yields about 3 quarts.

Warming Winter Wassail

When the weather outside is frightful . . .

2 quarts apple cider
2 cinnamon sticks
½ cup lemon juice
1 cup light corn syrup
1 (12-ounce) can pineapple juice
½ teaspoon nutmeg

In a large pot, boil, then simmer cider and cinnamon sticks 7 minutes. Stir in remaining ingredients. Remove cinnamon sticks; serve hot. Serves 12–16.

The beverage typically served as "wassail" at modern medieval-themed feasts most closely resembles mulled cider.

Historical wassail was completely different, more likely to be mulled beer. Then, sugar, ale, ginger, and cinnamon would be placed in a bowl, heated, and topped with slices of toast as sops.

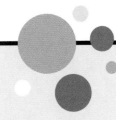

Even though it is estimated that only one out of 20,000 commercially produced eggs might contain salmonella bacteria (meaning the average consumer might encounter a contaminated egg once every 84 years), many people are uncomfortable using raw eggs in recipes. (www.laeggs.com) To pasteurize them: Place eggs in simmering water for 1–2 minutes, then submerge in ice water. Or, break the egg(s) called for in recipe into a small glass bowl, and microwave on HIGH 15 seconds. This will slightly cook the eggs, yet they will still have a runny consistency. A third method is to cook eggs with 2 tablespoons per egg of a liquid called for in recipe, till it reaches 150°.

Hot Buttered Rum

6 (½ tablespoons) confectioners' sugar
6 (¼ cups) rum
6 tablespoons butter
6 (⅓ cups) boiling water
Sprinkles of nutmeg and/or cinnamon

Into 6 mugs or glasses with handles, divide each of the ingredients in order; stir and serve at once. Sprinkle each with nutmeg and/or cinnamon.

A Noggin of Good Cheer

4 large eggs, separated
⅓ cup plus 1 tablespoon sugar, divided
1 cup heavy cream
1 pint milk
1 teaspoon grated nutmeg
3 ounces bourbon

Beat egg yolks; slowly add ⅓ cup sugar. Pour cream into milk; add to mixer. Add grated nutmeg. Beat egg whites till soft peaks; gradually add remaining tablespoon sugar. Mix in bourbon. Refrigerate. Serves 5–6.

Editor's Extra: Can use pasteurized egg whites. Easy to put in ice cream maker, then into freezer.

Crunchy Munchies

Crackers

Chips

Toasts

Wafers

Nuts

Popcorn

Snack Mixes

Roll-Out-The-Barrel Crackers

So quick . . . so great to take! This is a taste explosion in your mouth. Fun to watch people's expressions when they eat one . . . then two . . . then three . . . .

1 box low-sodium Ritz Crackers, divided
1 (1-ounce) package dry ranch dressing mix
2½ tablespoons Mrs. Dash Extra Spicy Seasoning
   Blend
¾ cup canola oil

Put half the crackers in a large jug or container with a tight-fitting lid; add seasonings, then rest of crackers, then oil last. Put lid on and roll gently to distribute. They're delicious right now! But do this about 3 times in an hour to be sure all crackers are coated. That's it! After crackers have soaked up all the seasoning, transport to a clean tin or jug for taking or serving.

Editor's Extra: Okay to use oval crackers; the square ones get broken too easily. But they work!

Fun-To-Munch Oyster Crackers

1 (1-ounce) package dry ranch dressing mix
¾ cup canola oil
½ teaspoon dill weed
¼ teaspoon lemon pepper
¼ teaspoon garlic powder
5 cups plain oyster crackers

Preheat oven to 250°. Combine dressing mix, oil, and dill weed. Pour over crackers; stir to coat. Sprinkle with lemon pepper and garlic powder; toss to coat. Crisp in 350° oven for 20 minutes. Stir halfway through baking.

It's Party Time!

Homemade Tortilla Chips

These crunchy chips can be flavored with an endless number of spices; use your imagination.

4 soft flour tortillas
Vegetable oil for deep-frying
Coarse sea salt for sprinkling
Paprika, Cajun seasoning, or chili powder for sprinkling (optional)

Cut each tortilla into 8 wedges. Add tortilla wedges in batches to hot oil and deep-fry until light golden brown. Remove from oil, drain on paper towels, and sprinkle with salt and paprika, if desired. Makes 32 chips.

> Tortilla chips are usually considered to be a Mexican food, but did you know that they were actually first mass-produced in Los Angeles, California, in the late 1940's?

Full-Of-Flavor Pita Chips

¼ cup olive oil
1½ tablespoons dry seasoning of choice (ranch or Italian dressing; barbecue or taco seasoning)
3 (6-inch) pita rounds, split
½ cup grated cheese of choice

Mix oil and seasoning mix in a small bowl. Cut each pita round into 8 wedges. Brush rough side of each wedge with oil mixture. Place on baking pan; lightly sprinkle with cheese of choice. Bake at 350° for 15 minutes or until crisp. Remove from oven; transfer to wire racks to cool. Makes 48 wedges.

Let's Celebrate!

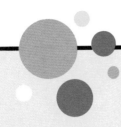

Crispy dippers to accompany your zesty, creamy, chunky, and smooth dips may come in all shapes and sizes.

Homemade crispies are always a welcome change from those available in the super-market.

Crispy Pita Wedges

10 (6-inch) pita rounds
½ cup butter, melted
Salt (optional)
Seasonings: dried herbs, spice powders, or flavored salt blends
Toppings: sesame, caraway, poppy seeds, grated Parmesan or Romano, or bacon bits

Split pita breads horizontally. Cut each round into 6 wedges. Brush wedges with melted butter on both sides and sprinkle with salt, if desired. Sprinkle wedges with desired seasonings and toppings. Bake on cookie sheet in 400° oven for 10–12 minutes, until golden. Chips will become crispier as they cool. Makes 120 chips.

Toasted Parmesan Triangles

Bread
Butter
Parmesan cheese

Trim crust from bread, and cut into 4 triangles. Dip in melted butter, and coat with Parmesan cheese. Toast in 250° oven until crispy, 15–20 minutes.

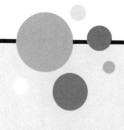

Toasties

Great go-with-everything crispy bread slices.

1 (6-roll) package baguettes
1½ sticks butter
1 teaspoon garlic powder
1 teaspoon Tabasco (or to taste)
1 tablespoon parsley flakes

Preheat oven to 225°. Slice bread into ¼-inch rounds (partially frozen bread slices best). Melt butter; add remaining ingredients. Brush both sides of bread very lightly with butter mixture. Bake 40–50 minutes till dry, but not brown. Turn heat off and leave in oven 30 minutes or more. Store in airtight container. Makes 120–150 rounds.

Crispy Cheese Wafers

Best double this recipe. Great make-ahead treat.

1 cup grated sharp Cheddar cheese, room
  temperature
1 stick margarine, softened
1 cup all-purpose flour
½ teaspoon salt
⅛–¼ teaspoon red pepper (optional)
1 cup crispy rice cereal

Combine all ingredients well. Shape into small balls. Bake at 350° in ungreased pan 2 minutes. Remove and flatten with fork. Bake 18–20 minutes longer— do not let brown. Makes 40–50 crisps.

Cheddar cheese manufacturers originated in the town of Cheddar in Somerset, England, in the 16th century. There are hundreds of different kinds of cheeses produced all over the world. About 150 are recognized by the USDA. Almost 90% of all cheese sold in the United States is classified as a Cheddar-type cheese.

Let's Celebrate!

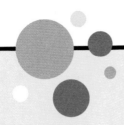

Wild pecans were well-known among colonial Americans as a delicacy. Commercial growing of pecans in the United States did not begin until the 1880s. Today the nation produces 80–95 percent of the world's pecans. Pecan trees may live and bear edible nuts for more than 300 years.

Although Georgia is the largest producer of pecans in the United States, followed by Texas, New Mexico, and Oklahoma, the world's largest pecan nursery is in Lumberton, Mississippi.

Pecan Cheese Wafers

There is no party these don't like to go to.

4 cups finely shredded Cheddar cheese
2 sticks butter, softened
¼ teaspoon cayenne pepper
2 cups all-purpose flour, divided
2 cups finely chopped pecans
Paprika

Mix cheese in mixer 2 minutes; add butter and mix till blended. Add pepper and 3 tablespoons flour. Blend well. Continue adding flour until mixture becomes soft dough and can be rolled into balls without sticking. Add finely chopped nuts. Dust hands and fork with flour. Form small balls. Flatten with fork on cookie sheet. Bake at 325° for 20–25 minutes. Sprinkle with paprika while hot, after you remove from oven, or sprinkle lightly with onion powder. Better after the first day. Keep in tin. Yields approximately 100.

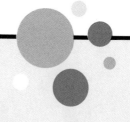

Buttery Sweet Toasted Pecans

These crisp bites are irresistible and will disappear when served as a nibble with cocktails.

3 tablespoons butter
3 cups pecan halves
2–3 teaspoons Cajun seasoning
3 teaspoons sugar

Melt butter in frying pan over medium heat. Stir pecans in butter for 1 minute. Sprinkle Cajun seasoning and sugar over nuts and cook, stirring constantly, until sugar has melted and nuts are glazed, about 2 minutes. Pour pecans onto a plate and cool slightly. Taste and season with salt, if needed. Serves 6–8.

Mother's Dry Roasted Pecans

Thanks, Mom. Love 'em.

2 cups water
¼ cup salt
2 cups pecan halves

Mix water and salt well. Add pecans and let soak 3 hours. Drain pecans well on paper towels. Spread evenly on cookie sheet. Bake in 325° oven for 25–30 minutes. Stir and check pecans after they have baked for 20 minutes. Cool.

Interesting . . .
Astronauts took pecans to the moon in two space missions. Guaranteed good in most any atmosphere.

Let's Celebrate!

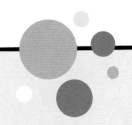

Okmulgee, Oklahoma, holds the world's record for largest pecan pie, pecan cookie, and pecan brownie. The town holds an annual pecan festival each June.

It's Party Time!

Mother's Toasted Pecans

Buttery delicious! Thanks again, Mom.

½ cup margarine
3 cups pecan halves
Salt to taste

Melt margarine on cookie sheet. Pour pecan halves onto cookie sheet and stir to coat well. Arrange in a single layer and lightly salt. Bake in 275° oven for 1 hour, stirring every 15–20 minutes. Yields 3 cups.

Sweet Toasted Pecans

. . . always popular.

1 egg white
½ cup brown sugar
½ teaspoon vanilla
¼ teaspoon salt
4 cups pecan halves

Beat egg white until stiff; stir in sugar, vanilla, and salt. Coat pecans with mixture; pour onto a cookie sheet that has been lined with wax paper and sprayed with cooking spray. Bake 10–15 minutes at 350° till lightly browned. Yields 4 cups.

Persnickety Pesto Peanuts

1 envelope pesto sauce mix
3 tablespoons vegetable oil
¼ teaspoon cayenne pepper
5 cups salted dry roasted peanuts

Whisk pesto mix, oil, and cayenne. Pour into a large bowl; add peanuts. Stir well to coat. Pour into greased 9x13-inch baking pan. Bake at 350° for 15–20 minutes, uncovered, stirring once. Let cool. Store in airtight container. Yields 5 cups.

Kicked-Up-A-Notch Peanuts

These are tasty warm out of the skillet or totally cooled down.

2 teaspoons vegetable oil
1½ teaspoons Creole seasoning
2 cups dry roasted peanuts

Heat oil and seasoning in skillet over medium heat; add peanuts. Stir about 2 minutes to coat evenly. Cool slightly; pour into serving dish or jar. Store tightly covered up to 3 weeks. Yields 2 cups.

Editor's Extra: You can add a tad of red pepper, but better have plenty of cold beer.

Cowboy Popcorn

2½ quarts popped popcorn
½ cup butter, melted
2 tablespoons ranch salad dressing mix
2 tablespoons grated Parmesan cheese
2 teaspoons dried parsley flakes

Pour popcorn into ungreased 9x13-inch baking pan. Mix remaining ingredients; pour over popcorn; toss to coat. Bake uncovered at 350° for 10 minutes uncovered. Toss again. Serve warm. Yields 8 servings.

Some people may not want to reach their fingers into a bowl of nuts or candies. Try putting them in wine glasses for guests to pour out into their hands. Or serve nuts with a small scoop, and have foil mini-cupcake liners alongside for individual servings.

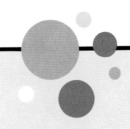

Snack mixes are ideal for make-and-take occasions. Nice for travel, too . . . in the car, on the plane, in a condo, on a hike . . . . From two to ninety-two, everybody loves these nibbles.

It's Party Time!

Crazy Craisin Party Mix

8 cups mixed Chex cereal (corn, rice, wheat)
1 cup sliced almonds
½ cup butter
¼ cup brown sugar
¼ cup frozen orange juice concentrate, thawed
½ cup craisins or dried cranberries

In large bowl, mix cereal and almonds; set aside. Microwave butter, brown sugar, and juice concentrate in glass measure uncovered on HIGH 30 seconds; stir. Pour butter mixture over cereal mixture, stirring until evenly coated. Pour into large roasting pan. Bake at 300° uncovered 30 minutes, stirring after 15 minutes. Stir in craisins or cranberries; cool. Store in airtight container or plastic food-storage bag. Makes 9 cups mix.

Climb-A-Mountain Mix

Who says you can't have a party on a mountainside?
Or this could see you through a mountain of homework.

¼ cup pepper jelly
3 tablespoons butter
¼ teaspoon five-spice powder
½ teaspoon Tabasco
3 cups dry roasted peanuts or cashews
2 cups dried tropical fruit mix
1 cup Crispix cereal or chow mein noodles

Heat first 4 ingredients in large saucepan over low heat. When jelly is melted, stir in remaining ingredients until well coated. Pour into roasting pan. Bake in 300° oven 30 minutes, stirring once. Cool; store tightly covered. Makes 6 cups. Put in zipper bag to go in backpacks.

Lite 'n Crunchy Party Mix

1 tablespoon Butter Buds
¼ cup water
3 tablespoons cooking oil
2 tablespoons Worcestershire
1 tablespoon Cajun seasoning
12 cups crispy cereal
4 cups broken lower-sodium pretzels

In a small pot, heat Butter Buds, water, cooking oil, Worcestershire, and seasoning till dissolved. Spray a large roasting pan with nonstick coating. Mix cereals and pretzels in pan. Pour on heated butter mixture and toss to coat. Bake at 300° for 45 minutes, stirring every 15 minutes. Spread out to cool. Store in airtight container. Makes 32 (½-cup) servings.

Super-Duper Snack Mix

The best!

¾ stick margarine
2 tablespoons Cajun seasoning
2 tablespoons Worcestershire
2 (12-ounce) cans mixed nuts
10 cups crispy cereal*

Melt margarine in saucepan with seasoning and Worcestershire. Mix nuts and cereal* in 11x15x2-inch baking pan. Pour margarine mixture over and stir gently to coat. Bake at 250° for 40 minutes, stirring twice during baking time. Cool before storing in airtight containers.

*Mix cereals like Chex and oat or wheat squares. Maybe add some sugared cereals like Cookie Crisp or Sugar Pops or Honeycomb—no more than ¼ of total—for a hint of sweet.

Considered a holiday staple in many American homes, homemade snack mixes have been around for more than fifty years. The original "Chex Mix" recipe hit the party circuit in 1955. When you have some cereal that has been opened for awhile, there's your incentive for making a snack mix! The yummy variations just keep getting yummier.

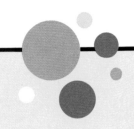

Chocolate Peanut Butter Chow

1 (12-ounce) bag chocolate chips
1 stick butter
1 cup chunky peanut butter
1 (12-ounce) box Chex cereal
3 cups powdered sugar

Microwave chips, butter, and peanut butter 1½–2 minutes; stir till creamy. Mix well with Chex until well coated. Put powdered sugar in large bag. Shake with cereal until coated. Serves 10–12.

Wonderful White Trash

So fun to your taste buds, you can't stop picking up just one more bite.

4 cups Graham Squares cereal
4 cups Chex cereal
2 cups broken pretzel sticks
3 cups pecan halves
1⅓ (12-ounce) packages almond bark
1 tablespoon vegetable oil

Mix cereals, sticks, and nuts together. Melt almond bark with oil over hot water. Pour over cereal mixture and stir to coat. Pour out onto wax paper to harden in bite-size clumps. Serves 12–16.

It's Party Time!

Big Dippers

Dips

Dunks

Salsas

Scoops

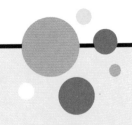

Collinsville, Illinois, is the self-proclaimed "Horseradish Capital of the World," and hosts an annual International Horseradish Festival each June.

Collinsville produces 60% (and the surrounding area of southwestern Illinois, 85%) of the world's commercially grown horseradish.

It's Party Time!

You-Won't-Believe-How-Good-It-Is Mustard Dip

Bring on the pretzels! Great on just about anything!

1 (8-ounce) carton sour cream
1 cup mayonnaise
1 cup yellow mustard
¼ cup onion flakes
1 package ranch dressing mix
⅓ cup sugar
1 tablespoon creamy horseradish

Mix all together well. That's it! Yields about 3 cups.

Note: Try this with veggies, pretzels, pita chips, tostitos, or even as a sandwich spread. Keeps well in fridge.

Greener Pastures Dip

2 (14½-ounce) cans whole artichoke hearts, drained, rinsed
½ cup olive oil
2 teaspoons fresh lemon juice
2 garlic cloves, minced
1 cup finely chopped green olives
Pepper to taste
¼ cup finely chopped fresh parsley

Purée artichokes, olive oil, lemon juice, and garlic in food processor until smooth. Transfer to a bowl and add green olives and pepper; stir well. Refrigerate at least 2 hours. Mix in chopped parsley before serving. Serve with crackers, pita triangles, or your favorite "dipper." Yields about 3 cups.

Editor's Extra: This is good on muffalettas as well, as it resembles an olive salad.

Irene's Shrimp Dip

Everybody enjoys a good shrimp dip. Here it is!

1 (7-ounce) can shrimp, rinsed, drained
1 (3-ounce) package cream cheese, softened
¼ cup sour cream
1 tablespoon lemon juice
1 tablespoon ketchup
¼ teaspoon Worcestershire
⅛ teaspoon onion powder
Dash of hot pepper sauce (optional)

Mix all ingredients together. Chill and serve with chips, crackers, celery or carrot sticks, broccoli or cauliflower florets. Makes about 1½ cups.

Quicker-Than-Quick Shrimp Dip

1 (8-ounce) package cream cheese, softened
⅛ cup mayonnaise
1 package ranch salad dressing mix
1 (7-ounce) can shrimp, rinsed, drained

Mix all in blender or food processor. Serve with crackers or veggies. Makes about 2½ cups.

Goodness Gracious Good Veggie Dip

1 (8-ounce) package cream cheese, softened
1 cup mayonnaise
1 cup sour cream
2 tablespoons lemon juice
2 tablespoons tarragon vinegar
1–2 teaspoons garlic salt
½ cup chopped green onions
½ cup chopped fresh parsley

Mix all ingredients and serve as a dip with fresh vegetables. Yields about 3½ cups.

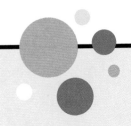

Garbanzo beans, also known as chickpeas, are an excellent source of calcium, containing almost as much as milk, and equally as much as yogurt.

It's Party Time!

Quick Chick Blender Hummus

1 (15-ounce) can garbanzo beans, half drained
2 tablespoons tahini paste (optional)
¼ cup lemon juice
2 tablespoons olive oil
2 garlic cloves, minced
Salt, pepper, and cayenne to taste

Blend all in blender or food processor. Yields about 2 cups.

Editor's Extra: Tahini is generally used in hummus, so do add some if you have it, but this is pretty good without it. Try throwing in several tablespoons sliced jalapeño to sub for the cayenne.

Waldorf Spinach Dip in a Bread Bowl

The apples add a different twist to an all-time favorite.

1 (10-ounce) package frozen chopped spinach, thawed, squeezed dry
1 (1-ounce) package vegetable dip mix
1 (6-ounce) container lemon yogurt
1 cup sour cream
1 cup mayonnaise
1 cup chopped apple
1 cup chopped celery
1 (3-ounce) package real bacon bits
1 large sourdough or Hawaiian bread round

Combine ingredients except bread; refrigerate till serving. Hollow out bread loaf and fill with dip. Serve with bread cubes from hollowing, and fresh veggies. Yields about 5 cups.

Easy Breezy Veggie Dip

2 cups sour cream
1 package dry Italian dressing mix
1 tomato, peeled, chunked
1 avocado, peeled, chunked

Blend or process all till well mixed. Serve with Frito Scoops, tostadas, or veggies. Makes about 3 cups.

Fiesta Dip

1 package dry ranch dip mix
1 (16-ounce) carton sour cream
1 (4-ounce) can sliced black olives, drained
2 cups grated Cheddar cheese
1 (10-ounce) can Ro-Tel tomatoes, drained

Mix together dip mix and sour cream. Stir in remaining ingredients. Serve with tortilla chips. Yields about 4½ cups.

Bacon and Tomato Layer Dip

1 (8-ounce) package cream cheese, softened
1½ cups mayonnaise
4 green onions, thinly sliced
4 medium tomatoes, chopped
1 green bell pepper, chopped
2 cups shredded Cheddar cheese
½ pound sliced bacon, cooked, crumbled

Beat cream cheese and mayonnaise in a bowl. Spread in an ungreased oval casserole dish or platter. Sprinkle onions, tomatoes, and green pepper over cream cheese. Sprinkle with Cheddar cheese. Refrigerate. Just before serving, sprinkle with bacon. Serve with Fritos Scoops or Tostitos. Serves 10–16.

Make your own wavy dippers. Cut won ton skins into wedges and place on Pam-sprayed, slightly crumpled foil on a baking sheet. Spray won tons with additional Pam. Bake at 400° about 5 minutes.

Let's Celebrate!

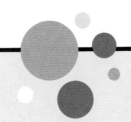

Rainbow Corn Dip

Also great on lettuce leaves as a salad. Add some tomato and/or egg wedges. Beautiful.

2 (11-ounce) cans Mexicorn, well drained
1 cup grated Cheddar or Jack cheese
1 (8-ounce) carton sour cream
3 green onions, diced
1 (2-ounce) jar pimentos, drained

Mix all together and chill. Offer chips or crackers for dipping. Makes about 5 cups.

Sedona Sun-Dried Tomato Dip

Great with tortilla or bagel chips, or on crackers or crisp bread.

⅔ cup toasted walnuts or pine nuts
⅓ cup oil-packed sun-dried tomatoes, drained
3 tablespoons chopped jarred roasted red peppers, drained
2 green onions, diced
2 tablespoons balsamic vinegar
3 tablespoons water
⅓ cup vegetable or olive oil

Blend all but oil in food processor. Slowly add oil. Makes about 1½ cups.

It's Party Time!

Sombrero Dip

1 (15-ounce) can refried beans
1 pound ground beef
1 tablespoon taco seasoning
1½ cups shredded lettuce
¾ cup chopped onion
1 cup diced tomatoes
1½ cups sour cream
1 (16-ounce) package shredded Cheddar cheese
Guacamole (optional)

In a large pie plate, spread refried beans. Brown ground beef; drain, and add taco seasoning. Layer ground beef, lettuce, onion, tomatoes, sour cream, cheese, and guacamole, if desired. Chill and serve with tortilla chips or scoops. Serves 10–16.

Don't get stuck on one kind of cheese. Experiment. Sub Monterey Jack for Cheddar, or provolone for Swiss, etc. The taste will be a little different, and the texture may vary slightly, but it'll work fine and you may like it better.

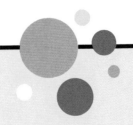

Carl G. Sontheimer developed the Cuisinart food processor from an industrial blender he had seen at a food show in 1971. His final product came out in 1973.

Cloud Nine 'Cado Dip

Nine ingredients, with cloud-nine results.

2 tablespoons lemon juice
1 tablespoon Dijon mustard
½ cup olive oil
4 tablespoons chopped green onions, divided
½ teaspoon sugar
1 teaspoon garlic salt
1 (8-ounce) package cream cheese, softened
1 large ripe avocado, peeled, pitted
2 tablespoons chopped fresh parsley

In food processor, mix lemon juice, mustard, olive oil, 2 tablespoons green onions, sugar, and garlic salt till smooth; set aside. Process cream cheese and avocado till smooth. With machine still running, add lemon juice mixture very slowly to cream cheese mixture, and blend till smooth. Garnish with parsley and remaining green onions. Offer fresh veggies, tortilla chips, crisp bagel chips, or Ritz Chips for dipping. Yields 2½ cups.

Guacamole Dunk

1 ripe avocado, mashed
½ cup finely chopped cucumber
½ cup finely chopped onion
1 (3-ounce) package cream cheese, softened
2 tablespoons lemon juice
½ teaspoon salt
1 teaspoon paprika
Dash of Tabasco

Beat ingredients until fluffy. Chill. Serve with chips or crackers. Yields 2 cups.

It's Party Time!

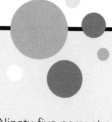

Avocado Salsa

This is seriously good.

2 ripe avocados, finely chopped
2 tomatoes, seeded, finely chopped
1 tablespoon chopped jalapeño
2 green onions, finely sliced
2 tablespoons chopped fresh cilantro
Salt to taste
Juice of ½ small lime

Mix all but lime juice in a bowl. Squeeze lime juice over mixture and stir. Put in serving dish and serve right away. If refrigerating for a short time, cover surface with plastic wrap to avoid discoloring. Serve with firm chips or pita wedges.

Ninety-five percent of United States avocado production is located in California, and 80% occurs in San Diego County. Fallbrook, California, claims the title of "Avocado Capital of the World."

Today's supermarkets offer avocados all year round in various stages of ripeness so you can use them today or in several days. Nice.

Serve salsas and dips in interesting vessels such as hollowed-out cabbage, bread, or pumpkins, pineapple, pepper, or melon halves.

Kicky Layered Dip

3 cups shredded lettuce
1 (15-ounce) can black beans, rinsed, drained
¾ cup chopped red and/or yellow sweet pepper
2 (8-ounce) cartons sour cream
1 fresh jalapeño chile pepper, seeded, chopped
1 (16-ounce) jar chunky salsa, drained
1 medium avocado, seeded, peeled, coarsely chopped
⅔ cup shredded Cheddar cheese
⅓ cup sliced pitted ripe olives

On platter or shallow dish, layer lettuce, beans, sweet pepper, sour cream, jalapeño pepper, and salsa. If desired, cover and chill for up to 6 hours. Before serving, sprinkle with avocado, cheese, and olives. Serve with tortilla chips or tostadas. Serves 12–16.

Easy-As-Can-Be Salsa

1 (6-ounce) can chopped ripe olives, drained
1 (4-ounce) can chopped green chiles, undrained
3 or 4 green onions, chopped
2 tomatoes, finely chopped
1 tablespoon oil
2 teaspoons seasoned rice wine vinegar
1 teaspoon garlic salt

Combine olives, chiles, onions, and tomatoes in bowl. Combine oil, vinegar, and garlic salt, and pour over olive mixture. Refrigerate several hours or till ready to serve. Serve with scoops. Makes about 2 cups.

It's Party Time!

Bodacious Salsa

It's pretty, delicious, and keeps exceptionally well.

1 (10-ounce) can Ro-Tel (hot, if you like)
2 (14-ounce) cans petite diced tomatoes
1 bunch green onions, chopped
Fresh cilantro, chopped, to taste
1 tablespoon chili powder
2 teaspoons cumin
Salt to taste
2 tablespoons canola oil

Combine all ingredients and refrigerate an hour or longer for flavors to marry. Serve with scoops or Tostito chips. Makes about 3 cups.

Corny Bean Salsa

1 (8¾-ounce) can whole-kernel corn, drained
1 (15-ounce) can black beans, rinsed, drained
4 green onions, sliced
⅓ cup chopped red bell pepper
2 tablespoons snipped fresh cilantro
2 tablespoons lime juice
1 teaspoon ground cumin
½ teaspoon Cajun seasoning

Combine corn, beans, green onions, sweet pepper, and cilantro in container with cover. In glass measure, stir together lime juice, and seasonings. Pour over bean mixture; toss gently to coat. Cover and chill. Serve with corn chips. Serves 12–15.

Let's Celebrate!

Nancy's Country Caviar

1 (15-ounce) can black-eyed peas, rinsed
1 (15-ounce) can black beans, rinsed
1 (15-ounce) can shoepeg corn, drained
1 (10-ounce) can mild Ro-Tel tomatoes, not drained
2 green onions, chopped
⅔ cup Italian dressing

Mix all together and put in refrigerator overnight, stirring twice. Serve with Fritos Scoops. Makes about 6 cups.

Mellow Mallow Fruit Dip

1 (7-ounce) jar marshmallow crème
1 (8-ounce) package cream cheese, softened
¼ teaspoon almond extract
Apple wedges, seedless grapes, cherries, strawberries, or fruit of your choice

Blend marshmallow crème, cream cheese, and almond extract well. To serve, place fruits on plate around bowl of dip. Makes 1½ cups.

Editor's Extra: Sprinkle a little lemon or pineapple juice over apples to discourage browning.

Caramel Fruit Dip

A favorite that's easy to make.

1 (8-ounce) package cream cheese, softened
¾ cup brown sugar, packed
½ cup marshmallow crème
1 teaspoon vanilla
½ cup chopped dry roasted peanuts (optional)

Mix all together in mixer. Serve with any firm cut fruit. Good with graham sticks, too. Yields about 1½ cups.

It's Party Time!

Touch of Spice Fruit Dip

¼ cup whipped cream cheese
1 (6-ounce) carton vanilla yogurt
½ teaspoon ground ginger
¼ teaspoon ground cinnamon

Mix cream cheese, yogurt, ginger, and cinnamon till smooth. Cover and refrigerate for at least an hour. Serve with fresh fruit. Yields 1 cup.

Creamy Amaretto Dip

Great on fruit or ice cream.

1 cup sour cream
¼ cup confectioners' sugar
¼ teaspoon almond extract
3 tablespoons amaretto liqueur

Mix till smooth. Add more powdered sugar, if needed, for consistency. Pour into serving cup surrounded by cut fresh fruit and toothpicks. Makes 1¼ cups.

Tropical Fruit Dip

1 (8-ounce) package cream cheese, softened
¼ cup frozen limeade concentrate, partially thawed
2 tablespoons orange juice
½ cup thawed Cool Whip

Mix first 3 ingredients until well blended. Gently fold in whipped topping; cover. Chill at least 1 hour. Serve with cut-up fresh fruit. Makes about 1¼ cups.

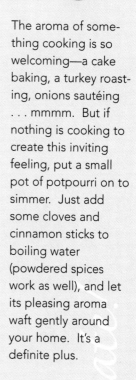

The aroma of something cooking is so welcoming—a cake baking, a turkey roasting, onions sautéing . . . mmmm. But if nothing is cooking to create this inviting feeling, put a small pot of potpourri on to simmer. Just add some cloves and cinnamon sticks to boiling water (powdered spices work as well), and let its pleasing aroma waft gently around your home. It's a definite plus.

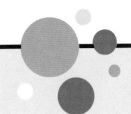

Pumpkin Cheesecake Dip

Not just for fall . . . nice anytime.

1 (8-ounce) tub ready-made cheesecake filling
1 (15-ounce) can pumpkin pie mix
1 (3-ounce) package vanilla instant pudding

Mix well and serve with gingersnaps or graham cracker sticks. Makes about 2 cups.

Pretty Cranberry Cream Cheese Centerpiece

Looks good and tastes even better.

2 (8-ounce) packages cream cheese, softened
⅓ cup powdered sugar
1 (6-ounce) package sweetened dried cranberries, divided
1 (15-ounce) can crushed pineapple, drained
1 cup chopped pecans, toasted
1 (3.5-ounce) can shredded coconut, divided
1 (11-ounce) can Mandarin oranges, drained
9 toasted pecan halves

Mix cream cheese and sugar; add cranberries, reserving ¼ cup. Stir in pineapple, chopped pecans, and coconut. Spoon mixture into flat serving bowl. Sprinkle reserved dried cranberries around edges of bowl. Drain oranges and spread on paper towels. Arrange sections around inside edge of cranberries. Sprinkle reserved ¼ cup coconut in center; top with pecan halves. Dip with pita crisps or spread on gingersnaps or Wheat Thins. Serves 12–16.

It's Party Time!

Some Like It Hot

Hot Dips

Chafing Dishes

Fondues

Hot Bread Bowls

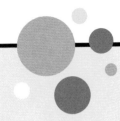

Reuben Kulakofsky, a grocer from Omaha, first served a reuben in a poker game at the Blackstone Hotel (1920–1935). The hotel's owner, Charles Schimmel, put it on the menu, and it became famous. But wait! Descendants of Arnold Reuben, owner of now defunct Reuben Restaurant on 58th Street in NYC, also claim it. Jacob Reuben, a butcher and deli owner in Brooklyn claims the invention as well. And further, the Dundee Dell restaurant in Omaha, who still serve it, say they invented it. The first, however, is most widely accepted.

Variations abound, but most include meat, cabbage, cheese, and dressing.

Sweet Georgia Onion Dip

How can something so easy taste so good?

1 cup real mayonnaise
1 cup chopped Vidalia onions
1 cup shredded Swiss cheese

Combine ingredients and place in Pam-sprayed baking dish. Bake at 350° for 20 minutes. Serve with scoops, crackers, Fritos, bread, anything! Yum! Makes 3 cups.

Reuben, Reuben Dip

Sing it! "Reuben, Reuben, I been thinkin' what a great dip this would be . . ." and is!

1 (14-ounce) can sauerkraut
4 ounces cooked corned beef
1 small onion
1 cup mayonnaise
1 cup sour cream
1 cup shredded Swiss cheese
1 tablespoon prepared horseradish
1 teaspoon Dijon mustard

Drain and squeeze excess moisture from sauerkraut. Process it with corned beef and onion until finely chopped. Pour corned beef mixture in a bowl and mix in mayonnaise, sour cream, cheese, horseradish, and Dijon mustard. Place in Pam-sprayed 1-quart baking dish. Bake in preheated 350° oven 30–40 minutes or until bubbly. Serve with party rye bread. Makes 5 cups.

Awesome Artichoke Dip

The title says it all.

1 cup mayonnaise
1 cup grated Parmesan cheese
1 (4-ounce) can chopped green chiles
1 (14-ounce) can artichokes, drained, chopped
1 garlic clove, minced
1 green onion, sliced
1 tomato, chopped

Mix and place in a 9-inch pie plate all ingredients except onion and tomato. Microwave on MEDIUM 6–8 minutes. Sprinkle with onion and tomato. Serve with crackers. Makes 3–4 cups.

Editor's Extra: If using an oven, set at 350° and bake 20–25 minutes.

The Famous Crab & Artichoke Dip

Famous because it's fabulous!

1 (15-ounce) can artichoke hearts, drained
1 cup mayonnaise
1 cup fresh lump crabmeat
2 garlic cloves, minced
Red and black pepper to taste
¾ cup grated Parmesan cheese

Mix artichoke, mayonnaise, crabmeat, garlic, and pepper in oven-proof casserole dish. Sprinkle Parmesan on top. Cover and bake at 350° for 20 minutes. Remove excess oil with large spoon; bake another 10 minutes. Sprinkle with paprika for color. Good with bagel chips or Fritos Scoops. Makes 3½ cups.

Let's Celebrate!

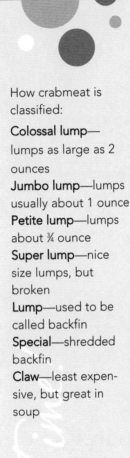

How crabmeat is classified:

Colossal lump—lumps as large as 2 ounces
Jumbo lump—lumps usually about 1 ounce
Petite lump—lumps about ¾ ounce
Super lump—nice size lumps, but broken
Lump—used to be called backfin
Special—shredded backfin
Claw—least expensive, but great in soup

Delectable Crabmeat Mornay

The best chafing dish you can possibly serve! Also great in patty shells for a sit-down luncheon or dinner.

6 green onions, chopped
1 stick butter (no sub)
2 tablespoons flour
½ bunch parsley, finely chopped
1 (6-ounce) carton half-and-half
½ pound sliced Swiss cheese
1 tablespoon sherry wine
½ teaspoon Cajun seasoning
1 pound lump crabmeat

Sauté onions in butter. Stir in flour, parsley, half-and-half, and cheese; stir till cheese is melted. Add sherry and seasoning; fold in crabmeat. Heat till thickened, do not boil. Serve in chafing dish over low heat with Melba rounds. Makes 4–5 cups.

Quick Hot Crab Dip

1 stick butter, softened
1 (8-ounce) package cream cheese, softened
1 pound fresh lump crabmeat
2–3 tablespoons soy sauce
Sprinkle of red pepper

Blend butter and cream cheese. Heat in microwave or over low heat. Fold in crabmeat, soy sauce, and pepper. Serve in chafing dish with crackers or crisp toast. Makes 2½–3½ cups.

French Fried Onion Crab Dip

2 (8-ounce) packages cream cheese, softened
1 (8-ounce) package imitation king crabmeat
2 tablespoons chopped green onions
2 teaspoons Worcestershire
4–5 drops Tabasco
½ can French fried onions, crumbled

Combine all ingredients, except onions, in 9-inch pie plate or casserole dish. Top with crumbled onions and bake at 375° for 20–25 minutes. Great served with toasted bread wedges. Yields about 2½ cups.

Easy Spicy Corn Dip

2 cups frozen corn, thawed, well drained
1 (8-ounce) package cream cheese, softened
1 cup chopped tomato
½ cup shredded Cheddar cheese
1 tablespoon finely chopped pickled jalapeño
  peppers
¼ teaspoon chili powder

Preheat oven to 350°. Blend all ingredients except chili powder. Spread into pie plate or 1-quart baking dish; sprinkle with chili powder. Bake 20 minutes or until golden brown. Serve hot with crackers or scoops. Makes 4–5 cups.

Let's Celebrate!

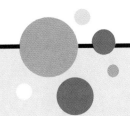

Mighty Meaty Mexican Dip

A slow cooker does the work . . . keeps it warm.

1 pound ground sausage
2 (15-ounce) cans pinto beans
2 cups salsa
1 (4-ounce) can diced green chiles, undrained
3 cups finely shredded Cheddar Jack cheese, divided
1 tablespoon chopped jalapeño

In a large skillet, brown sausage; drain. In a slow cooker, combine meat, beans, salsa, and green chiles. Stir in 2 cups cheese. Cover; cook on LOW setting 3–4 hours or on HIGH setting 1½–2 hours. Sprinkle with remaining 1 cup cheese. Great with Tostitos Scoops. Makes 6 cups.

Amigos Bean Dip

Call your friends—this is terrific!

3 cups shredded Colby Jack cheese, divided
1 (16-ounce) can refried beans
1 (10-ounce) can Ro-Tel tomatoes
1 (8-ounce) package cream cheese, cubed small
½ cup sour cream
1 tablespoon taco seasoning

In a large bowl, combine 2 cups cheese, beans, tomatoes, cream cheese, sour cream, and taco seasoning. Pour into a 2-quart baking dish; sprinkle with remaining 1 cup cheese.

Bake, uncovered, at 350° for 20–25 minutes or until edges are bubbly. Serve warm with tortilla chips, scoops, or vegetables. Makes 5 cups.

Editor's Extra: This can be made with reduced-fat ingredients with little loss of great taste.

It's Party Time!

Mexican Bean Scoop

1 (16-ounce) can refried beans
1 (8-ounce) package cream cheese, softened
1 (8-ounce) carton sour cream
1½ cups salsa or picante sauce
1 cup shredded Mexican cheese

Combine first 4 ingredients; place in casserole; sprinkle cheese over top. Bake at 350° until cheese is melted. Serve with corn scoops. Makes about 3 cups.

Mexican Nacho Dip

This feeds hungry partygoers.

2 pounds ground beef
2 pounds Mexican Velveeta cheese, cubed
1 (10¾-ounce) can cream of celery soup
1 (8-ounce) jar mild picante sauce

Brown and drain beef. Add cheese and melt on medium heat. Stir in soup; add picante. Serve hot with tortilla chips. Crockpot works well. Makes a whole lot.

Bought dips can be quite good, but usually recognizable. It may take a wee bit more time to put a few ingredients together, but the "made-it-myself" taste and pride is worth it.

Some dips are hearty enough to stand on their own, or maybe with fruit, nuts, and drinks, whereas before-dinner dips or other appetizers are meant to just whet the appetite, but not completely satisfy. Save room for dinner . . . and dessert!

Bang-Bang Buffalo Chicken Dip

Make it as hot as you dare . . . but not quite explosive. This is awesome.

4 boneless chicken breasts
¼ cup buffalo wing sauce or to taste
1 (8-ounce) package cream cheese
1 (8-ounce) bottle ranch dressing
1 (8-ounce) package shredded Cheddar cheese

Boil chicken breasts 15–20 minutes till cooked. Dice and put in 9x13-inch casserole dish. Sprinkle hot sauce—like Frank's—all over chicken. Mix cream cheese with ranch dressing; pour over chicken. Cover with cheese. Bake 20 minutes at 350° or till cheese is melted. Use Fritos Scoops or Tostitos as dippers. Makes about 5–6 cups.

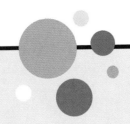

It's Party Time!

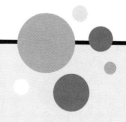

Chicken Enchilada Dip

This is the absolute best dip you can serve.

1 (8-ounce) package cream cheese, softened
2 (6-ounce) packages fajita seasoned pre-cooked chicken strips, chopped
1 (7-ounce) can chopped green chiles
¼ cup chopped pickled jalapeño slices
¾ (16-ounce) tub French onion dip (1½ cups)
1 (16-ounce) tub white queso cheese sauce
1 cup shredded sharp Cheddar cheese

Spread cream cheese in a 9x13-inch baking dish. Spread chopped chicken over cream cheese, evenly. Sprinkle chopped green chiles and jalapeños over all. Spread French onion dip over chile layer. Top with queso cheese sauce and sprinkle with shredded Cheddar. Bake at 350° for 20–30 minutes or until bubbly and slightly browned on top. Serve with white tortilla chips. Makes 5–6 cups.

Editor's Extra: Okay to sub plain cooked chicken tenders sprinkled with some seasoning.

Not everybody has chafing dishes and warming trays. For informal parties, it's handy to serve warm dips in fondue pots or small slow cookers.

Let's Celebrate!

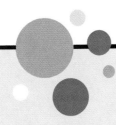

Chips and crackers come in many flavors. Be sure to taste to be sure they compliment your dip. Think about choosing unflavored chips or crackers that do not interfere with the flavor of the dip.

It's Party Time!

Easy Cheesy Chili Dip

1 (10-ounce) can chili without beans
1 (4-ounce) can chopped green chiles, drained
1 tablespoon chili powder
1 (8-ounce) package cream cheese, softened
1 (4-ounce) can chopped black olives

Bring chili to a boil in saucepan. Stir in green chiles, chili powder, cream cheese, and olives. Stir over medium heat until cheese is melted. Keep hot in a chafing dish. Serve with tortilla chips. Makes 2½ cups.

Green Chile Cheese Dip

1 (10¾-ounce) can cream of chicken soup
1 (4-ounce) can chopped green chiles
1 cup grated Mexican blend cheese
2 teaspoons instant minced onion

Heat all ingredients in saucepan; stir over low heat till cheese melts. Serve with Tostitos, Fritos Scoops, or other chips. Makes 2½ cups.

Speedy Gonzales Chili Dip

1 (8-ounce) package cream cheese, softened
1 (15-ounce) can chili without beans
¾ cup shredded taco cheese
1–1½ tablespoons chopped cilantro

Spread cream cheese onto bottom of glass pie plate. Layer with chili then cheese. Microwave on HIGH for 1 minute, or until cheese is melted. Sprinkle with cilantro. Serve with chips or crackers. Makes about 3 cups.

Hot Tamale Dip

So good, you can eat it with a fork!

1 (10½-ounce) package corn chips
2 (16-ounce) cans chili
1 (20-ounce) can tamales
12–14 slices Velveeta cheese

Spread corn chips in lightly buttered 9x13-inch casserole. Pour chili over chips; slice tamales over chili; top with cheese slices. Bake in preheated 350° oven 20–30 minutes till cheese is melted. Serve with scoops. Serves 12–20.

Bread Bowl of Beef Dip

1 (8-ounce) package cream cheese, softened
1 (8-ounce) carton sour cream
1 (4-ounce) can chopped green chiles
1½ cups grated Cheddar cheese
1 (4-ounce) package dried beef, chopped
1 sourdough bread loaf

Combine well all ingredients except bread. Hollow out inside of bread loaf; reserve for dipping. Spoon filling into hollow. Bake at 350° for 45 minutes. Serve with reserved bread pieces, baked pita chips, or your favorite crackers. Serves 10–12.

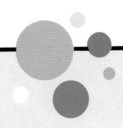

Gather all ingredients for a recipe before beginning. Not only is it convenient to have everything in front of you, but it negates leaving something out. Also it eliminates hurried trips to the grocery when you're halfway into it and discover you are out of something you thought you had! Of course many a new recipe has been created from on-hand substitutions. Go for it!

Bread Boat Sausage Dip

This will be the hit of the party!

2 pounds ground sausage
1 (8-ounce) package cream cheese
1 (16-ounce) carton sour cream
1 (4-ounce) can green chiles
1 (10-ounce) can Ro-Tel tomatoes
4 cups shredded Mexican blend cheese
2 French bread loaves

Brown sausage; drain. Stir in cream cheese, sour cream, green chiles, Ro-Tel, and cheese. Remove from heat. Cut top off French bread, and scoop out center. Fill with dip, wrap in foil, and bake at 350° for 35–45 minutes. Serve with Frito Scoops. Serves 12–20.

Wheel o' Brie Bread Bowl

1 round sourdough bread
2 tablespoons butter, softened
½ teaspoon sugar
½ teaspoon dry mustard
1½ teaspoons chili powder
½ teaspoon garlic powder
1 (8-ounce) wheel brie cheese, rind removed

Cut circle in top of bread and remove bread center to make room for brie wheel.

Spread butter on bread. Mix sugar with spices. Sprinkle 2 tablespoons spice mixture over bread. Using a serrated knife, make 2-inch cuts in 1-inch intervals around edge of bread. Place brie in bread. Sprinkle cheese with remaining spice mixture. Place top of bread over cheese. Bake in 350° oven 20–25 minutes. Remove bread top and tear into small pieces. Dip bread pieces in hot cheese. Serves 8–10.

Zippy Spinach Dip

Add a little zip to your spinach dip.

1 (1-pound) package regular bulk sausage
1 (10-ounce) package frozen chopped spinach,
   drained
1 (8-ounce) package cream cheese, softened
1 cup shredded Cheddar cheese
1 cup sour cream
½ cup chopped green onions
1 (10-ounce) can Ro-Tel tomatoes, well drained
1 teaspoon garlic powder
1 round loaf bread

Cook sausage until done; drain. Add remaining
ingredients. Cook until cheese is melted. Keep
warm. Cut top off bread and hollow the inside. Fill
hollow with warm dip. Serve with your favorite chips,
crackers, or bread chunks. Serves 10–12.

Editor's Extra: You can use regular tomatoes and hot
sausage . . . or both hots . . . or nots.

Cheesy Salsa Spinach Dip

2 (10-ounce) packages creamed spinach, thawed
1½ cups chunky-style salsa
½ cup sour cream
½ cup shredded Parmesan cheese
2 cups mozzarella cheese

Mix first 4 ingredients. Pour into greased 9x9-inch
casserole. Top with mozzarella. Bake at 350° for 25 minutes or until cheese starts to brown. Serve with crackers, Fritos Scoops, or veggies. Makes about 6 cups.

Let's Celebrate!

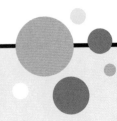

Velveeta is a processed cheese product first made in 1918 by Swiss immigrant Emil Frey of the Monroe Cheese Company in Monroe, New York, then sold to Kraft Foods in 1927. The product is made, in part, of whey, a by-product of cheese-making. Velveeta is noted for its easy melting and long shelf life and does not need to be refrigerated until after opening. Jarred cheese (like Cheez Whiz) is likewise easy to spread and melt.

Easy Breezy Broccoli Dip

Dip anything in this!

1 (10-ounce) package frozen chopped broccoli
1 (1-pound) box Mexican Velveeta
1 (10¾-ounce) can cream of mushroom soup
2 tablespoons Worcestershire
½ teaspoon garlic powder (optional)

Cook frozen broccoli according to package directions for microwave. Drain well. Add all other ingredients. Cook an additional 5 minutes on full power. Stir halfway through cooking time. Makes 3½ cups.

Glorious Green Dip

A great combination of ingredients guaranteed to please.

1 (10-ounce) package frozen chopped spinach,
  thawed, drained
1 cup grated Parmesan cheese
1 cup mayonnaise
1 garlic clove, minced
8–10 artichoke hearts, coarsely chopped
1 green onion, minced

Squeeze excess moisture from spinach. Combine it with cheese, then mayonnaise, garlic, and artichokes in a bowl, mixing well after each addition. Place in ungreased baking dish and press lightly. Bake at 325° in a preheated oven for 25–30 minutes or until brown and bubbly. Sprinkle with chopped green onion. Serve warm with crackers. Makes about 4 cups.

A Heart-Melting Dip

2 tablespoons butter
2 tablespoons all-purpose flour
1 tablespoon dry mustard
1 cup milk
3 (4-ounce) rounds Brie cheese, cubed
1 (6-ounce) jar marinated artichoke hearts, drained, chopped
¼ cup chopped roasted red sweet peppers
Toasted baguette slices

Melt butter over medium heat; stir in flour, mustard, and milk, and whisk until smooth. Cook until thickened and bubbly, stirring occasionally. Add Brie, stirring till smooth. Stir in artichoke hearts and roasted peppers, and heat through. Serve with toasted baguette slices. Yields 3 cups.

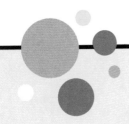

Easy Cheese Bowl

1 round sourdough loaf
1 (8-ounce) package cream cheese, softened
1 (8-ounce) carton sour cream
1 (7-ounce) can chopped green chiles
1 cup frozen chopped seasoning blend
¼ teaspoon Tabasco
2 cups shredded cheese of choice

Slice off top of sourdough loaf; set aside. Hollow out loaf to 1 inch of edges reserving bread cubes to toast for serving with dip. Mix cream cheese and remaining ingredients till smooth. Fill bread bowl with dip mixture; replace top; wrap in foil. Bake at 350° for 30–40 minutes. Serve with toasted bread cubes or crackers.

Editor's Extra: Seasoning blend is a package of frozen chopped onions, celery, bell pepper, and parsley. Ask for it if you don't find it—saves a lot of prep time.

Good-To-The-Last-Drop Cheeseburger Dip

¾ pound ground beef
1 (1-pound) box Velveeta cheese, cubed
1 cup shredded mozzarella cheese
1 (14-ounce) can diced tomatoes with green pepper, celery, and onion, undrained
2 tablespoons dill pickle relish
1 tablespoon mustard

Brown beef in large skillet; drain. Add cheeses; heat on medium, stirring till smooth. Add remaining ingredients. Serve warm in chafing dish or crockpot with your favorite scoops. Makes about 3 cups.

It's Party Time!

Pigs in a Cheese Trough

An ideal and delicious way to use left-over ham.

2 eggs
1 tablespoon milk
1⅓ cups dry bread crumbs
½ cup grated Parmesan cheese
1 tablespoon dried parsley flakes
**1½ pounds boneless cooked ham, cut into ¾-inch
  cubes**
Oil for frying

Whisk eggs and milk in a shallow bowl. In another bowl, mix bread crumbs, Parmesan, and parsley. Dip ham cubes in egg mixture, then roll in crumb mixture. In a large skillet, heat ¼ inch of oil to 375°. Fry ham cubes, a few at a time, about 2 minutes on each side or till golden brown. Drain on paper towels.

CHEESE SAUCE:
5 ounces Velveeta cheese, cubed
¼ cup milk
½ cup salsa

Heat cheese and milk over medium heat until cheese is melted. Remove from heat; stir in salsa. Serve with ham cubes. Serves 8–12.

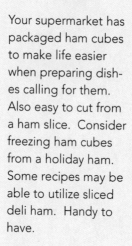

Your supermarket has packaged ham cubes to make life easier when preparing dishes calling for them. Also easy to cut from a ham slice. Consider freezing ham cubes from a holiday ham. Some recipes may be able to utilize sliced deli ham. Handy to have.

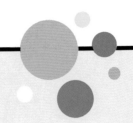

Pizzazzy Fondue

Do something exciting at a fondue party besides cheese and chocolate sauces. Yum!

½ pound hot ground sausage
¾ cup chopped onion
2 (26-ounce) jars spaghetti sauce
1 (3-ounce) package sliced pepperoni, finely chopped
1 pound mozzarella cheese, cut into ¾-inch cubes
1 loaf Italian or French bread, cut into 1-inch cubes

Brown sausage and onion in skillet over medium-high heat until sausage is no longer pink, stirring to break up meat. Drain fat. Put in crockpot. Stir in pasta sauce and pepperoni. Cover; cook on LOW 3–4 hours. Serve with cheese and bread cubes. Serves 16–24.

It's Party Time!

Cheese, Please

Balls

Squares

Cubes

Crisps

Nachos

Quesadillas

Cheese Spreads

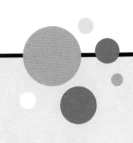

Deep-Fried Cheese 'n Pepperoni Balls

1 (16-ounce) package hot roll mix
¼ pound mozzarella cheese, cubed
¼–½ pound pepperoni, thinly sliced

Prepare roll mix by package directions, omitting egg and using 1 cup water (no need for dough to rise). Place 1 cheese cube on 1 pepperoni slice. Shape pieces of dough carefully around cheese and pepperoni, forming balls. Fry in deep hot oil 5 minutes or till brown, turning once. Makes about 32.

Amigo Cheese Squares

Simple prep . . . simply great taste.

2 pounds shredded Monterey Jack cheese
2 (4-ounce) cans chopped green chiles
1 (12-ounce) can evaporated milk
2 eggs
1 cup all-purpose flour

Spread cheese in greased 9x13-inch pan. Sprinkle chopped chiles on top. In blender, mix milk, eggs, and flour; pour over cheese. Bake at 350° for 30–40 minutes. Cool slightly before cutting. Makes 36–40.

It's Party Time!

Cheese 'n Chile Cubes

1 pound grated Cheddar cheese, divided
1 (4-ounce) can chopped green chiles
6 eggs
Paprika to taste

Spread half the cheese in a greased 8-inch square baking dish. Drain chiles, reserving liquid. Sprinkle green chiles over cheese; add remaining cheese. Beat eggs with reserved liquid; pour over cheese; sprinkle with paprika. Bake in preheated 350° oven for 35–40 minutes. Cut in small squares. Serve with toothpicks. Okay to freeze and reheat. Makes 25.

Cheesy Chile Bites

Can be served hot or cold.

4 eggs, beaten
1 (4-ounce) jar sliced pimentos, drained
1 (4-ounce) jar chopped green chiles
2 cups shredded sharp Cheddar cheese
¼ teaspoon red pepper (optional)

Combine all ingredients and mix well by hand. Pour into greased 8-inch square baking dish. Bake 20 minutes at 400°, or until set. Cool slightly before cutting into bite-size squares. Serves 8.

Be creative with cheeses, as so many recipes call for Cheddar. In just one supermarket, we found the following selection of shredded cheeses: Mild Cheddar, Sharp Cheddar, Colby-Jack, Nacho & Taco, Taco, Fancy Swiss, Fancy Mozzarella, Pizza Double Cheese, Mozzarella & Provolone, Cheddar Jack, Monterey Jack, 4-Cheese Italian, and 4-Cheese Mexican. And as soon as somebody can think of another combination, there'll be more.

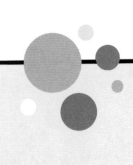

Avocado Cheese Crisps

1 cup finely shredded Cheddar Jack cheese with
  jalapeño peppers
1 ripe avocado, pitted, peeled, chopped
1 tablespoon lime juice
1 garlic clove, finely chopped
¼ cup sour cream
¼ cup chunky salsa

Heat oven to 400°. Line a baking pan with parchment paper. Spoon 2 teaspoons cheese per crisp onto paper; pat into 2-inch circles. Bake 6–8 minutes or until edges are light golden brown. Remove to wire rack. Cool 5 minutes.

Mix avocado, lime juice, and garlic; mash avocado and mix with ingredients. Spoon ½ tablespoon avocado mixture on each cheese crisp; top with ½ teaspoon each sour cream and salsa. Makes 16.

One-Ingredient Crispies

You must use freshly grated Parmesan. So easy and good. These keep well for several days.

1½ cups freshly grated Parmesan cheese

Preheat oven to 400°. Spoon little mounds of cheese spaced well apart on 2 parchment-lined baking sheets; flatten with back of a spoon. Bake 5 minutes, until golden. Leave on baking sheets for a minute to firm up. Remove slowly from paper; curl crispies over a rolling pin until set. Cool on a wire rack. Makes about 12.

It's Party Time!

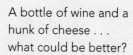

Cheesy Party Pastries

Okay, it's not really fast. . . .but undeniably fabulous!

1 sheet puff pastry
6 ounces crumbled blue cheese
½ (8-ounce) package cream cheese, softened
¼ cup heavy cream
1 teaspoon lemon juice
¼ cup chopped pecans
Chopped fresh parsley
1 firm apple, cored, cut into 18 slices, soaked in
**   pineapple or lemon juice**

Thaw pastry sheet for 20–30 minutes. Preheat oven to 400°. Unfold pastry on lightly floured surface. Cut along fold marks into 3 strips. Cut each strip into 6 rectangles. Place 2 inches apart on baking sheet. Bake 15 minutes or until golden. Cool on wire rack.

Beat blue cheese, cream cheese, cream, and lemon juice until smooth. Split pastries into 2 layers. With 1 tablespoon cheese mixture spread each of half the pastries. Top with remaining halves and spread with remaining cheese mixture. Sprinkle with pecans and parsley. Top each pastry with 1 apple slice. Refrigerate until ready to serve. Makes 18.

Ring Around the Berries

Easy to make ahead . . . serves a large crowd.

4 green onions, finely chopped
Salt and red pepper to taste
3 cups grated Cheddar cheese
¾ cup mayonnaise
1 cup finely chopped nuts
1 cup strawberry preserves

Combine all, except preserves. Form into bowl shape and place on serving dish. Fill with preserves. Serve with club crackers. Serves 18–20.

A bottle of wine and a hunk of cheese . . . what could be better?

A cheese board is easy, yet elegant. It requires only unwrapping the cheese. Put an assortment of your favorites on a pretty platter or board along with appropriate crackers or bread. Add grapes or sliced apples or pears . . . nuts make a nice accompaniment as well.

Separate cheeses so they don't touch. Serve at room temperature. Have a knife for each cheese —wide blade for soft, sharp knife for hard.

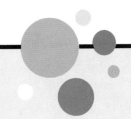

Crescent-Wrapped Pepper Jelly Brie

1 (8-ounce) can crescent rolls
1 (8-ounce) round Brie cheese, about 4 inches in diameter
2 tablespoons hot pepper jelly
2 tablespoons chopped fresh cilantro
1 egg, beaten
1½ cups seedless red or green grapes
1 kiwi, unpeeled, sliced
¾ cup fresh strawberry halves
1 orange, cut into wedges

Unroll crescents onto baking pan, and press firmly to seal perforations. Cut cheese horizontally into 2 equal layers. Place bottom half of cheese on center of crescent rectangle; spread jelly over cheese. Sprinkle with cilantro. Top with remaining cheese. Gather dough evenly around cheese and over top; twist to form bow. Brush dough with beaten egg. Bake at 350° for 20–25 minutes. Cool slightly before serving. To serve, arrange fruit around Brie. Serves 12.

Sweet Bacon-y Brie

So easy . . . so yummy . . . .

1 (8-ounce) round Brie
¼ cup chutney
2 tablespoons real bacon bits

Preheat oven to 400°. Place cheese in ungreased oven-proof dish. Top with chutney and bake, uncovered, 10–12 minutes, or till softened. Sprinkle bacon bits on top. Serve with assorted crackers. Serves 8–12.

It's Party Time!

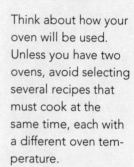

A Sweet Bite of Brie

1 (17¼-ounce) package frozen puff pastry, thawed
¼ cup green or red pepper jelly
1 (5-inch) brie round

Cut puff pastry sheets into 16 squares. Spread ½ teaspoon jelly on each square. Cut brie into 32 chunks, placing a cube on one side of each square; fold over opposite edge, using fork to seal completely. Place 1 inch apart on ungreased cookie sheets. Bake at 400° for 10–13 minutes or until golden brown.

Editor's Extra: Good with plum or apricot preserves, too.

Fried Cheese with Marinara Sauce

½ pound block mozzarella cheese
2 eggs
1½ cups Italian seasoned bread crumbs
Salt and pepper to taste
2 cups vegetable oil
½ cup marinara sauce

Cut cheese into 8–10 blocks. Beat eggs in a shallow bowl. Mix bread crumbs with salt and pepper in another bowl. Dip cheese blocks into eggs and then into bread crumbs, coating all sides. Repeat to add a second layer of crumbs and place on wax paper.

Heat oil in medium-size saucepan over high heat to 375°. Fry cheese for 1–2 minutes, until golden brown on all sides. Heat marinara sauce and serve with cheese cubes for dipping. Serves 8.

Think about how your oven will be used. Unless you have two ovens, avoid selecting several recipes that must cook at the same time, each with a different oven temperature.

Utilize electrical appliances such as a toaster oven, skillet, grill, roaster, or crockpot. There's more than one way to cook just about anything.

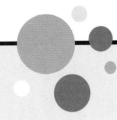

It's a Snowman Cheese Ball

2 cups shredded 4-cheese blend
1 (8-ounce) package cream cheese, softened
¼ cup finely chopped fresh chives or green onions
1 (2-ounce) package slivered almonds, toasted
⅛ teaspoon ground red pepper, or to taste
¼ cup grated Parmesan cheese
Peppercorns
1 baby carrot

Mix cheese, cream cheese, chives, almonds, and red pepper well. Cover and refrigerate 1 hour. Divide mixture into 3 balls—small, medium, and large. Roll in Parmesan cheese. Arrange on serving dish small to large, like a snowman lying down. Decorate with peppercorns for eyes, mouth, and buttons, and carrot for nose. A green onion skin strip around his neck makes a scarf. Surround with crackers or cut-up fresh vegetables. Serves 16–20.

A cheese snowman can also have raisin eyes, sliced black olive buttons (a sliver for a crescent mouth), and two pretzel sticks for arms. Cute to give him a vanilla wafer-marshmallow hat that sticks together with some of the cheese mixture. Your snowman may not melt, but he'll disappear as he is spread on surrounding crackers.

It's Party Time!

Mini Cheese Balls

What a great idea! No more breaking your cracker trying to spread some cheese on it.

2 (8-ounce) packages cream cheese, softened
⅓ cup minced green onions
1 (2½-ounce) package thinly sliced deli ham, finely chopped
2 tablespoons Worcestershire
1 cup finely chopped pecans

Mix cream cheese, green onions, ham, and Worcestershire. Shape into walnut-size balls. Roll in chopped nuts. Refrigerate until serving. Serve on crackers or toothpicked vegetables. Makes about 36.

Beefy Cheese Ball

Make a day or two ahead to allow the onions to season the cream cheese.

1 (4-ounce) jar dried beef, chopped finely
10 green onions, minced
3 (8-ounce) packages cream cheese, softened
Paprika for garnish

Mix all but paprika in bowl. Shape into a ball and sprinkle with paprika. Serve in center of dish surrounded by crackers. Serves 20–30.

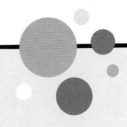

It is easy to round a cheese ball if you do it with plastic wrap. Just pile the cheese mixture onto the wrap, pull up the sides, and begin shaping.

Olive-Cheese Balls

½ (9-ounce) jar pimento stuffed olives
3 tablespoons butter, softened
½ cup all-purpose flour
Salt and pepper to taste
¼ teaspoon Cavender's Greek Seasoning
½ teaspoon mustard
3 tablespoons water, more if needed
Few drops Tabasco
Sprinkle of paprika

Drain olives; set aside. Mix remaining ingredients until mixture can be handled. Add more water if needed. Make a small disk in your hand of dough (about 1 fat teaspoon); place olive in center and press dough around olive. Repeat till all olives are covered. Place olives on cookie sheet and bake at 450° for 15–20 minutes. May be frozen and baked at a later time. Serve hot. Makes about 25.

Sweet Cha Cha Cheese Ball

1½ (8-ounce) packages cream cheese, softened
¼ cup butter, softened
1 teaspoon vanilla extract
¾ cup confectioners' sugar
2 tablespoons brown sugar
1 cup chocolate chips
½ cup finely chopped pecans

Beat cream cheese, butter, and vanilla until fluffy. Gradually beat in sugars; stir in chocolate chips. Cover and refrigerate 2 hours. Shape into a ball; refrigerate another hour. Just before serving, roll in pecans. Serve with gingersnaps or graham crackers. Serves 10–16.

It's Party time!

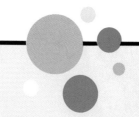

Almond Chip Cheese Ball

A welcome sweet taste among the savory.

3 (8-ounce) packages cream cheese, softened
1 teaspoons almond flavoring
1 cup powdered sugar
1 (12-ounce) bag mini-chocolate chips
½–1 cup toasted sliced almonds

Mix all together except almonds. Form into a large cheese ball or 2 small ones. Roll in almonds. Refrigerate overnight. Serve with ginger snaps and/or vanilla wafers. Serves 20–30.

Editor's Extra: Toast almonds in skillet briefly while stirring. Or toast 2–3 minutes in toaster oven.

Nutty Olive Cheese Ball

½ stick butter, softened
1 (8-ounce) package cream cheese, softened
1 (8-ounce) package blue cheese, crumbled
1 (8-ounce) can chopped ripe olives
2 tablespoons snipped fresh chives
⅓ cup coarsely chopped pecans or almonds,
**   toasted**

Beat butter cream cheese, and blue cheese with electric mixer on low speed until smooth. Stir in olives and chives. Cover and chill.

When firm, shape cheese mixture into a ball; cover and chill until ready to serve. Roll in toasted nuts. Serve with crackers, celery sticks, or apple slices. Serves 20–30.

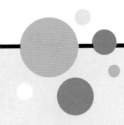

Music can be an important element of your party. But unless you're playing with a karaoke machine or having a dance, background music should be appropriate, and not so loud your guests cannot carry on a conversation. The younger crowd often equates loud with more fun, so you may have to try to police the volume lest the neighbors invite the police to do so.

Smoky Bar Cheese

2 pounds grated Cheddar cheese (½ sharp)
2 garlic cloves, minced
3 tablespoons Worcestershire
½ teaspoon salt
2 teaspoons dry mustard
⅛ teaspoon cayenne pepper
1 teaspoon liquid smoke
1 cup warm beer

Stir cheeses and garlic in mixing bowl. With a wooden spoon, mix in remaining ingredients except beer. Slowly add enough beer blending to make a smooth paste. Store, covered, in crock(s) in refrigerator. Serve at room temperature. Makes about 6 cups.

Jack Cheese Tortilla Wedges

(8-inch) flour tortillas
¼ teaspoon sea salt
1 cup grated Monterey Jack cheese
⅔ cup grated Cheddar cheese
½ cup chopped, canned green chiles, drained
⅔ cup chopped onion

Heat ¼-inch oil in a large skillet. Fry tortillas till golden on each side, 30–60 seconds. Poke bubbles with a fork to keep tortillas flat. Drain, then sprinkle with salt. Place 2 tortillas on a baking pan. Sprinkle each with ½ the cheese, ½ the chiles, and ½ the onion, covering the surface completely. Top with remaining tortillas, pressing down lightly. Bake at 375° about 8 minutes, till cheese is melted. Remove from oven, and cut into wedges. Serve hot. Makes 12–14 wedges.

Quick Mozzarella Tortillas

Roasted red bell peppers are a tasty surprise.

1 teaspoon olive oil
2 (10-inch) soft flour tortillas
5 ounces mozzarella cheese, thinly sliced
2 tablespoons chopped roasted red bell peppers
Salsa

Brush a 12-inch, nonstick frying pan with olive oil and heat on medium 1 minute. Lay 1 tortilla in pan and place cheese slices cut to fit on top. Scatter roasted peppers on cheese; cover with other tortilla. Cook 1–2 minutes until golden underneath, then carefully flip it and cook another 1–2 minutes, until crisp and golden on second side. Slide onto cutting board, and slice into 12 wedges. Serve with salsa.

Pepperoni Tortillas on the Grill

Good for a quick lunch or after-school snack.

4 (8-inch) flour tortillas
2 teaspoons olive oil
1½ cups shredded pizza cheese, divided
24 (1-inch) slices pepperoni
1 (6-ounce) can sliced black olives, drained
⅔ cup diced tomato, well drained

Heat grill. Place tortillas on baking pans; brush with oil; sprinkle with 1 cup cheese over all. Top with divided pepperoni, olives, and tomato, and remaining cheese.

With broad spatula, slide pizzas onto grill over medium heat. Cook covered 3–6 minutes till cheese is melted and crust is crisp. Slide pizzas back onto baking sheets to cut and serve. Serves 6–8.

Editor's Extra: These can be baked in 425° oven about 7–9 minutes till edges are crispy.

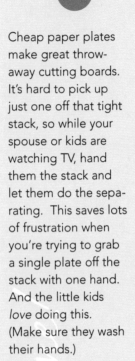

Cheap paper plates make great throwaway cutting boards. It's hard to pick up just one off that tight stack, so while your spouse or kids are watching TV, hand them the stack and let them do the separating. This saves lots of frustration when you're trying to grab a single plate off the stack with one hand. And the little kids *love* doing this. (Make sure they wash their hands.)

Super Nachos

1 (8-ounce) bag Fritos, divided
1 (8-ounce) package shredded nacho and taco
cheese, divided
1 (15-ounce) can chili
⅓ cup guacamole
⅓ cup sour cream
1 (7-ounce) can jalapeños, drained, minced
2 green onions, thinly sliced
Salsa

Spread half the Fritos in a 9x13-inch dish and sprinkle with half the cheese; top with remaining Fritos and cheese. Bake at 450° for 12 minutes or till cheese is melted.

Heat chili over medium heat. Spoon pockets of chili here and there over mound of hot baked Fritos. Dot guacamole and sour cream over chips, scatter jalapeños and green onions over all, and serve with salsa on the side. Serves 8–10.

Game-Time Nachos

1 (1-pound) block Mexican Velveeta cheese, cubed
½ cup shredded sharp Cheddar cheese
⅓ cup milk
1 tablespoon taco seasoning mix
1 (7-ounce) bag bite-size tortilla chips (about 75
chips)
2 cups finely chopped plum tomatoes
1 (3-ounce) package real bacon bits

In small saucepan, combine Velveeta, Cheddar, milk, and taco seasoning mix. Cook over medium-low heat until cheeses are smooth, stirring frequently.

Arrange chips on 1 or 2 large serving plates. Pour warm cheese mixture over chips. Top with tomatoes and bacon. Serve immediately. Serves 8.

Editor's Extra: Nice to sprinkle a little chopped cilantro or parsley on top.

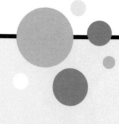

Cheesy Hot Quesadillas

6 (6-inch) white corn tortillas
¾ cup shredded Monterey Jack cheese
1 fresh jalapeño chile pepper, seeded, chopped
1 firm tomato, chopped
2 tablespoons snipped fresh cilantro
Sour cream

Brush one side of tortillas with oil. Divide cheese, then jalapeño, tomato, and cilantro evenly over other side of 3 tortillas. Cover with remaining tortillas, oiled sides up. Cook quesadillas in heavy skillet or griddle over medium heat, one at a time, for 2–4 minutes or until cheese is melted and tortillas are lightly browned, turning once. Cut quesadillas into quarters. Serve with sour cream. Makes 6 servings.

Cheesy Chili con Queso Cups

Good warm or at room temperature.

4 eggs
½ cup chunky salsa
¼ cup all-purpose flour
2 teaspoons chili powder
1⅔ cups shredded Cheddar cheese
1 green onion, chopped

Preheat oven to 400°. Grease 24 (3-inch) muffin pan cups. Mix all ingredients in bowl. Spoon about 1 tablespoon cheese mixture into each cup. Bake about 10 minutes until golden brown. Serve with sour cream and additional salsa, if desired.

To keep warm dishes warm on the serving table, fill a small cloth bag halfway with raw rice. Microwave for 2–3 minutes till hot to touch. Place on serving platter and cover with napkin. Nestle dish into warm "nest."

Let's Celebrate!

Savory Pepper Jelly Cheesecake

This recipe deserves a blue ribbon. Get ready . . . your guests are going to want the recipe!

1 cup crushed Ritz Crackers or crushed pretzels
1 stick butter, melted
2 (8-ounce) packages cream cheese, softened
1¼ cups sour cream
2 eggs
2 cups shredded Cheddar cheese
1 tablespoon minced garlic
½ cup chopped green onions
1 teaspoon white pepper
2 teaspoons Worcestershire
1 jar green pepper jelly
1 jar red pepper jelly
1 cup toasted pecan chips

Combine crackers with melted butter; press into bottom of springform pan. Combine cream cheese, sour cream, and eggs in a bowl until smooth. Stir in cheese, garlic, onions, pepper, and Worcestershire. Pour over crust. Bake at 350° for 30 minutes or until cheesecake is set and firm in the middle. Allow to cool on wire rack. Refrigerate until serving time.

When ready to serve, remove from springform pan and transfer to serving platter. Make an outer ring of green pepper jelly and fill center with red pepper jelly. Top green jelly outer ring with toasted pecans. Cut into wedges. Serve with Ritz Crackers.

It's Party Time!

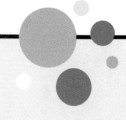

5-Minute Boursin Cheese

You'll be proud to serve this inexpensive cheese that has expensive taste.

1 (8-ounce) package cream cheese, softened
1 teaspoon minced onion
1 teaspoon minced garlic
1 teaspoon basil
1 teaspoon caraway seed
1 teaspoon dill weed
Coarse black pepper

Mix cream cheese with onion, garlic, basil, caraway, and dill weed. Shape into a round, flat shape. Put on serving plate and cover top and sides with coarse black pepper. Good right away or several days later. Surround with crackers and serve with a festive spreading knife. Serves 8–10.

Good, Good Gouda Spread

1 (7-ounce) Gouda cheese with red wax coating
1 (3-ounce) package cream cheese, softened
¼ cup powdered sugar
2 teaspoons lemon juice
¼ teaspoon curry powder

Hollow out Gouda with sharp knife, leaving wax coating intact to form shell. Process Gouda cheese, cream cheese, sugar, lemon juice, and curry powder in food processor until smooth. Mound cheese mixture into shell. Cover; refrigerate 3 hours or overnight.

Place cheese on serving tray 1 hour before serving; surround with fresh fruit wedges or assorted crackers. Serves 6–8.

Interesting . . .

There is an old superstition that a thief would not be able to steal anything that had a caraway seed in it, nor would the thief be able to leave the house!

Also thought to keep lovers and pigeons from straying, caraway seed was used as an ingredient in love potions, and to tame pigeons.

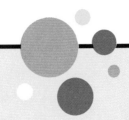

A Pine Cone Made of Cheese

It's a delicious show piece.

2 cups shredded 4-cheese blend
1 (8-ounce) package cream cheese, softened
2 tablespoons spicy mustard
½ (4-ounce) can diced green chiles, drained
¼ cup sliced almonds, toasted

Place cheeses and mustard in food processor; blend well. Stir in chiles; place on wax paper and shape into oval. Insert almonds in rows all over to look like a pine cone. Cover and refrigerate 2 hours or more. Let return to room temperature before serving on dish surrounded by crackers. Serves 8 or more.

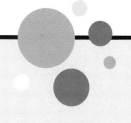

Zesty Beefy Cheese Log

2 cups shredded sharp Cheddar cheese, room temperature
1 (8-ounce) tub cream cheese with chives, room temperature
¼ cup dry white wine or apple juice
1 teaspoon prepared horseradish
½ cup finely chopped dried beef

Mix Cheddar, cream cheese, wine, and horseradish in mixer. Cover and chill 2 hours. Shape into log. Roll log in chopped beef. Wrap in plastic wrap; refrigerate. Serve with any crackers. Serves 10 or more.

Jalapeño Cheese in a Jar

It's spicy, creamy, and always ready to serve.

2 pounds Velveeta cheese
1 medium onion, grated or processed
1 (5-ounce) can evaporated milk
2 cups Miracle Whip
1 (4-ounce) can chopped jalapeño peppers, drained

Microwave cut-up cheese in 8-cup measure 5 minutes on HIGH, stirring halfway through cooking. Add onion, milk, Miracle Whip, and peppers; stir till smooth. Jar, cool, cap and refrigerate. Makes 6–7 (½-pint) jars.

Editor's Extra: Want some cheese grits? Just put a spoonful of this cheese on a serving of plain grits and turn it into a "wow." Outstanding on baked potatoes, too.

If you make a dish to take to the party ahead of time and put it in the frig, you surely don't want to get to the party and realize your dish is still in the frig! Here's a sure-fire way to remember it: Put your car keys in the refrigerator on top of the dish. Can't leave home without it!

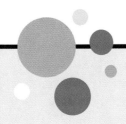

The best hostess gift? Pay for cleanup! Maybe go in with other guests to hire someone for the duration or just after the party . . . or the next day.

Second best: Stay and help cleanup yourself (and that might be first best).

Pineapple Almond Cheddar Spread

Sound delicious? It is!

½ (8-ounce) package cream cheese, softened
⅓ cup mayonnaise
2 teaspoons soy sauce
2 cups shredded Cheddar cheese
1 (8-ounce) can crushed pineapple, drained
½ cup chopped toasted almonds
¼ cup finely chopped green pepper
2 tablespoons finely chopped green onion

Mix cream cheese, mayonnaise, and soy sauce until smooth. Beat in remaining ingredients. Good with celery or crackers. Makes about 4 cups.

It's Party Time!

Garden Goodies

Raw Veggies

Platters

Stuffed Veggies

Salads

Fruit

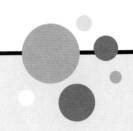

Zucchini Stix Dippers

These are quite good! Better double the recipe.

¼ cup buttery cracker crumbs
2 tablespoons grated Parmesan cheese
1 egg white
1 teaspoon milk
2 small zucchini, cut lengthwise into quarters
Chili sauce, spaghetti sauce, or salsa

Combine cracker crumbs and Parmesan cheese in a shallow dish. Whisk egg white and milk in another shallow dish. Dip zucchini wedges first into crumb mixture, then into egg white mixture, letting excess drip back into dish. Roll again in cracker crumb mixture to coat. Place zucchini sticks on Pam-sprayed baking sheet. Bake at 400° for 15–18 minutes or till golden brown. Serve with sauce of choice. Serves 8–10.

Spicy Grilled Corn Cobbies

½ cup tomato paste
2 tablespoons pancake syrup
Salt and red pepper to taste
¼ cup soy sauce
1 teaspoon chopped garlic
2 tablespoons balsamic vinegar
3 tablespoons olive oil
8 ears shucked corn, halved

Preheat grill to medium-high. Whisk all but corn in mixing bowl. Brush marinade over ears and place on grill. Grill all sides, turning until cooked, about 3 minutes per 3 sides. Remove to serving plate and brush with extra sauce. Serves 8.

It's Party Time!

Cocktail Garden Platter

Crudités fit for a queen. This is a hit with everybody!

½ pound fresh whole green beans
1½ cups fresh baby carrots
¾ cup fresh cauliflower florets
¾ cup fresh broccoli florets
½ cup honey mustard salad dressing
¼ teaspoon dried dill weed
1 cup fresh small whole mushrooms
1 red bell pepper, cut lengthwise into thin strips
Lettuce leaves

In large saucepan, boil green beans in plenty of water; cook 3 minutes. Add carrots, cauliflower, and broccoli. Return to a boil for 2–3 minutes until blanched. Drain; rinse with cold water to cool.

In large bowl, combine salad dressing and dill; add blanched vegetables, mushrooms, and bell pepper. Toss to coat. Cover; refrigerate.

Line platter with lettuce leaves. Arrange vegetables over lettuce. Serve with cocktail forks. Serves 8.

Crudité (kru-di-tay) is a fancy word for the raw or lightly cooked vegetables that are usually served on platters and accompanied by a dip.

Let's Celebrate!

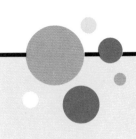

Better-With-Butter Veggie Platter

1 bunch broccoli, cut into florets
1 head cauliflower, broken into florets
2 zucchini, cut into ¼-inch slices
1 stick butter
¾ teaspoon parsley flakes
¾ teaspoon thyme
½ teaspoon onion salt
2 tomatoes, cut into wedges
⅓–½ cup grated Parmesan cheese

Cook broccoli, cauliflower, and zucchini until tender-crisp; drain. Melt butter with parsley, thyme, and onion salt. Arrange vegetables in microwave-safe platter or serving bowl and drizzle butter mixture over top. Sprinkle with Parmesan. Microwave, uncovered, on HIGH until heated through, 1–2 minutes. Serves 8.

Popeye Popovers

A tasty way to pop in veggies.

1 (8-ounce) jar artichoke hearts, drained, chopped
1 (10-ounce) box frozen chopped spinach, thawed, drained
½ cup ricotta cheese
1 egg, beaten
1 garlic clove, minced
¼ cup minced red onion
¼ cup shredded mozzarella cheese
½ teaspoon Cavendar's Greek Seasoning

Combine all ingredients; mix well. Spray mini-muffin cups with nonstick cooking spray; fill with popover batter. Bake in 350° oven 25–30 minutes. Makes 36 mini popovers.

It's Party Time!

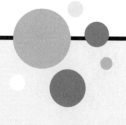

Perfected Baked Beans

Fifteen minutes prep, then let these flavors "marry" in the oven.

3 slices bacon, cooked, crumbled
2 (15-ounce) cans baked beans
1 small onion, chopped
½ cup ketchup
¼ cup dark brown sugar
1 tablespoon mustard
Salt and pepper to taste

Combine all ingredients and bake in greased casserole in 350° oven 1 hour. Serves 6.

Bundles of Sweet Beans

Not just for a sit-down occasion, these are pretty, and add elegance to your heavy hors d'oeuvres buffet.

1 cup firmly packed brown sugar
1 stick butter
1 tablespoon Worcestershire
2 teaspoons garlic powder
3 (15-ounce) can whole green beans, drained
½ pound sliced bacon, halved

Melt sugar, butter, Worcestershire, and garlic powder in small saucepan over medium-high heat; set aside. Bundle 6 beans together with ½ strip of bacon; secure bacon with a toothpick; place on a baking sheet. Spoon butter mixture over bundles. Cover baking sheet and allow to marinate overnight in refrigerator. Uncover bean bundles and bake 40 minutes at 350°. Serves 10–16.

Editor's Extra: Consider bundling fewer beans in ½ strips of bacon. Or cut the beans in half for a smaller bundle, then tie with small strips of bacon cut both ways.

Can't get all the wrinkles out of your tablecloth? Let gravity "iron" it. Put it on your table over a pad, then lightly spray with water the night before your party. Next morning, it is magically smooth!

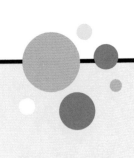

Peppered Peppers

Use any color peppers you like. These are good!

1 green bell pepper
1 red bell pepper
1 cup shredded Monterey Jack cheese
3 tablespoons chopped ripe olives
¼ teaspoon crushed red pepper flakes

Cut peppers into strips. Place skin side down on ungreased cookie sheets; sprinkle with cheese, olives, and pepper flakes. Broil 3–4 inches from heat for 5–7 minutes or until cheese is melted. Serves 6–10.

Terrific Tomato Tarts

Fresh basil and Parmesan are best, but dried work almost as well.

1 (15-ounce) package refrigerated pie crusts
2 teaspoons canola oil
1½ cups grated Cheddar or Swiss cheese
4 tomatoes, sliced
Salt and pepper
2 tablespoons basil
Grated Parmesan cheese

Cut pastries with 2½-inch biscuit cutter and place rounds on Pam-sprayed baking sheets; prick with fork. Brush rounds lightly with oil; top rounds with cheese. Place a slice of tomato on cheese. Sprinkle with salt, pepper, basil, and Parmesan. Bake at 400° about 15–17 minutes. Makes about 30.

It's Party Time!

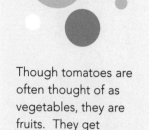

'Maters in Shells

Simply smashing!

⅔ cup chopped tomatoes
⅓ cup mayonnaise
¼ cup shredded mozzarella cheese
¼ cup shredded Parmesan cheese
1 tablespoon prepared pesto
Dash of red pepper
1 (12-count) package frozen miniature phyllo tart
   shells

Lightly mix tomatoes, mayonnaise, cheeses, pesto, and pepper. Divide into tart shells and place on ungreased baking sheet. Bake at 350° for 8–12 minutes or until lightly browned. Yields 12 appetizers.

Though tomatoes are often thought of as vegetables, they are fruits. They get "mealy" in the frig, so leave 'em out.

Classic Party Potatoes

An old favorite that is always popular.

1 (2-pound) package frozen hash browns
1 (10¾-ounce) can cream of celery soup
8 ounces shredded 4-cheese blend
¾ cup chopped onion
1 (8-ounce) carton sour cream
1 stick butter, melted
1 sleeve Ritz or other crackers, crushed

Blend all together but butter and crackers. Pour into a 9x13-inch dish. Pour melted margarine over and distribute crushed crackers evenly over top. Bake at 350°, uncovered, for one hour. Serves 10–12.

Let's Celebrate!

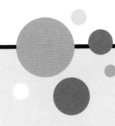

Party Timesavers:

- Decorate and set the table the night before.

- Prepare as many dishes ahead as possible to freeze or refrigerate.

- Preslice, chop, and refrigerate ingredients for party-day dishes.

- Make and bag extra ice cubes. (You'll need about a pound for every 5 guests.)

Potato Salad Boats

A delicious conversation piece.

10 small red potatoes
¼ cup chopped pimento-stuffed olives
2 teaspoons minced fresh parsley
1 teaspoon finely chopped onion
½ cup mayonnaise
1¾ teaspoons Dijon mustard
¼ teaspoon salt
⅛ teaspoon pepper
Paprika

Cook potatoes in water to cover 12–15 minutes till tender. Drain; place potatoes in ice water; drain and pat dry. Peel 2 potatoes; finely dice and place in a small bowl. Cut remaining potatoes in half. With a melon baller, scoop out pulp, leaving a ⅜-inch shell; set shells aside. Add pulp to bowl. Stir in olives, parsley, onion, mayonnaise, mustard, and pepper; stir to combine. Stuff potato shells with potato salad. Sprinkle with paprika. Chill for an hour before serving. Makes 20.

Potluck Potato Salad

No picnic should be without one!

6 medium potatoes, peeled, cubed
1 cup chopped celery
⅔ cup finely chopped green onions
¼ cup sweet pickle relish
¾ teaspoon salt
1⅓ cups mayonnaise
4 hard-boiled eggs, chopped

Cook potatoes in boiling water to cover until tender; drain. Cool slightly, then combine with celery, green onions, pickle relish, and salt. Fold in mayonnaise and eggs. Chill before serving. Serves 12.

French Fried Onion Potato Bites

2 cups left-over mashed potatoes
1¼ cups shredded pizza cheese
1 egg, beaten
½ onion, finely chopped
¾ teaspoon Cavender's Greek Seasoning
2 tablespoons bacon bits (optional)
1 (2.8-ounce) can French fried onions

Combine potatoes, cheese, egg, onion, seasoning, and bacon bits, if desired. Roll into balls and flatten into cakes. Turn over into crushed onion rings, then place on greased baking pan. Bake about 20 minutes at 375°. If you like them toasty brown, turn over and bake an additional 5 minutes. Makes about 24–30.

Editor's Extra: Okay to use instant potatoes. Also okay to freeze and bake from frozen. And really okay to try different varieties of crushed chips and crackers for coating.

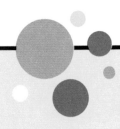

It's Party Time!

Though flowers are the first thought for a centerpiece, think of around-your-house alternatives. My daughter makes frozen sculptures with autumn leaves or holly leaves, berries, and nuts by freezing them in water in a half-gallon milk carton or round ice cream carton, then unmolding onto a tray with ample lip for melting. Candles spaced on either side make a unique fire-and-ice conversation piece that continues to re-sculpture itself as it very slowly melts. The cost? Nothing.

—Gwen

Caviar Party Potatoes

For discriminating tastes . . . .

60 new potatoes, unpeeled, boiled until tender
Oil for deep frying
1 (8-ounce) carton sour cream
1 (2-ounce) jar caviar, rinsed, drained

Slice off bottom of each potato and hollow out a "bowl" in other end with a melon baller or small spoon. (Use centers of potatoes for something else.) Heat oil in deep fryer to 375°. Carefully drop potato "bowls" into hot oil and fry until crisp; drain on paper towels. Fill warm potatoes with sour cream, then top with a little caviar. Serve immediately. Makes 60 potatoes.

Editor's Extra: Sub diced, cooked, seasoned shrimp for caviar if you like, but you'll have to call it something else.

Cajun-Style Packet Potatoes

2 pounds small new potatoes
¼ cup butter or margarine, melted
2 garlic cloves, minced
2 teaspoons Cajun seasoning

Place scrubbed potatoes in center of large piece of heavy-duty foil. Mix butter, garlic, and seasoning, and pour over potatoes. Seal foil packet, allowing room for expansion. Place potatoes on grill over medium heat. Cook 35–45 minutes or until potatoes are tender, turning foil packet several times during cooking. Serves 8.

Savory Stuffed 'Shrooms

Scrumptious!

½ pound spicy bulk sausage
30 large mushrooms
½ cup chopped green onions
3 garlic cloves, minced
1 stick butter
1 cup Italian bread crumbs
1 cup shredded Pepper Jack cheese, divided

Brown sausage; drain. Remove stems from mushrooms and chop finely; leave caps whole. Sauté stems, onions, and garlic in butter. Add sausage, bread crumbs, and ½ cup cheese. Spoon mixture evenly into each mushroom cap. Place on a greased baking sheet. Sprinkle with remaining cheese. Bake at 350° for about 25 minutes, or till browned. Serve warm.

Stuffed Portobellos Supreme

2 (5-ounce) portobellos, stems removed
1 garlic clove, minced
2 tablespoons olive oil
1 (6-ounce) can crabmeat, drained, flaked, cartilage
　removed
2 tablespoons mayonnaise
2 roasted sweet red pepper halves
2 slices provolone

Place portobellos on a greased cookie sheet. Combine garlic and oil; brush over portobellos. Broil on top rack about 5 minutes. Mix crabmeat and mayonnaise. Place a red pepper half on each portobello, then top with crab mixture. Broil about 3 minutes, until heated through. Top with provolone, and broil 1–2 more minutes until cheese is melted. Cut in wedges. Serves 6–8.

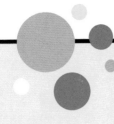

Keep several mixed seasonings—Cajun, seafood, Greek—on your spice shelf for handy one-shaker flavoring. There are quite a few seasonings that are produced locally that are especially fun to pick up when you travel. If you simply love it, chances are you can find it online.

Porto Mushroom Fries

4 cups fresh bread crumbs
1 teaspoon mixed seasoning
12 ounces portobello mushrooms, sliced ½ inch thick
3 large eggs, beaten
4 cups vegetable oil
Salt to taste

Season bread crumbs with seasoning. Dip mushroom slices in beaten eggs, then into bread crumbs, pressing firmly. Deep-fry mushrooms in 350° oil in small batches for 1–2 minutes, or until mushrooms are browned. Drain and sprinkle with salt. Serves 8–10.

Note: Can be made ahead, then reheated in a 350° oven about 10 minutes before serving.

Stuffed MMMMMushrooms

Easy and delicious!

1 (8-ounce) package cream cheese, softened
1 tablespoon minced green onion
¼ cup real bacon bits
¼ teaspoon garlic powder
1 pound whole fresh mushrooms, stems removed

Combine cream cheese, green onion, bacon, and garlic powder until smooth. Fill mushroom caps with cream cheese mixture. Broil on top rack about 5 minutes until heated through. Serve immediately. Serves 8–10.

Mama Mia Mushrooms

Mama Mia Marvelous!

1 pound medium-size mushrooms, cleaned
¼ cup Italian dressing
½ cup Italian sausage, cooked, crumbled
½ cup shredded mozzarella cheese

Break stems off mushrooms. Preheat broiler. Brush mushroom caps with dressing and place on rack of broiler pan; broil 5 minutes. Press ½ teaspoon sausage into mushroom caps; sprinkle each with cheese. Broil 5 more minutes or until cheese is melted. Serve right away. Serves 8–10.

Sweet Tater Won Ton Stars

1 cup diced peeled sweet potato
½ cup diced red bell pepper
4 medium green onions, sliced
3 tablespoon butter, melted, divided
2 teaspoons curry powder
¼ teaspoon salt
1 egg
2 teaspoons all-purpose flour
½ cup vanilla yogurt
24 won ton wrappers

Cook sweet potato, bell pepper, and onions in 1 tablespoon butter 3–5 minutes, stirring occasionally, until sweet potato is tender. Stir in curry powder and salt. Cool slightly. Stir together egg, flour, yogurt, and sweet potato mixture. Brush one side of each won ton with remaining melted butter. Press each won ton, buttered side up, into greased muffin cup. Spoon sweet potato mixture into won tons. Bake at 350° for 12–15 minutes or until golden brown. Makes 24.

Let's Celebrate!

117

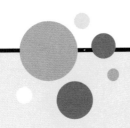

Haystack of Onion Rings

Make ahead . . . ten-minute finish. Yum!

ONION RINGS:

2 large yellow or sweet onions
1 cup pancake mix
1 cup soda water
1 tablespoon chili powder
1 teaspoon Greek seasoning
3 cups vegetable oil

Cut peeled onions into very thin slices; separate into rings. In bowl, combine pancake mix, soda water, chili powder, and seasoning; beat well. In large saucepan or deep fat fryer, heat oil to 375°. Stir onions into batter. With 2 forks, lift onions in small portions and drop into hot oil; fry 1–2 minutes or until crisp and browned. Remove onions with slotted spoon; drain on paper towels. Repeat with remaining onions. Spread fried onions on ungreased cookie sheet; cover; refrigerate.

Before serving, heat oven to 375°; bake 10 minutes or until crisp. Stack onion rings on serving platter; serve with Taco Dip. Serves 8.

TACO DIP:

1½ cups sour cream
1 (1¼-ounce) package taco seasoning mix

Blend sour cream and taco seasoning mix in pint jar or small bowl. Refrigerate, covered, until ready to serve.

It's Party Time!

Cool Garden Pizza Rounds

1 (10-count) can refrigerated flaky biscuits
2 teaspoons cornmeal
1 (8-ounce) container refrigerated spinach dip
½ cup finely chopped red bell pepper
½ cup shredded carrots
3 green onions, thinly sliced

Preheat oven to 400°. Separate each biscuit into 3 layers. Arrange 15 rounds on each of 2 ungreased baking sheets. Sprinkle all with cornmeal. Bake 8–10 minutes until golden brown. Remove and place on wire rack. Cool completely. Spread each round with 1½ teaspoons spinach dip. Sprinkle each evenly with bell pepper, carrots, and onions. Cover and refrigerate at least an hour. Makes 30.

When a recipe becomes a make-again favorite, tape a copy of it to the inside of a cabinet door near your work area. Nobody can see it when the cabinet is closed, but it's really handy when you need it.

Garden Pizza Wedges

½ cup cream cheese with garden vegetables
4 (7-inch) ready-to-serve Italian pizza crusts
2 cups fresh spinach leaves
8 thin slices tomato
1 medium yellow or orange bell pepper, cut into rings
16 thin slices cucumber

Spread cream cheese evenly on tops of 2 pizza crusts and bottoms of 2 of them. Layer spinach, tomato, bell pepper, and cucumber over creamed tops. Top with remaining pizza crusts, cream cheese side down. Cut each into 4 wedges.

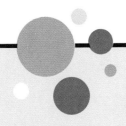

Use cooking spray on graters and processor bowls and blades when grating cheese. Also handy to spray measuring cups before putting sticky items in—they slide right out!

Pesto Pizza Wedges

1 (10-ounce) jar basil pesto
2 (7-inch) ready-to-serve pizza crusts
⅓ cup grated Parmesan cheese

Preheat oven to 450°. Spread pesto over pizza crusts. Sprinkle each with Parmesan cheese. Bake about 8 minutes, until crust is brown and cheese melts. Cut into 8 wedges each and serve hot. Makes 16 wedges.

Veggie Ponies

Use low-fat cheese, dressing, crackers, and cream cheese, if desired. Just as good!

1 small tomato, finely chopped
3 tablespoons sliced green onions
½ cup finely shredded mozzarella cheese
2 tablespoons zesty or creamy Italian dressing
Ritz, Triscuits, or other crackers
1 (8-ounce) package cream cheese, softened

Mix tomato, onions, cheese, and dressing. Spread each cracker with a teaspoon or more of cream cheese; top with a teaspoon of tomato mixture. Makes about 45.

Banana Pepper-Ronies

16 small sweet banana wax peppers
½ cup chive-and-onion cream cheese spread
⅓ cup finely chopped pepperoni

Cut small slice from flat side of each pepper, keeping stem intact; remove seeds; drain on paper towels. Mix cream cheese and pepperoni; spoon into peppers. Wipe any cheese mixture from skin of peppers. Broil until cheese is bubbly. Makes 16.

It's Party Time!

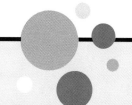

Pepper Canoes

16 fresh jalapeño or banana peppers
1 (8-ounce) package cream cheese, softened
1 (1-ounce) package chili seasoning
16 slices bacon, cut in half

Cut peppers in half lengthwise; hollow out seeds; wash. Mix cream cheese and seasoning together in a bowl. Fill pepper halves with mixture; wrap with bacon slices. Secure with toothpicks. Cook on grill (or broil) till cheese is bubbly.

Mexican Mix-Up

A dip? A salsa? A dressing? A burrito filling? Absolutely.

1 (12-ounce) can whole-kernel corn, drained
1 (15½-ounce) can black beans, drained
⅓ cup Italian salad dressing
1 (16-ounce) jar medium picante sauce

Mix all together and chill. Serve with Baked Tostitos. Yields about 4 cups.

Pepperoni Tomato Pops

18 cherry tomatoes
¼ cup shredded mozzarella cheese
18 slices pepperoni

Cut a thin slice off stem end of tomatoes; save tops. Hollow tomatoes using small melon baller or coffee spoon. Fill tomatoes with cheese; top with slice of pepperoni. Cover with reserved tomato top; secure with toothpick. Place on baking sheet. Broil 6 inches from heat source for about 3 minutes or till cheese is melted. Remove toothpicks before serving. Drain on paper towels. Best served warm.

Let's Celebrate!

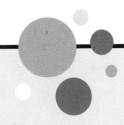

Cutting a corner tip off a zipper bag works well for piping soft fillings onto canapés. It's handy for decorating a plate with a sauce, too, and also for decorating with frosting.

It's Party Time!

Cuke and Cream Canapés
A delicate appetizer that's big on taste.

2 large cucumbers
Salt and pepper to taste
1 (8-ounce) package cream cheese, softened
⅔ cup mayonnaise
1 teaspoon minced garlic
2 teaspoons dried parsley
2 green onions, chopped
Dash of Tabasco
Crackers
½ cup finely minced red bell pepper

Peel and cut cucumbers into slices; salt and pepper to taste. In a food processor or blender, process all remaining ingredients except crackers and red peppers until finely mixed. Spoon a small amount of mixture onto each cracker; add a cucumber slice, then add a dollop of mixture on top. Place on a serving platter, garnish with minced red pepper, and refrigerate until ready to serve. Makes about 36 pieces.

Editor's Extra: This sauce is delicious as a dip with crackers. Or dip the cucumber slices in it!

Delicious Deli Roll-Ups

24 fresh asparagus spears, trimmed
½ cup prepared pesto
24 thin slices Swiss or provolone cheese
24 thin slices deli ham or turkey

Bring ½ inch of water to a boil in a large skillet. Add asparagus; cover and boil 4 minutes. Drain; plunge asparagus immediately in ice water. Drain and pat dry. Spread 1 teaspoon pesto over each slice of cheese; top with an asparagus spear; roll up tightly. Place each on a slice of ham or turkey; roll up tightly. Refrigerate until serving.

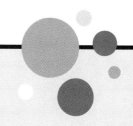

Perky Pea Pods

1 cup ginger dressing
1 pound large shrimp, peeled, cooked deveined
(about 35)
6 ounces fresh snow pea pods (30–35)

Pour dressing evenly over shrimp in medium bowl; stir to coat. Cover; refrigerate 1 hour.

Remove stem and strings from pea pods. Place in boiling water about 1 minute or until pea pods turn bright green. Drain; rinse with cold water and dry with paper towels.

Drain dressing from shrimp. Wrap a pea pod around each shrimp; secure with toothpick. Cover; refrigerate until serving time.

Easy Corn and Tomato Salad

2 (11-ounce) cans shoepeg corn, drained
½ cup chopped sweet onion
2 large tomatoes, chopped
⅓–½ cup mayonnaise
Salt and pepper to taste

Combine corn, onion, and tomatoes; mix with mayonnaise and season. Chill before serving. Serve on lettuce as a salad, or with scoops as a dip. Serves 6–8.

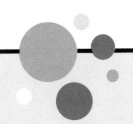

Colorful Corn Salad

2 (14-ounce) cans shoepeg corn, drained
3 green onions, chopped
¾ cup chopped bell pepper
½ cup chopped celery
⅓ cup chopped black olives
1–2 teaspoons Cajun seasoning
¾ cup mayonnaise
1 tomato, chopped, drained

Drain corn well; add remaining ingredients. Just before serving, add chopped tomato. Serves 6–8.

Miracle Red Grape Broccoli Salad

No matter when you serve this, it just seems to fit.

4 cups chopped broccoli florets, cut small
1 cup halved seedless red grapes
¼ cup chopped red onion
1 cup Miracle Whip
2 tablespoons rice wine vinegar
12 slices bacon, cooked, crumbled
¼ cup coarsely chopped pecans or walnuts

Mix broccoli, grapes, and onion in bowl. Combine Miracle Whip and vinegar; toss with veggies and grapes. Chill. Before serving, add bacon and nuts. Toss well. Serves 6–8.

It's Party Time!

King Crab Louie

A salad for a king! Or queen!

1 head lettuce
1 pound fresh lump crabmeat
8 king or snowcrab legs, cooked and cracked
  (optional)
3 tomatoes, cut in wedges
4 eggs, hard-boiled, quartered
Asparagus spears, cooked
Black olives, pitted
Dill pickles, sliced
King Louie Dressing

Arrange 2 or 3 big leaves of lettuce on 6 chilled salad plates. Shred more lettuce leaves and mound in center of each plate. Mound fresh lump crabmeat on the shredded lettuce, then divide crab legs on top. Arrange tomato wedges, egg quarters, asparagus spears, olives, and pickles. Serve with King Louie Dressing. Boiled shrimp or lobster can be substituted for crabmeat. Serves 6.

KING LOUIE DRESSING:
¾ cup mayonnaise
¼ cup chili sauce
2 teaspoons fresh lemon juice
1 teaspoon minced onion
⅓ cup whipping cream

Mix together mayonnaise, chili sauce, lemon juice, and onion. Whip heavy cream and fold in. Chill. Makes 1½ cups.

To help to remember really good recipes, write notes in your cookbooks. Put the date by the recipe you are preparing, and the occasion. Later record comments.

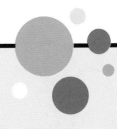

Toasted nuts add so much taste and crunch to salads. But beware, you can burn them easily while trying to get them toasted. Try putting them on a toaster oven tray and toast for 2½–3 minutes, just till slightly browned. *Use a timer.* Remove immediately to cool.

9x13 Chicken Salad

1 (10-ounce) bag torn romaine lettuce
¼ cup chopped red onion
1 cup chopped celery
1½ cups halved cherry tomatoes, divided
2 cups chopped, cooked, seasoned chicken
2 teaspoons red pepper sauce
1 (8-ounce) bottle ranch dressing
6 slices bacon, cooked, crumbled

In 9x13-inch glass baking dish, layer lettuce, onion, celery, ½ the tomatoes, and the chicken. Sprinkle red pepper sauce over chicken. Pour dressing evenly over salad. Sprinkle with bacon and remaining tomatoes. Serves 6–8.

Strawberry and Chicken Salad Trifle

1 head romaine lettuce, torn
2 (6-ounce) packages cooked chicken strips
1 cup crumbled feta cheese
1 cup toasted pecan halves
1 quart fresh strawberries, sliced
⅔ cup red wine vinegar dressing

In trifle bowl, layer lettuce, chicken, cheese, pecans, and strawberries. Refrigerate. Just before serving, pour dressing over salad. Serves 6–8.

Watermelon Cube Salad

Cool, tasty, and refreshing, this is a great summertime salad.

6 cups seeded watermelon cubes
1 tablespoon sugar
½ teaspoon salt
½ red or sweet onion, thinly sliced
⅓ cup red wine vinegar
¼ cup olive oil
½ teaspoon cracked black pepper to taste

Put watermelon cubes in a large bowl; sprinkle with sugar and salt; stir gently to coat. Stir in onion, vinegar, oil, and pepper. Good right now, but better chilled for a couple of hours. Great served over shredded lettuce. Good to marinate with tomato cubes, too. Serves 10–12.

Sunshine Stuffed Strawberries

Refresh your guests with this sweet appetizer, or use as a light dessert.

1 pint strawberries
1 (8-ounce) package cream cheese, softened
¼ cup confectioners' sugar, or to taste
2 tablespoons Grand Marnier, curaçao, or Triple Sec

Cut stems from berries so that berries stand points up. Cut an X through pointed end of each berry ⅓ way down. Sit berries on a serving dish. Beat cream cheese with sugar and liqueur until well blended. Place mixture into a pastry bag with a star tip. Pipe cream cheese mixture into center of each berry. If desired, surround fruit with attractive greenery, such as fresh mint, watercress, or well-cleaned greens from the garden. Makes about 15.

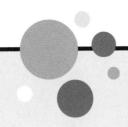

Fruits like apples and bananas will stay "whiter" if you squeeze a little lemon juice over slices. Or dip them in pineapple juice.

It's Party Time!

Pearly Whites

A giggly way to get kids to eat apples.

2 red apples
⅓ cup peanut butter
12–15 mini-marshmallows

Core apples; cut each into 8 slices. Make mouths by spreading a teaspoon of peanut butter on half the apple slices. Add 4 or 5 marshmallows for teeth. Spread remaining apple slices with a teaspoon peanut butter; press gently on top of first apple slice at an angle, leaving space for teeth to show.

Mango-Stuffed Celery Bites

Spicy, sweet, and delightfully delicious.

1 (8-ounce) package cream cheese, softened
1 teaspoon vinegar
1 teaspoon curry powder
2 tablespoons milk
6 tablespoons mango chutney
Salt and pepper to taste
12 celery stalks, cleaned

Mix well the cream cheese, vinegar, curry powder, milk, chutney, salt and pepper. Stuff into celery stalks. Cut celery into 2-inch pieces. Chill until serving time. Yields 48 pieces.

Deep-Fried Banana Logs

Bananas, halved, sliced lengthwise
Eggs, beaten
Cornflakes, crushed

Dip banana slices in beaten eggs, then coat with crushed cornflakes. Deep-fry in hot oil until golden, about 35–40 seconds.

Just a Bite

Nuggets

Pinwheels

Meaty Bites

Crab Bites

Shrimp Bites

It's Party Time!

Coconut Chicken Bites

2 cups shredded coconut
1 large egg
1 tablespoon vegetable oil
½ teaspoon red pepper flakes, or to taste
1 pound chicken tenders, cut bite-size

Preheat oven to 400°. Spread coconut on large baking sheet. Bake 5 minutes till lightly browned, stirring every 2 minutes. Process coconut in food processor until finely chopped (not pasty). Beat egg with oil and red pepper flakes in small bowl; add chicken bites; toss to coat; roll in coconut; arrange on foil-lined baking sheet. Bake 16–18 minutes till no longer pink in center. Serve with spicy mango salsa. Serves 6–8.

Pretzel-Crusted Chicken Nuggets

4 boneless chicken breasts
¼ cup egg beaters
1 tablespoon mustard
¼ teaspoon sugar
¼ cup flour
2 cups pretzel crumbs

Cut chicken into ¾-inch cubes. Blend egg, mustard, and sugar. Shake nuggets in bag with flour. Dip in egg mixture; coat with pretzel crumbs. Put on baking sheet. Bake at 400° for 9–11 minutes. Serve with honey mustard for dipping. Makes 20–24.

Toasted Almond Chicken Nuggets

This not only sounds good...it is good!

6 skinless chicken breast halves
1 cup all-purpose flour
1 cup almonds, toasted, ground
Salt and pepper to taste
1 large egg, beaten
1 cup buttermilk
⅓ cup butter, melted

Cut chicken into chunks. Combine flour, almonds, salt and pepper; set aside. Combine egg and buttermilk. Dip chicken in milk mixture and dredge in flour mixture. Pour butter in large baking pan. Add chicken, turning to coat in butter. Bake at 375° for 30 minutes. Serves 8–10.

Crispy Onion Chicken Nuggets

1½ pounds boneless, skinless chicken breasts
¾ cup honey mustard, divided
2 (3½-ounce) cans French fried onions

Preheat oven to 400°. Cut chicken into 1½-inch pieces; stir chicken with ⅓ cup mustard in medium bowl. Crush onions finely in plastic food bag. Toss chicken in onions a few pieces at a time, pressing gently to adhere. Spread chicken on baking sheet. Bake 15 minutes or until chicken is no longer pink in center. Serve with remaining honey mustard. Serves 8–10.

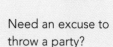

Need an excuse to throw a party?

- Throw a block party to meet your neighbors.
- Have a bring-a-brew party to sample each other's favorite beers.
- Everybody bring a salad! Or salad makings. A salad soirée!
- Have a cookie swap . . . why wait for Christmas?

Let's Celebrate!

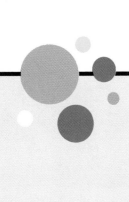

Buttery Chicken Nuggets

6 boneless chicken breast halves
1½ cups fine bread crumbs
¾ cup grated Parmesan cheese
2 tablespoons Greek seasoning
1 stick butter, melted

Cube chicken into 1¼-inch pieces. Combine crumbs, cheese, and seasoning. Dip chicken in butter, then in bread-crumb mixture. Place on Pam-sprayed baking sheet. Bake at 400° about 12–15 minutes. Serves 12–16.

Pop-In-Your-Mouth Chicken Nuggets

3 boneless chicken breasts
¾ stick butter, melted
¾ cup finely crushed Cheez-Its
½ teaspoon Cajun seasoning

Cube chicken; dip in melted butter. Combine remaining ingredients; roll chicken pieces in crumb mixture. Place on nonstick cookie sheet. Bake in 400° oven 10–15 minutes. Serves 6–8.

It's Party Time!

Baked Parmesan Chicken Nuggets

¾ cup grated Parmesan cheese
¼ cup chopped fresh parsley
1 cup crushed herb-seasoned stuffing mix
1½ sticks butter
1 large garlic clove, crushed
5 boneless chicken breasts, cubed bite-size

Mix cheese, parsley, and crumbs in bowl. Melt butter with garlic in small skillet. Dip chicken cubes in butter, then roll in crumbs. Place on Pam-sprayed baking pan. Bake at 375° for 20–25 minutes, or until chicken is done. Okay to refrigerate several hours before baking. Serves 8–10.

Microwave Chicken Nuggets

These are so easy and good, you'll want to make a meal of them.

⅓ cup grated Parmesan cheese
½ cup grated Cheddar cheese
½ cup seasoned bread crumbs
3 chicken breasts, cut in ¾-inch cubes
½ cup butter or margarine, melted

Combine cheeses and crumbs. Dip chicken into melted butter and roll in crumbs. Arrange chicken in single layer in a microwave-safe dish. Pour remaining butter and crumbs over chicken. Cover with plastic wrap; vent on one side. Cook on full power for 5–5½ minutes. Freezes well. Serves 6–8.

When recipes call for butter or margarine, unless specified "no substitute," use whichever you like. Butter tends to burn easier, so watch it carefully. When sautéing, a little oil added to the butter tames the tendency to burn. Both work fine in baking . . . but you can't beat the taste of real butter.

Let's Celebrate!

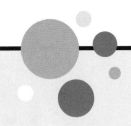

It's Party Time!

Betsy's Tomato Crackers

Too good to be so easy. Delicious!

1 cup Hellmann's mayonnaise
¼ cup real bacon bits
Wheat Thins
1 pint cherry tomatoes, sliced

Mix mayonnaise and bacon bits. Place mayo-mixture on Wheat Thins; top with tomato slices. Makes about 25–30.

Tasty Parmesan Tomato Bites

Small fresh tomatoes, sliced ¾ inch thick
Salt
Parmesan cheese
Italian bread crumbs

On foil-lined pan, sprinkle tomatoes with salt, Parmesan cheese, and Italian bread crumbs. Broil until cheese melts and bread crumbs slightly brown. Watch closely! Serve hot.

BLT Bites

Serve on lettuce-lined tray for the total BLT.

12 slices bacon, fried, crumbled
½ cup mayonnaise
2 tablespoons minced green onions
1 tablespoon chopped parsley
20–24 cherry tomatoes

Mix bacon with mayonnaise, onions, and parsley. Take thin top off each tomato. With a teaspoon or melon baller, hollow out tomato; fill with mixture.

'Bello Beef Bites

Heat up the grill and get out the grill basket.

½ **pound fresh portobello mushrooms, cut bite-size**
½ **pound beef sirloin steak, cut in ¾-inch cubes**
1 **cup frozen pearl onions, thawed**
½ **cup plus 2 tablespoons balsamic vinaigrette,**
   divided
½ **cup halved cherry tomatoes**

Marinate mushrooms, beef, onions, and ½ cup vinaigrette in large bowl for 10 minutes; toss to coat; drain. Put all in grill basket and place 4–6 inches from medium-high heat about 8 minutes, shaking twice, till vegetables are tender and beef done like you like it. Spoon mixture into serving dish; stir in tomatoes and remaining 2 tablespoons vinaigrette. Serve with toothpicks. Serves 8.

Tiny Quiche Bites

1 **pound bulk hot pork sausage**
1 **cup shredded Cheddar cheese**
1 **cup shredded Colby Jack cheese**
½ **cup finely chopped onion**
1 **(4-ounce) can chopped green chiles**
10 **eggs**
1 **teaspoon garlic salt**
½ **teaspoon pepper**

Brown sausage; drain. Pour into a greased 9x13-inch baking dish. Layer with cheeses, onion, and chiles. Beat eggs with seasonings; pour over cheese. Bake, uncovered, at 375° for 18–22 minutes or until knife inserted near center comes out clean. Cool slightly; cut into 1-inch squares. Insert toothpicks in squares. Serves 12–20.

Let's Celebrate!

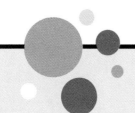

Fried Pasta Bites

Different . . . and sure to get attention.

7 ounces rotini, mostaccioli, or shell pasta, cooked
Vegetable oil
2 tablespoons grated Parmesan cheese
½ teaspoon Creole seasoning
½ teaspoon chili powder
⅛ teaspoon garlic powder

Drain and rinse cooked pasta with cold water, and drain thoroughly. Heat oil to 375°. Fry about 1 cup well-drained pasta at a time in oil about 2 minutes, stirring to separate, until crisp and light golden brown; drain on paper towels. Mix remaining ingredients in large bowl. Add pasta and toss until evenly coated. Store tightly covered up to 2 weeks. Serves 15–20.

Veggie Ranch Pinwheels

2 (8-ounce) packages cream cheese, softened
1 (1-ounce) package dry ranch salad dressing mix
2 green onions, minced
4 (12-ounce) flour tortillas
1 (4-ounce) jar diced pimentos
1 (4-ounce) can diced green chiles
1 (2¼-ounce) can sliced black olives (optional)

Combine first 3 ingredients; spread on tortillas. Drain vegetables and blot with paper towels. Spread equal amounts of remaining ingredients on top of cream cheese. Roll tortillas tightly; chill at least 2 hours. Cut into 1-inch pieces. Makes 3 dozen.

It's Party Time!

Deli-Licious Party Wheels

1 (8-ounce) package cream cheese, softened
½ cup grated Cheddar cheese
2 tablespoons picante sauce
⅛ teaspoon garlic powder
4–6 flour tortillas
½ pound deli sliced ham or turkey

Combine cream cheese, Cheddar cheese, picante, and garlic powder; mix well. Spread mixture on flour tortillas, covering completely. Top with slices of ham or turkey; roll up tightly. Wrap in plastic wrap and freeze several hours. Slice, thaw, and serve. Makes 40–60 wheels.

Guests will appreciate your making appetizers small enough to be eaten in one bite preferably, but no more than two bites.

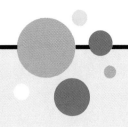

Ham and Cheese Pinwheels

1 (5-ounce) jar pineapple cheese
4 (10-inch) flour tortillas
1 (6-ounce) bag fresh baby spinach
8 ounces thinly sliced ham
8 ounces thinly sliced Swiss cheese
1 (7-ounce) jar roasted red bell peppers, drained, sliced

Spread ¼ jar cheese on each tortilla. Cover with ¼ of spinach, meat, and cheese. Place red bell pepper strips down center. Roll tightly. Repeat with remaining tortillas. Cut rolls into 1½-inch slices; secure with toothpicks. To serve, stack slices on serving plate. Serves 16–18.

Roast Beef Roll-Ups

¾ cup mayonnaise
2 tablespoons ranch salad dressing mix
¼ cup finely chopped green onions
4 (10-inch) flour tortillas
½ pound thinly sliced lean roast beef

Mix mayonnaise and dressing mix; stir in onions. Spread on tortillas; divide beef over all. Roll tortillas up tightly. Cut into ¾-inch pieces; secure with toothpicks. Chill. Makes 48–60.

Pepperoni Party Pinwheels

1 (8-ounce) can refrigerated crescent rolls
½ cup diced pepperoni
½ cup shredded mozzarella cheese
½ teaspoon Cajun seasoning
1 egg, separated

Separate dough into 4 rectangles; seal perforations. Mix pepperoni, cheese, seasoning, and egg yolk in a bowl. In another bowl, whisk egg white until foamy; set aside.

Divide pepperoni mixture over each rectangle, spreading to within ¼ inch of edges. Roll up jellyroll-style; pinch seams to seal. Cut each into 6 pinwheels.

Place cut side down on greased baking sheets; brush tops with egg white. Bake at 375° for 12–15 minutes till golden brown. Serve warm. Makes 24.

Savory Stuffing Bites

½ cup butter, melted
4 eggs, beaten
2 tablespoons chopped fresh parsley (or 2 teaspoons dried)
1 garlic clove, minced
2 cups chopped mushrooms
1 cup chopped onion
½ cup grated Parmesan cheese
2½ cups herb-seasoned stuffing mix

Mix well all but stuffing mix; add stuffing. Mix lightly and shape into 1-inch balls; place 2 inches apart on cookie sheet. Bake at 350° for 15 minutes or until golden. Makes about 32 appetizers.

Let's Celebrate!

People generally enjoy seeing pictures of themselves and others having fun. Consider hanging a bulletin board of past party photos—you might ask repeat guests to bring some of previous get-togethers. You can also leave photo albums on the coffee table. Or put a mute slide show on the TV—photos always spark conversation.

But do resist the temptation to show numerous pictures of your vacation or grandkids . . . choose through the eyes of your guests.

Tasty Tortilla Bites

1 (8-ounce) package cream cheese, softened
1 (4-ounce) can chopped green chiles
3 green onions, chopped
½ teaspoon garlic salt
3 large flour tortillas

Mix cream cheese, chiles, onions, and garlic salt. Spread on each tortilla, roll up, wrap in plastic wrap, and refrigerate. When chilled, cut into bite-size pieces. Serve with toothpicks, and salsa for dipping. Makes 40–50.

Quesadilla Bean Bites

4 (8-inch) flour tortillas
¾ cup shredded nacho/taco blend cheese, divided
½ cup canned black beans, rinsed, drained
2 green onions, sliced
2 tablespoons chopped fresh cilantro
½ teaspoon ground cumin
Salsa and sour cream

Place 2 tortillas on greased baking sheet; sprinkle each with divided cheese. Combine beans, green onions, cilantro, and cumin in bowl; mix lightly. Spoon bean mixture evenly over cheese; top with remaining tortillas. Spray tops with cooking spray.

Bake 10–12 minutes at 450° till cheese melts and tortillas are light brown. Quarter. Transfer to serving plate, then top each wedge with salsa and sour cream. Makes 8. Or cut again to make 16.

Sweetie Meat Bites

These will disappear as appetizers. Also great for breakfast or brunch.

1 pound sliced bacon, halved
1 (16-ounce) package miniature smoked sausage links
1 cup packed brown sugar

Wrap a bacon half slice around each sausage. Place in foil-lined baking pans. Sprinkle brown sugar over bites. Bake, uncovered, at 400° for 30–40 minutes or till bacon is crisp. Makes about 36.

Bacon and Tamale Bites

6 hot tamales, shucked, cut into thirds
12 slices bacon, halved

Wrap each tamale piece with ½ slice bacon. Broil until bacon is crisp, turning frequently. Serve hot. Makes 18 bites.

Dog Bites Everybody Likes

You'll be amazed at how easy and delicious these are!

10 slices raw bacon, halved
5 hot dogs, quartered
1½ cups powdered sugar

Wrap bacon around hot dogs; secure with tooth-picks. (Can be refrigerated at this point.) Put in baking dish, cover with powdered sugar, and bake at 350° for 1 hour. Makes 20.

Editor's Extra: For easy cleanup, line baking dish with foil, and spray lightly with cooking spray.

Let's Celebrate!

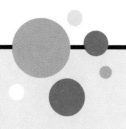

Vienna claims the weinerwurst (1480) and Frankfurt the frankfurter wurst (later weiners and franks). Around 1870, Charles Feltman, a German immigrant, began selling sausages in rolls on Coney Island. There are many stories and myths about how they eventually came to be called hot dogs, but none has been authenticated as first.

It's Party Time!

Dogs in Coats

Kids will love these dogs.

1 (11-ounce) can refrigerated breadsticks
8 hot dogs
Wooden craft sticks

Separate breadstick dough and roll into pieces 15 inches long. Put craft sticks into one end of each hot dog. Wrap bread "ropes" around dogs from one end to the other, pinching to seal. Spray Pam on baking sheet before placing dogs 1 inch apart. Bake in 350° oven for 18–20 minutes. Offer mustard, ketchup, or ranch dressing in bowls for dipping. Serves 8.

Jellyroll Reubens

1 medium onion, diced
2 tablespoons vegetable oil, divided
1 cup rinsed, drained sauerkraut
6 large flour tortillas
1½ cups grated Swiss cheese, divided
12 ounces thinly sliced pastrami, divided

Sauté onion in 1 tablespoon oil. Add sauerkraut and cook 2 minutes. Spread each tortilla with ¼ cup cheese. Lay ⅙ pastrami down center, and spread ¼ cup sauerkraut mixture over.

Roll tortillas up jellyroll-style, so that pastrami and sauerkraut run down the length of middle. Brush rolls with vegetable oil. Bake on cookie pan until lightly browned, about 10 minutes. Cut each roll on diagonal into 6 pieces. Serve with Russian dressing for dipping. Makes 36 pieces.

Crab English Muffin Bites

Still a favorite.

1 stick butter, softened
1 jar Old English cheese spread
1½ teaspoons mayonnaise
½ teaspoon garlic salt
1 pound fresh lump crabmeat
6 English muffins

Mix first 5 ingredients. Add crabmeat. Spread on open English muffin. Cut in fourths, then freeze on baking sheet. Put in zipper bags to keep frozen several days. When ready to use, broil frozen for 10 minutes or until bubbly. Makes 24.

Fried Crab Puffs

What could be better!

1 cup fresh lump crabmeat
2 cups biscuit mix
¼ cup chopped green onions
¼ cup grated Parmesan cheese
½ teaspoon dill weed
¼ cup milk
1 large egg
Cajun seasoning to taste

Mix all well, and drop by teaspoon into deep fryer at 350°. When they float to the top, they're done. Good with sweet and sour sauce and/or hot mustard sauce. Serve with toothpicks. Serves 18–20.

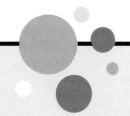

Favorite Scallops Appetizer

1 pound sea scallops
10 slices maple-flavored smoked bacon
Greek seasoning
¼ cup pure maple syrup, divided

Rinse and drain scallops; pat dry. Cut into 20 pieces; halve each bacon slice crosswise. Cook bacon, but not crisp. Drain on paper towels till cool enough to handle.

Preheat oven to 425°. Wrap each scallop piece with a slice of bacon. Secure with wooden toothpicks. Place in shallow baking pan and season. Brush with some maple syrup. Bake 8–10 minutes or until scallops are opaque and bacon is cooked (it may not be crisp), turning once and brushing with remaining maple syrup halfway through cooking. Serve warm. Makes 20.

Wasabi Salmon

Worth swimming upstream for!

2 tablespoons soy sauce
2 teaspoons white wine vinegar
1 teaspoon vegetable oil
½ teaspoon grated gingerroot
½ pound salmon fillet
½ cup wasabi mayonnaise
16 wheat crackers
1 green onion, thinly sliced

Combine soy sauce, vinegar, oil, and gingerroot in shallow bowl and marinate salmon in mixture, skin side up, for 10 minutes. Cook salmon in skillet, skin side down, on medium heat 8–12 minutes, brushing once with marinade, until salmon flakes easily with fork. Spread mayonnaise on crackers and top each with about 1 tablespoon flaked salmon and additional mayonnaise. Garnish with green onion. Yields 16.

Soy sauce is one of the world's oldest condiments and has been used in China for more than 2,500 years.

Wasabi is the Japanese version of horseradish. In Japan sushi is often served with a mixture of wasabi and soy sauce. It adds a little zing.

Shrimp in Circles

2 (8-ounce) cans crescent rolls
1 teaspoon garlic salt
2 cups shredded Monterey Jack cheese
1 cup chopped cooked shrimp
¼ cup finely chopped green onions

Press dough into 4 long rectangles. Sprinkle with garlic salt and cheese, then shrimp and onions; press in gently.

Roll tightly from short side, pressing edge to seal. Cut each roll into 8 slices. Place cut side down, on sprayed cookie sheet and bake at 350° for 15–20 minutes till browned. Serve warm. Makes 32.

Red Pepper Shrimp

So good, it doesn't need a sauce.

½ cup Dijon mustard
½ cup rice wine vinegar
1 teaspoon Cajun seasoning
2 teaspoons crushed red pepper, or more
2 pounds large shrimp, peeled, deveined, tails on
½ cup olive oil, divided

Shake all ingredients except 2 tablespoons olive oil in a large resealable plastic bag till shrimp are coated, and marinate in refrigerator 4–6 hours.

Sieve to shake off excess marinade. Coat a large skillet with remaining 2 tablespoons olive oil, and heat over medium heat; place shrimp in one layer (cook shrimp in 2 batches). Cook, shaking pan occasionally to turn shrimp, until shrimp turn pink and are cooked through, 3–5 minutes. Serve warm or at room temperature. Serves 10–15.

Note: Can marinate up to 2 days ahead. Cook day of party and refrigerate till serving time.

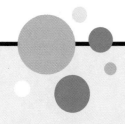

How to boil eggs:

Put eggs into a deep saucepan and cover with water. On high heat, bring water to a full boil, then turn off heat and cover the pot. In six minutes, drain eggs. If using right away, rinse under cool water, drain again, then shake eggs against sides of pot. Shells will practically fall off. (For soft-boiled eggs, take out of hot water in three minutes.)

Dare Deviled Eggs

6 eggs, boiled, peeled
¼ cup sandwich spread or mayonnaise
1 teaspoon mustard
1 teaspoon vinegar
Tabasco to taste
¼ teaspoon salt
Paprika for garnish

Cut eggs in half. Remove yolks and mash with remaining ingredients, except paprika. Stuff mixture into egg whites; dust with paprika. Cover and refrigerate. Makes 12.

Editor's Extra: Add sliced pimento-stuffed olives to tops for pretty garnish.

Coconut Shrimp Caribe

You'll think you're in the islands.

Vegetable oil for frying
24–30 large shrimp
½ cup cornstarch
¼ teaspoon white pepper
¼ teaspoon cayenne pepper
2 egg whites
3 cups shredded sweetened coconut
½ teaspoon salt

Heat oil to 350°. Peel, devein, butterfly, and wash shrimp; dry with paper towels. Combine cornstarch, salt, pepper, and cayenne in a bowl. In a separate bowl, whisk egg whites until foamy. Put coconut in a third bowl. Dredge shrimp in cornstarch mixture, shaking off any excess. Dip in egg whites and then press into shredded coconut. Fry in small batches for about 3 minutes. Drain on paper towels and sprinkle with a little salt (which reduces some of the greasiness from frying). Serve with a dipping sauce such as chutney, curry, apricot or peanut sauce. Serves 6–10.

Heavy Hors D'Oeuvres

Meatballs

Wings

Weiners

Brisket

Turkey

Ham

Skewers

Kabobs

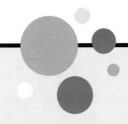

Baking meatballs in the oven rather than frying is so much easier and less messy . . . and no need to turn them at all. Best to make them small for quicker and more even cooking.

It's Party Time!

Gwen's Baked Sausage Meatballs

An old recipe for a brand-new audience.

1 (1-pound) roll hot ground sausage
1 pound ground chuck
1 egg
⅔ cup seasoned bread crumbs
¼ cup minced onion
½ teaspoon salt
¼ cup Worcestershire

Mix all ingredients, except Worcestershire, together with hands. Form into small (1-inch) balls and put on baking sheets. Bake at 325° for 22 minutes or till nicely browned. Remove meatballs to chafing dish or crockpot to keep warm, saving 3 tablespoons drippings. Mix with Worcestershire and a little water. Pour over meatballs. You want just enough liquid to keep them from sticking to pot. Sooooo good. Serves 10–20.

Kicky Sausage Balls

1 pound hot seasoned sausage
3 cups biscuit mix
¼ cup water
12 ounces shredded sharp Cheddar cheese
½ teaspoon onion powder

Combine all ingredients and mix well. Shape into 1¼-inch balls and place on baking sheets. Bake at 375° for 15 minutes. Serve hot. Makes about 36.

Editor's Extra: These can be frozen. When taking from freezer, place in 300° oven 10 minutes, then bake at 375° for 15 minutes.

Meatball Penguins

16 onion strips, ½ x 3 inches
1 carrot
1 (16-ounce) package frozen cooked meatballs,
  thawed
Pimento, diced

Blanch onion strips in boiling water for 20 seconds; cool in ice water immediately. Drain; set aside. Cut carrot into 16 diagonal slices. Cut a small triangle from each carrot slice for "beaks"; set aside. Place carrot pieces in microwaveable bowl; cover and microwave on HIGH 30 seconds.

In 16 "head" meatballs, make a small hole for carrot "beak" to go into. Press small pimento dots for eyes. Place small skewer through meatball "head" into carrot "beak" to secure. Push skewer with "head" attached through onion strip "breast" on 16 "body" meatballs and into carrot "feet." Have cutout in feet facing forward. Makes 16.

Okay, here it is: head, beak, eyes, onion breast, body, feet all on a small skewer. Place penguins in ungreased shallow pan. Bake 10–12 minutes until hot. Place on serving platter standing up.

149

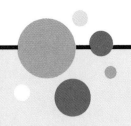

Instead of toothpicks, spear soft hors d'oeuvres—like meatballs—with pretzel sticks. Guests may enjoy eating the stick as well.

Can't Beat These Meatballs

MEATBALLS:

¾ pound ground beef
¾ pound ground pork
⅓ cup plain bread crumbs
⅓ cup finely chopped onion
⅓ cup finely chopped red bell pepper
¾ teaspoon garlic powder
Salt and pepper to taste
1 egg, slightly beaten

Combine all ingredients until well blended. Shape into 1½-inch meatballs. Place in greased pan and bake at 375° for 30 minutes or till browned and thoroughly cooked.

SAUCE:

⅔ cup apple juice
1 cup jalapeño jelly
½ teaspoon ground ginger
½ teaspoon garlic powder
2 tablespoons cornstarch
1 teaspoon salt

Mix ingredients well. Cook in large skillet over medium heat 2–3 minutes or until thickened, stirring constantly. Add Meatballs and stir to coat. Cook and stir over medium heat 5–7 minutes or until thoroughly heated. Transfer to chafing dish or crockpot to keep warm. Serves 12.

It's Party Time!

Jalapeño Crockpot Meatballs

4 dozen frozen meatballs
1 cup apple jelly
2 cups barbecue sauce
2 jalapeño peppers, coarsely chopped
½ cup chopped onion
¼ teaspoon chile powder (optional)

Combine all ingredients in a crockpot. Cover and cook on LOW 4–6 hours. Easy to double. Serves 14–20.

Crockpot BBQ Balls

If you need about a hundred meatballs that are easy and delicious, this is it!

3 pounds frozen meatballs
1 large onion, chopped
1 cup beer
1½ cups ketchup
2 tablespoons seasoned rice wine vinegar
½ teaspoon garlic powder
¼ cup brown sugar
Salt and pepper to taste

Combine all ingredients in crockpot. Cover; cook on LOW 8–12 hours. Serves 20 or more.

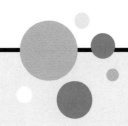

Shape and Bake Meatballs

Everybody loves these.

MEATBALLS:

1½ pounds lean ground beef or turkey
1 egg, slightly beaten
½ cup finely chopped onion
⅓ cup bread crumbs
¼ teaspoon garlic powder
¼ teaspoon salt
⅛ teaspoon red pepper

Heat oven to 375°. In large bowl, combine ingredients well. Shape into 1-inch balls; place on ungreased baking pan. Bake for 20–25 minutes until browned.

SAUCE:

¾ cup grape jelly
½ cup chili sauce
3 medium bell peppers, (1 green, 1 yellow, 1 red), cut into 1-inch pieces

Combine grape jelly and chili sauce in large saucepan. Boil over medium heat till dissolved. Add bell peppers. Reduce heat; simmer 5 minutes. Add meatballs; simmer 5 more minutes. Serve warm from chafing dish or fondue pot. Serves about 30.

It's Party Time!

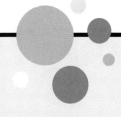

Queso Meatballs

1½ pounds frozen meatballs
2 tablespoons vegetable oil
1 (1-pound) package Velveeta cheese, cubed
1 (4-ounce) can chopped green chiles
1 envelope taco seasoning mix
½ cup water

Put frozen meatballs in large skillet or pot, and cook, covered, on medium heat 10–15 minutes till heated. Remove to bowl and wipe skillet clean. Now add oil, cheese, chiles, taco seasoning mix, and water. Over low heat, stir till melted. Add meatballs; simmer; cover, stirring occasionally, till all is heated. Keep warm in crockpot or chafing dish. Serves 10–12.

Cheese can burn easily if you're in too much of a hurry. Melt it on low heat and stir a lot. It helps to cut cheese as small as you can, as the more edges exposed to the heat, the quicker it will melt.

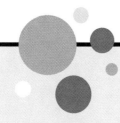

Here's a tip! Save those wing tips and boil with your favorite seasonings, then strain and freeze. Great way to start your soup.

Juicy Sauced Chicken Wings

2 pounds chicken wings
¾ cup chopped onion
½ cup soy sauce
½ cup brown sugar
1 teaspoon minced fresh ginger
2 garlic cloves, minced
2 tablespoons dry sherry
Sesame seeds (optional)

Separate chicken wings at joints with knife, and discard tips; place in a baking dish. Process onion, soy sauce, brown sugar, ginger, garlic, and sherry in a food processor until blended. Pour over wings. Bake in 350° oven 1 hour. Sprinkle with sesame seeds, if desired. Serve hot. Serves 15–20.

Ritzy Hot Wings

These bake beautifully. Men especially love them.

1 sleeve Ritz Crackers, finely crushed
2 teaspoons Greek seasoning
½ teaspoon garlic powder
2 pounds chicken wings, tips discarded
½ cup wing sauce

Preheat oven to 350°. Mix cracker crumbs with seasonings in shallow dish. Coat chicken with wing sauce; dip in crumb mixture, turning to coat both sides of each piece. Place on greased baking sheet. Bake 35–40 minutes or until golden brown and cooked through, turning pieces after 20 minutes. Serves 15–20.

It's Party Time!

Cranberry Barbecue Wings

2 pounds chicken short wings (drummettes)
1 cup barbecue sauce
⅓ cup whole cranberry sauce
⅓ cup orange marmalade
¼ cup chopped fresh chives
¼ teaspoon dry mustard

Heat oven to 375°. Spray foil-lined pan with cooking spray. Place wings on foil and cover with more foil. Bake at 375° for 20–30 minutes.

Meanwhile, in small bowl, combine all remaining ingredients; mix well. Remove wings from oven. Uncover; turn wings over; pour off any drippings. Spoon sauce mixture over wings. Bake, uncovered, an additional 20 minutes, turning once and brushing with sauce. Serve wings warm with sauce from pan. Serves about 16.

Smoky Red Wingers

A delicious crockpot wing thing. Fall-off-the-bone delicious!

1 (10¾-ounce) can condensed tomato soup
¾ cup water
¼ cup brown sugar
3 tablespoons rice wine vinegar
3 tablespoons chopped green pepper
½ teaspoon onion powder
½ teaspoon Tabasco or to taste
½ teaspoon cayenne
1 teaspoon liquid smoke
16 chicken wings

Combine all ingredients except chicken wings in slow cooker; mix well. Add chicken wings; stir to coat with sauce. Cover; cook on LOW 5–6 hours until cooked and glazed with sauce. Stir gently. Serve warm.

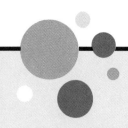

The time of your party dictates the food and amounts. If it is right after work, better have plenty, offering at least a few heavy hors d'oeuvres. Early afternoon, or after 8 p.m. can justify lighter snacks.

Crockpot Hot Wing Things

It just doesn't get much easier than this. Throw the wings and things in the crockpot and git 'r' done!

5 pounds whole chicken wings (about 25)
½ cup Karo syrup
½ cup buffalo wing sauce
2 teaspoons granulated garlic

Discard wing tips. Put all in crockpot. Stir to coat wings. Cover and cook on LOW 6 hours or until tender. Makes 50.

Editor's Extra: Leftover warmed meat (off the bone) is excellent on a bun.

Cracker-Crusted Drummettes

¾ cup crushed club crackers
1 cup grated Parmesan cheese
1 teaspoon garlic salt
36 chicken drummettes
¼ cup butter, melted

In a small bowl, combine cracker crumbs, Parmesan cheese, and garlic salt. Dip drummettes in butter, then roll in crumbs. Arrange on greased baking sheets. Bake at 375° for 35–40 minutes till golden brown. Serves a party of 8–12.

It's Party Time!

Dippy Drummettes with Sassy Sauce

1 tablespoon brown sugar
1 tablespoon dried thyme leaves
3 garlic cloves, minced
2 teaspoons allspice
1 teaspoon salt
2 tablespoons cider vinegar
2 tablespoons Tabasco
1 (3-pound) package frozen chicken wing drum-
    mettes, thawed

In glass bowl, combine brown sugar, thyme, garlic, allspice, salt, vinegar, and Tabasco; mix well. Add drummettes; toss to coat. Marinate covered in refrigerator 1 hour.

Line 2 (10x15x1-inch) baking pans with foil; spray with nonstick cooking spray. Place drummettes on foil, discarding any remaining marinade. Bake at 425° for 45 minutes till chicken is no longer pink. Serves a party of 10–16.

SASSY SAUCE:
1 teaspoon dried ranch salad dressing mix
½ cup sour cream
½ cup mayonnaise

Mix all ingredients well. Serve with drummettes.

Editor's Extra: Can be made day before, covered, and refrigerated. Reheat at 350° about 20 minutes.

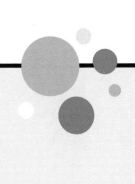

Taco Chicken Drummettes

4 pounds fresh or frozen chicken drummettes,
** thawed**
1 envelope taco seasoning
3 tablespoons vegetable oil
2 tablespoons balsamic vinegar
2 teaspoons hot pepper sauce, divided
1 cup ranch salad dressing

Toss drummettes in zipper bag with taco seasoning, oil, vinegar, and 1 teaspoon hot pepper sauce. Grill chicken over medium heat 5 minutes covered. Uncover and grill 10–15 minutes longer till juices run clear, turning occasionally. Combine ranch dressing and remaining hot pepper sauce. Serve chicken with sauce. Serves a party of 16–20.

Crockpot Teriyaki Drumsticks

½ cup teriyaki sauce
1 (8-ounce) can tomato sauce
¼ cup packed brown sugar
1 teaspoon minced garlic
3 pounds skinless chicken drumsticks
3 tablespoons cornstarch
¼ cup cold water

Combine teriyaki sauce, tomato sauce, brown sugar, and garlic. Place chicken in crockpot, and pour sauce over. Cover, and cook on LOW 5–6 hours until tender. Remove chicken and keep warm.

Strain cooking juices into a pot. Combine cornstarch and cold water in a cup until smooth. Bring juice from cooker to a boil; add cornstarch mixture and cook and stir until thickened. Serve over chicken. Serves a party of 8–12.

It's Party Time!

Drummette Lollipops

Fun and delicious.

36 chicken wing drummettes
2 cups buttermilk
½ teaspoon salt
3 tablespoons butter
2 cups bread crumbs
½ teaspoon coarsely ground black pepper
1 teaspoon paprika
¼ teaspoon cayenne pepper
1 teaspoon garlic powder

With a sharp paring knife, separate skin and tendons from bone at narrow end of drummettes. With fingers, push meat down to form a ball . . . lollipop! Marinate chicken in buttermilk and salt in a bowl and toss to coat. Cover and refrigerate for 1 hour.

In 400° oven, melt butter on a large baking sheet in oven. Take out and set aside.

Combine crumbs with remaining ingredients in large plastic bag. Lift chicken pieces out of buttermilk, and 3 at a time, drop into bag and shake to coat. Put lollipops on pan, meat end down. Bake until golden, 20–25 minutes.

What's a "drummette?" People used to use chicken wings mostly for soup making till somebody in Buffalo came up with a dandy recipe for "wings." Now their popularity calls for "filet" of chicken wing, which is the larger, meatier part of the wing. Looks sort of like a drumstick, so now we have "drummettes."

Let's Celebrate!

Cocktail Weiners

1½ cups ketchup
½ cup firmly packed brown sugar
¾ cup water (or ½ cup water and ¼ cup bourbon)
2 tablespoons minced onion
2 pounds cocktail weiners

Combine all but weiners, and mix well. Add weiners and bring to a boil. Cover and reduce, and simmer 30 minutes, stirring occasionally. Serves 8–10.

Editor's Extra: You can sub regular weiners cut into ½-inch slices.

Easy-Do Crocked Barbecue

On a bun or a baked potato . . . . so good.

1 (3- to 4-pound) roast
1 (20-ounce) bottle ketchup
⅓ cup barbecue sauce
⅔ cup chopped onion
¼ cup brown sugar
Salt and pepper to taste
1 teaspoon chili powder

Trim roast, pat dry, and place in crockpot. Mix all other ingredients and pour over roast. Cook on LOW for 10–12 hours. Shred with 2 forks, or massage meat in a zipper bag. Serves 10.

It's Party Time!

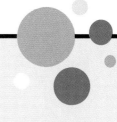

While-You-Sleep Italian Beef

A super easy way to serve a lot of hungry people great-tasting beef on a bun.

1 (4-pound) beef roast
1 jar pepperoncini peppers, with juice
1 (12-ounce) can beer
1 teaspoon beef bouillon granules dissolved in 1 cup
   hot water

Combine all ingredients in big crockpot. Cook on HIGH 30 minutes; then turn heat to LOW. Cook all day or all night. When done, slice roast thinly and return to pot juices. Serve on hoagie or hamburger or onion buns. The juicier the better. Serves 10–12.

Best Brisket Ever

1 (4- to 5-pound) brisket
1 (4-ounce) bottle liquid smoke
1 teaspoon onion salt
1 tablespoon brown sugar
1 teaspoon celery salt
1 teaspoon paprika
¼ teaspoon nutmeg
¼ teaspoon garlic powder

Cover brisket with liquid smoke. Refrigerate overnight, covered with foil. Next day, mix remaining ingredients and sprinkle all over brisket. Cover tightly with foil and bake 2 hours at 300°. Loosen foil, and bake 5 more hours at 200°. Remove meat to platter. Cover and refrigerate at least 1 hour. Remove grease from drippings. Slice brisket thinly across grain. Serve with hot drippings or barbecue sauce. Serves 10 or more.

Party Tray Prep:

Remember to put garnishes on your grocery list: lemons, limes, parsley, grapes, cherry tomatoes, olives, colorful peppers, cabbage, lettuce leaves . . . these help to make your party trays pretty and appetizing.

Let's Celebrate!

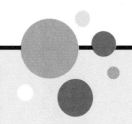

Can-Can Taco Soup

This can warm up a crowd.

2 pounds ground chuck
1 onion, chopped
1 (4-ounce) can chopped green chiles
1 (15-ounce) can hominy or corn or both
2 (15-ounce) cans pinto beans
3 (14½-ounce) cans diced tomatoes
1 package dry Hidden Valley Salad Dressing Mix
1 package dry taco mix
3 cups water

In a large, heavy pot, brown ground meat and onion together. Add remaining ingredients (cans undrained). Stir; bring to boil; simmer 25 minutes. Offer sour cream, shredded Jack cheese, small Fritos, and/or chopped green onions when serving, if desired. Serves 12–15.

Editor's Extra: Sub one can of Ro-Tel tomatoes for a spicier soup.

Gotta-Love-The-Juice Brisket

Soppin' good juice . . . absolutely fantastic!

1 (5-pound) brisket or London broil
1 tablespoon Cajun seasoning
1 (10¾-ounce) can cream of mushroom soup
1 (10¾-ounce) can French onion soup

Season brisket to taste. Pour mushroom soup into heavy pan with lid. Put brisket on rack on top of soup, then spoon onion soup over meat. Cover and bake one hour at 350°, then 3 hours at 200°. Leave covered whole time. Serve with sesame or onion hamburger buns. Serves 10–14.

It's Party Time!

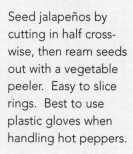

Some-Like-It-Hot Crockpot Tailgate Chili

Satisfies hungry appetites.

12 ounces bulk sausage

1½ pounds stew meat, cubed small

1 (12-ounce) package frozen seasoning blend (chopped onions, celery, bell pepper)

2 (15-ounce) cans kidney beans

2 (14½-ounce) cans diced tomatoes

1 (12-ounce) can tomato paste

2 tablespoons real bacon bits

2–4 fresh jalapeño peppers, seeded, chopped (optional)

4 cups water

Brown sausage and meat in large skillet; transfer to large crockpot with slotted spoon. Sauté frozen seasoning blend veggies in drippings; transfer to crockpot with slotted spoon. Add remaining ingredients. Cover and cook on LOW 8–10 hours or on HIGH 4–5 hours. Serve with your choice of sour cream, sliced green onions, corn chips, or Cheddar cheese for toppings. Serves 12 or more.

Seed jalapeños by cutting in half cross-wise, then ream seeds out with a vegetable peeler. Easy to slice rings. Best to use plastic gloves when handling hot peppers.

Let's Celebrate!

When having a seated dinner, consider your guests by not having a centerpiece so big and tall that people have to look around or over it to see one another.

For an interesting low centerpiece, place rock salt or glass vase marbles on a plate or tray, then place one or more fat candles (ones that stand up by themselves) of different heights in the center. Arrange tiny ornaments suitable for the occasion (confetti, beads, cranberries) around the candles. You may want to add greenery around the tray as well.

Quick Dinner Party Lasagna

1 pound ground beef
1 (10¾-ounce) can tomato soup
1 cup water
1 (10¾-ounce) can cream of mushroom soup
⅓ cup milk
2 cups shredded mozzarella cheese, divided
6 uncooked lasagna noodles

In skillet over medium-high heat, cook beef until browned; pour off fat. Stir in soup and water; heat through. In bowl, mix mushroom soup, milk, and ½ cup cheese.

Spoon half the meat mixture in a 2-quart shallow baking dish. Top with 3 lasagna noodles and soup mixture. Top with remaining 3 lasagna noodles and remaining meat mixture. Cover. Bake at 400° for 40 minutes. Uncover and top with remaining cheese. Bake 10 minutes more or until cheese is melted. Let stand 10 minutes. Serves 8.

Elegant Crabmeat Imperial

A main course with a baked potato and salad, or a rich thick dip/spread on toast points or crackers.

⅓ cup mayonnaise
¼ cup finely chopped green pepper
1 (1-ounce) jar chopped pimento
1 egg, beaten
Salt and pepper to taste
1 pound fresh lump crabmeat

Combine all ingredients except crabmeat, and stir well. Fold in crabmeat carefully so as not to break up lumps. Place in small casserole dish that has been sprayed with vegetable oil spray. Bake 15 minutes in 350° oven. Remove and put a thin layer of mayonnaise on top; broil for a few minutes until top is slightly tan. Serves 4–6.

Editor's Extra: After baking, spoon this into baked pastry shells. Elegantly delicious!

Easy Overnight Turkey Bake

This works beautifully. Juicy and fall-off-the-bone tender.

1 (14- to 18-pound) turkey
Cajun seasoning to taste

Preheat oven to 500°. Season turkey inside and out. Place in roaster with 6 cups of water. Cover tightly; bake for 1 hour. Turn off oven and DO NOT OPEN DOOR FOR 12 HOURS.

Turkey Lurkey Skewers

Serve these with your favorite dip or dressing. Delish.

1 (2-pound) turkey breast, cubed ¾ inch
16 small wooden skewers
¼ cup milk
¾ cup mayonnaise
3 cups crushed potato chips

Thread 3 turkey cubes on each wooden skewer. Mix milk and mayo. Coat cubes in mayo mixture, then crushed potato chips. Bake 15–20 minutes at 350°. Place on plate with assorted dips. Serves 12–16.

Sensational Salad Skewers

Your guests will love these.

40 pimento-stuffed olives
40 large pitted ripe olives
1 (9-ounce) package refrigerated cheese tortellini, cooked, drained, rinsed
¾ cup Italian dressing
40 thin slices pepperoni
20 thin slices hard salami, cut in half

Combine olives, tortellini, and Italian dressing in a large zipper bag. Close bag and refrigerate 4 hours or overnight.

Drain Italian dressing; discard. Skewer a stuffed olive, folded pepperoni slice, tortellini, folded salami slice, and ripe olive on a toothpick or short skewer. Makes 40 kabobs.

It's Party Time!

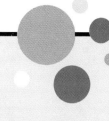

Caramelized Sirloin Skewers

1 pound beef sirloin steak, thinly sliced
¼ cup steak sauce, divided
¼ cup barbecue sauce
1 teaspoon Dijon mustard
1 teaspoon brown sugar

Place steak with 2 tablespoons steak sauce in zipper bag; toss, then marinate 10–15 minutes. Mix remaining 2 tablespoons steak sauce, barbecue sauce, mustard, and sugar; set aside. Preheat grill to medium-high heat. Thread steak onto 8 long soaked wooden skewers. Grill 6 minutes or until cooked through, turning after 3 minutes; brush each time with sauce mixture. Serves 4–6.

Try slicing thinly cut meat or chicken into long (4 inches or more) strips, then after marinating and seasoning, twist and thread onto 6- to 8-inch skewers. Broil or grill for an appetizing all-meat skewer.

Tangy Grilled Chicken Kabobs

½ cup raspberry vinaigrette dressing
2 tablespoons mayonnaise
1½ pounds boneless, skinless chicken tenders, cut into 1-inch pieces
1 red onion, cut into small wedges
1 lemon, halved

Mix dressing and mayonnaise; pour into large zipper bag. Add chicken; seal bag. Turn several times to evenly coat chicken. Refrigerate 20–30 minutes to marinate.

Preheat grill to medium-high heat. Remove chicken from marinade; thread chicken and onion alternately onto 16 soaked wooden skewers. Grill 8–10 minutes or until chicken is cooked, turning occasionally. Place lemon on grill, cut sides down. Squeeze lemon juice over kabobs before serving. Serves 10–12.

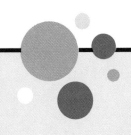

Sweet-And-Sour Meatball Kabobs

1 large green bell pepper, cut into 12 pieces
8 thin wedges red onion
12 small fresh mushrooms
½ teaspoon seasoned salt
16 frozen cooked meatballs, thawed
¾ cup sweet-and-sour sauce, divided

Heat gas or charcoal grill. In large bowl, mix bell pepper, onion, mushrooms, and seasoned salt.

Alternately thread meatballs, bell pepper, onion, and mushrooms onto 4 metal skewers. Place kabobs on gas grill over medium heat or on charcoal grill 4–6 inches from medium coals. Cook covered 10–15 minutes or until meatballs are thoroughly heated and vegetables are crisp-tender, brushing generously with half sweet-and-sour sauce and turning frequently. Heat remaining sweet-and-sour sauce to a boil; boil 1 minute. Serve sauce along side for dipping. Serves 4–6.

It's Party Time!

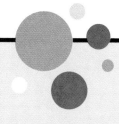

Veggie Kabobs with Honey Mustard Dip

KABOBS:
1 (6-inch) zucchini
1 red onion
1 medium red bell pepper
12 fresh button mushrooms
¼ cup Italian dressing

While coals or gas grill is heating, soak 12 (6-inch) wooden skewers in water 30 minutes. Cut all veggies into threadable pieces (about 1 inch), and place in bowl; toss with dressing. Thread alternate veggies on skewers. Cover and grill 4–6 inches from medium heat 8–10 minutes, turning once, until veggies are tender. Serve with Honey Mustard Dip. Serves 6–8.

HONEY MUSTARD DIP:
¼ cup honey mustard dressing
¼ cup mayonnaise
¼ cup sour cream
¼ teaspoon curry

Mix all ingredients in small bowl with spoon.

Kabobs do best when meat and veggies are cut uniformly in size. Leave a little space between them when threading for more even cooking. And do offer a fork and/or knife for easy removal onto plates.

Let's Celebrate!

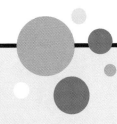

It's Party Time

Limes, as well as lemons, are wonderful to keep on hand . . . for drinks, for zests, for cleaning, for getting fish smell off your hands, and getting rid of odors, too. But did you know they might make a throbbing headache go away? Worth a try. Slice a lime in half and rub it on your forehead. Close your eyes and feel the throbbing slip away.

Gingered Shrimp Kabobs

Who doesn't love shrimp kabobs?

1 teaspoon grated fresh ginger
1 garlic clove, crushed
Grated zest of ½ lime
Juice of 1 lime
Salt and ground black pepper to taste
16–20 raw medium shrimp, peeled, deveined
Sweet chili sauce, for dipping
16–20 skewers, soaked in water

Combine ginger, garlic, lime zest, juice, and salt and pepper in a bowl with a lid. Add shrimp, toss to coat, and cover. Refrigerate for 10 minutes.

Preheat broiler. Thread a shrimp lengthwise onto end of each skewer. Place kabobs on broiler pan and broil 1 minute on each side, until cooked through. Serve with chili sauce for dipping. Makes 16–20 kabobs.

Easter Surprise Ham

1 (14- to 16-pound) ham, bone in
1 (6-ounce) can pineapple slices, juice reserved
Cherries
Brown sugar
Mustard
Cloves

Trim fat from ham. Mix pineapple juice with equal amount of brown sugar. Add mustard to taste. Coat ham and bake at 250° for 6 hours, uncovered, basting frequently. Score ham and place a clove in each diamond. Cover ham with pineapple slices. Place cherries inside holes of pineapple slices. Bake 30–40 minutes more. Serves 16–24. Beautiful.

Heavenly Sweet Party Ham

1 (6- to 8-pound) ham

Place ham in baking pan; cover tightly with foil. Place in 250° oven 5–8 hours, or overnight. Place ham (without juices) in a shallow baking dish and baste with Glaze. Bake at 350° until Glaze begins to harden on ham (20–30 minutes). Remove ham from oven and let sit at least 10 minutes before slicing. Serve with party bread. Serves 10–14.

GLAZE:
1 cup brown sugar
1 cup apricot preserves
½ cup honey Dijon mustard

Mix ingredients in medium saucepan. Heat till sugar dissolves. Baste ham with warm Glaze.

171

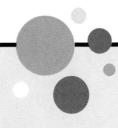

It's Party Time!

Sometimes chips lose their crispness after being opened a while. Revive them by putting a small amount on a paper plate and microwaving about 30 seconds. This works with crackers as well. It may not be quite the same as freshly opened chips, but what have you got to lose?

Party in a Bag

Fun, delicious, and easy cleanup! Kids love 'em.

2 pounds ground chuck
¾ cup chopped onion
1 envelope taco seasoning
12 (2¾-ounce) bags Fritos or Doritos
1½ cups shredded cheese
¼ head lettuce, shredded
2 tomatoes, chopped
1 cup sour cream
1 (4-ounce) can sliced black olives, drained
1 (8-ounce) jar taco sauce

Brown meat and onion; add taco seasoning. Cut ¼ inch off top of chip bags; squeeze bags to crush chips slightly. Fill bags with cooked meat mixture. Top with cheese, lettuce, tomatoes, sour cream, and olives offered on paper plates. Stick fork in bag and serve. Offer taco sauce. Serves 8–12.

Editor's Extra: Let guests start the bag with meat, then whichever lined-up remaining ingredients they desire. Stick a plastic fork in the bag. Easy cleanup.

Mad About Crab Puffs

1 (8-ounce) can refrigerated crescent rolls
1 tablespoon butter, melted
¼ teaspoon garlic powder
1 egg
½ cup mayonnaise
1 (6-ounce) can crabmeat, drained
¾ cup shredded sharp Cheddar cheese
1 plum tomato, finely chopped
2 tablespoons minced green onion
4 dashes Tabasco

Unroll dough on lightly floured surface; press perforations to seal. Press into 8x12-inch rectangle; cut into 2-inch squares; place on ungreased baking sheet. Brush with butter/garlic powder mixture. Bake in 375° oven 4–6 minutes till puffy.

In a bowl, beat egg and mayonnaise, then stir in remaining ingredients. Spoon tablespoons of mixture on baked squares. Bake 10–12 minutes longer or till slightly browned. Best served warm. Makes 24.

Bayside Mini Crab Cakes

1 pound crabmeat
5 green onions, finely chopped
½ cup seasoned dry bread crumbs
2 eggs
⅓ cup mayonnaise
1 teaspoon Old Bay Seasoning
3 tablespoons vegetable oil

Mix all in bowl except oil. Shape into small patties. Heat 1½ tablespoons oil in a large frying pan. Add crab cakes in batches, frying until golden brown on bottom, about 2 minutes. Turn over and cook until other side is golden brown, about 2 minutes more. Add more oil between batches. Nice with tartar or rémoulade sauce. Serves 10–12.

Mitch's Marvelous Marinade

This is a grill master's best friend. Great on pork loin or roast as well as chicken halves.

1 cup cider vinegar
4 teaspoons salt
⅓ cup corn oil
2 teaspoons Tabasco
1 tablespoon Worcestershire
4 garlic cloves, thinly sliced, or ¼ teaspoon garlic powder

Combine and heat to blend. Baste meat or chicken halves frequently throughout grilling. Makes 1½ cups, enough for 4 chicken halves.

It's Party Time!

Embellished Breads

Rolls

Stuffed Breads

Crostini

Bruschetta

Biscuits

Sticks

Muffins

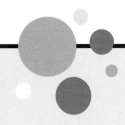

Mmmm . . . warm rolls . . . what's better? But we do prefer them warm. To keep rolls warmer longer, put a sheet of tin foil under the napkin in your bread basket.

Soft Sunrise Rolls

Sunrise, sunset . . . anytime.

2 (8-ounce) cans refrigerated crescent rolls
1 (8-ounce) package cream cheese, softened
2 tablespoons sugar
1 teaspoon lemon juice
1 cup powdered sugar
1 teaspoon vanilla extract
2 tablespoons milk

Separate crescents into 8 rectangles; press perforations to seal. Mix cream cheese, sugar, and lemon juice. Spread mixture evenly over each rectangle. Roll up jellyroll fashion, starting at long end. Cut each roll into 5 (1-inch) slices, using a serrated knife. Place on a lightly greased cookie sheet and bake at 375° for 15 minutes.

Meanwhile, combine powdered sugar, vanilla and milk. Drizzle over rolls. Serve warm. Makes 48 rolls.

Simple Sausage Rolls

Use mild or hot sausage. Easy and good.

2 (8-ounce) cans refrigerated crescent rolls
1 pound ground sausage

Separate crescents into 8 rectangles; press perforations to seal. Divide uncooked sausage into 8 pieces, spreading each piece as thin as possible onto each dough rectangle. Roll tightly from short end; wrap in plastic wrap; chill 25–30 minutes till firm. Slice each roll into 4; put on baking sheet and bake at 350° about 15 minutes till golden brown. Serves a bunch.

Editor's Extra: Easy to freeze dough rolls, defrost for a minute in the microwave (#3 power), and bake as directed above.

Rum Roll Bites

Great for breakfast or brunch.

½ cup sugar
¼ cup butter
¼ cup rum
⅛ teaspoon cinnamon
1 tray small party rolls

Cut through rolls in tray to make small bite-size pieces. Boil remaining ingredients for 1 minute. Pour over tray of rolls. Heat according to directions on package. Serves 10–12.

Cheesy Italian Garlic Bread

½ cup mayonnaise
½ cup butter, softened
1 tablespoon grated Parmesan cheese
2 teaspoons minced garlic
½ teaspoon Italian seasoning
⅛ teaspoon seasoned salt
½ cup shredded Monterey Jack cheese
1 loaf French bread, halved lengthwise

Mix mayonnaise, butter, Parmesan cheese, garlic, Italian seasoning, and seasoned salt until smooth. Stir in Monterey Jack cheese. Spread over cut sides of bread.

Bake on ungreased cookie sheet at 350° for 10–12 minutes, till cheese is melted. Slice and serve warm. Yields 12 servings.

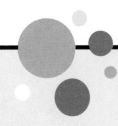

Fresh fruit is always welcome! It doesn't need a recipe. Just cut melons, pineapple, strawberries . . . any fresh fruit . . . and serve! It can be separated in a lazy susan with a dip in the middle, or with a small pitcher of poppy seed dressing alongside, or mixed together, or all by itself. If a friend asks what they can bring, say, "fresh fruit!" It goes with no matter what you are serving, and all your guests will love it.

N'Awlins Party Pull Bread

1 long loaf French bread
½ pound provolone or Muenster cheese, sliced thin
1 stick butter, softened
2 tablespoons grated onion
2 tablespoons Creole mustard
½ teaspoon Cajun seasoning

Cut Xs all over top of bread almost to bottom. Wrap foil halfway up sides of bread—don't cover top. Fold cheese and stuff into X cuts. Combine remaining ingredients and spread on top. Place on baking pan on bottom rack of oven. Bake at 400° until cheese melts, 10–15 minutes. Serve by letting guests pull off chunks of cheesy bread. Serves about 10.

Buttery Bacon and Cheese Bread

1 long skinny loaf French bread
2 cups grated mozzarella cheese
6–8 slices bacon, fried, crumbled
1 stick butter, melted

Preheat oven to 350°. Slice bread but not through bottom crust. Place on long sheet of heavy foil; stuff cheese and bacon into slices. Drizzle melted butter over bread. Wrap and bake about 25 minutes. Serves 8–10.

Editor's Extra: Other grated cheeses, cheese blends, or combos are good as well.

Hot 'n Bubbly Bread

1 loaf French bread
½ cup mayonnaise
2 cups shredded mozzarella cheese
½ cup butter, softened
6 green onions, chopped
½ teaspoon garlic powder
1 (4-ounce) can sliced black olives (optional)

Slice French bread lengthwise. Mix remaining ingredients by hand; spread on both halves of bread and bake in preheated 350° oven for 15 minutes or until hot and bubbly. Serves 8–12.

Lemony Garlic Bread

This goes with anything or by itself.

1 stick butter
1 tablespoon fresh lemon juice
3 green onion tops, chopped
¼ teaspoon Worcestershire
1 teaspoon minced garlic
Dash of Tabasco
1 loaf French bread, sliced lengthwise
Grated Parmesan cheese
Cayenne pepper (optional)

Melt butter in skillet and sauté all but the last 3 ingredients. When onions are soft, spoon mixture on both halves of bread. Sprinkle Parmesan cheese on bread, then dust with cayenne pepper, if desired. Bake on cookie sheet at 350° until lightly browned. Wrap heated bread in tin foil to take along.

Mexicali Shotgun Bread

1 loaf French bread
1 (4-ounce) can chopped green chiles
1 cup sour cream
1 (6-ounce) package southwestern-flavored cooked chicken strips, chopped
½ (16-ounce) package Mexican Velveeta, halved, sliced

Slice bread in half lengthwise. Make a ¾-inch trench in middle of top and bottom side. Put bread halves on long pieces of tin foil, folding up along sides. Mix chiles, sour cream, and chicken; fill trenches with mixture. Place Velveeta slices on top of filling. Bake in a 350° oven 20 minutes, or until cheese melts. Slice into sections and serve. Serves 8–10.

Pick-Apart Bacon-Ranch Bread Ring

12 bacon strips, diced
1 (1-pound) loaf frozen bread dough, thawed
2 tablespoons olive oil, divided
1 (1-ounce) package ranch salad dressing mix
1 cup shredded mozzarella cheese

Cook bacon over medium heat until partially cooked; drain. Roll out dough to ½-inch thickness. Brush with 1 tablespoon oil. Cut into 1-inch pieces, and put in large bowl with bacon, dressing mix, cheese, and remaining oil; mix well. Arrange pieces in a 9-inch oval on a greased cookie sheet, layering if needed. Cover and let rise in a warm place 30 minutes, until doubled.

Bake in 350° oven 15 minutes, then cover with foil and bake 5–10 minutes longer, till golden brown. Serves 8–10.

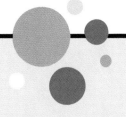

Pesto Crostini

½ loaf whole-wheat baguette
5 plum tomatoes
1 cup shredded part-skim mozzarella cheese
3 tablespoons prepared pesto

Slice baguette into 20 thin, diagonal slices. Slice tomatoes lengthwise into 4 slices. Place bread slices on ungreased nonstick baking pan. Put 1 teaspoon cheese, 1 slice tomato, then another teaspoon cheese on top. Bake at 400° for 8 minutes or until bread is toasted and cheese melted. Top each crostini with a dab of pesto sauce. Serve warm. Serves 4–6.

Partygoers seem to never tire of bread appetizers. Whether stuffed, crisped, hot baked, or sandwiched, they're always crowd pleasers.

Grilled Mozza-Roma Bites

1 loaf crusty Italian bread, cut into 16 slices
⅓ cup prepared pesto
16 fresh basil leaves
8 slices mozzarella cheese
24 thin slices Roma tomatoes
Olive oil

Spread half the bread slices with pesto. Top each slice with 2 basil leaves, 1 slice cheese, and 3 slices tomatoes; top with remaining bread slices.

Brush outsides of sandwiches lightly with olive oil. Grill sandwiches in indoor grill pan or skillet (both sides) about 5 minutes or till lightly browned and cheese is melted. Cut sandwiches into 4 pieces. Best served warm. Makes 24.

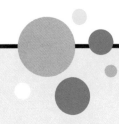

It's always a good idea to make a list of all you need to do before your party. It reduces stress and is fulfilling to check off each accomplishment. Don't hesitate to hand out chores and recipes to friends who are usually ready and willing to help. Remember: Party = fun. So don't forget to have a lot of it yourself.

BLT Bruschetta

½ cup canola oil
1 long loaf French bread, cut in ¼-inch slices
9 slices bacon, cooked crisp, crumbled
1 cup chopped green leaf lettuce
3 Roma tomatoes, seeded, chopped
2 tablespoons chopped fresh basil leaves
1 garlic clove, minced
¼ teaspoon salt
¼ teaspoon ground pepper
⅓ cup feta cheese

Brush oil on both sides of bread slices; place on baking sheet. Bake at 400° turning once, for 7 minutes, until crisp and golden brown; cool. In medium bowl, stir together remaining ingredients. Serve topping in small bowl surrounded by toast slices. Serves 10–12.

Colorful Crusty Bruschetta

1 long loaf crusty French bread, cut into 12 slices
3 tablespoons olive oil
1½ tablespoons fresh lime juice
2 teaspoons minced cilantro
½ cup chopped tomatoes
2 tablespoons chopped black olives
½ cup whole-kernel corn
½ cup minced green pepper
2 garlic cloves, minced

Preheat oven to 375°. Brush bread slices with oil, put on baking pan, and toast 8 minutes. Combine remaining ingredients in a bowl, and top each slice of bread with some of the mixture. Serves 6–10.

Pita Christmas Trees

4 pita bread pockets
16 pretzel sticks, halved
½ cup sour cream
½ cup guacamole
2 tablespoons minced parsley or green onion
¼ teaspoon Greek seasoning
¼ cup very finely chopped red bell pepper

Cut each pita pocket into 8 wedges. Insert pretzel half into center of bottom of each wedge to form a tree trunk.

In a bowl, mix sour cream, guacamole, parsley or onion, and seasoning. Spread about 1 teaspoon mixture on each pita wedge. Place pepper pieces all over for garland. Cover and refrigerate before serving. Makes 16.

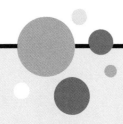

When cutting a roll into an even number of slices, you'll get more uniform slices if you cut it in half first, then in halves again, and so on till you have the desired number.

It's Party Time!

Crescent Roll Veggie Tree

Colorful and eye-catching.

1 (8-ounce) can refrigerated crescent rolls
2 ounces cream cheese
⅓ cup flavored dip or sour cream
Assorted diced veggies

Open crescent roll can, but do not unfold rolls. Cut roll into 12 slices. On greased baking pan, make tree by starting with one roll at top, then two underneath, three, four, then put two underneath for trunk. While baking per directions on can, mix cream cheese and dip or sour cream. When baked, spread with cream, then sprinkle with diced colorful veggies. Delicious!

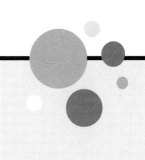

Quiche-y Crescent Cups

1 (8-ounce) can refrigerated crescent dinner rolls
⅓ cup shredded Gruyére cheese
4 green onions, sliced
1 tablespoon diced pimentos
1 large egg
3 tablespoons whipping cream

Unroll dough and press into a 9x12-inch rectangle; seal perforations. Cut into 12 equal squares. Press squares into 12 ungreased mini muffin cups, shaping edges to form rims ¼ inch high.

Evenly divide cheese into muffin cups. Top evenly with onions and pimentos. Whisk egg and whipping cream until blended. Spoon about 1 tablespoon mixture into each cup. Bake in 375° oven about 20 minutes till filling is set. Allow to cool 5 minutes before serving. Yields 12 appetizers.

Moo-Cow in a Blanket

1 (8-ounce) can refrigerated crescent dinner rolls
2 tablespoons Italian salad dressing
2 slices provolone cheese
3 ounces thinly sliced deli roast beef
2 tablespoons jarred chopped roasted red bell peppers

Heat oven to 350°. Spray cookie sheet with cooking spray. Separate dough into 8 triangles; press out and cut in half lengthwise to make 16 triangles. Brush with salad dressing. Cut each cheese slice into 8 strips; cut roast beef into 16 portions. Place cheese and beef pieces on mini triangles with a tad of red pepper. Roll from flat end to point. Bake 12–17 minutes till browned. Serve warm. Serves 16.

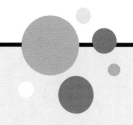

When serving a variety of buffet dishes, consider making tents to label what each dish is. This makes it easier for your guests to choose and move on.

It's Party Time!

Chicken Broccoli Pizza Spirals

1 (10-ounce) can chunk chicken, diced
½ (10-ounce) package frozen broccoli florets, thawed, chopped
2 cups shredded Pepper Jack cheese
¼ cup chunky salsa
2 green onions, chopped
1 (10-ounce) can refrigerated pizza dough

Combine chicken, broccoli, cheese, salsa, and green onions in small bowl.

Pat pizza dough into 10x15-inch rectangle. Sprinkle mixture evenly over top. Starting with long side, roll tightly. Pinch seam to seal. Place on baking sheet, seam side down. Bake at 400° for 15–20 minutes till golden brown. Cool slightly on wire rack. Slice and serve warm with extra salsa. Serves 6–8.

Crispy Pizza Dip Sticks

How to turn a frozen pizza into crispy dippers.

1 (1-pound) 4-cheese thin crispy pizza
2 tablespoons olive oil
5 tablespoons grated Parmesan, divided
¼ teaspoon red pepper flakes
Chunky salsa or marinara sauce

Brush edges of pizza crust lightly with oil. Drizzle remaining oil evenly over pizza. Mix 3 tablespoons Parmesan with pepper; sprinkle evenly over pizza. Place pizza directly on center oven rack. Bake 20 minutes or until edges are golden brown. Sprinkle with remaining Parmesan. Cut pizza into quarters; cut each quarter into 8 thin sticks. Offer as dippers with salsa or sauce. Makes 32.

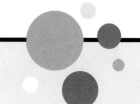

Quick Muffin Pizzas

1 (8-ounce) jar pizza sauce
6 English muffins, split, toasted
1 (4-ounce) package sliced pepperoni
1 cup shredded mozzarella cheese

Spread pizza sauce on muffin halves. Top each with 3 slices pepperoni, then cheese. Place 4 halves on microwave serving plate in circle. Cook on 70% power 3–4 minutes, or till cheese is melted. Repeat with remaining muffins. Makes 12.

Broccoli Cornbread Mini Muffins

Moist and delicious. Great with chili or soup, or to just pop in your mouth.

1 (10-ounce) package frozen chopped broccoli, thawed
1 cup shredded Cheddar cheese
1 (8½-ounce) package corn muffin mix
⅓ cup finely chopped onion
2 eggs
1 stick butter, melted

Combine broccoli, cheese, corn muffin mix, and onion in large bowl. Mix eggs and butter well; add to broccoli mixture, stirring just to moisten. Spoon into lightly greased miniature muffin pans, filling ¾ full.

Bake at 325° for 13–20 minutes or until browned. Let stand 2–3 minutes before removing from pans. Makes 36–40.

Let's Celebrate!

187

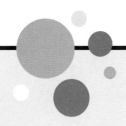

Always read through a recipe before you begin. Marinate . . . preheat the oven . . . grease the pans . . . make a day ahead . . . these are things you don't need to discover after you've begun.

It's Party Time!

Funny Face Muffins

⅓ cup ranch dressing
⅓ cup whipped cream cheese
4 English muffins, halved, toasted
Face decorations: American cheese slices; asparagus spears; shredded cheese; shredded carrots; red bell pepper; raisins; broccoli

Mix ranch dressing and cream cheese; spread even amounts over each muffin half. Have fun making faces. Be creative with whatever you have on hand: sliced black olives or raisins eyes, shredded cheese hair, red pepper strip mouth, broccoli nose, etc. Makes 8.

Editor's Extra: Good to sub bagel slices or toasted hamburger buns for muffins.

Pecan Muffinettes

Outstanding!

½ cup butter, melted
1 cup brown sugar
½ cup self-rising flour
2 eggs
1 teaspoon vanilla extract
1 cup chopped pecans

Mix all ingredients. Bake in well greased mini-muffin tins or Pam-sprayed paper cup liners at 350° for 13–15 minutes, till springy. Makes 3 dozen.

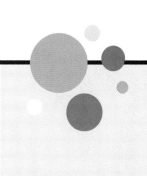

Bacon Blue Tartlets

1 (10-count) can biscuits
6 slices bacon, cooked, drained, crumbled
1 (4-ounce) package blue cheese, crumbled
¼ cup finely chopped walnuts
3 green onions, chopped
½ cup mayonnaise

Cut biscuit rounds into 3 triangles. Press each piece of dough into greased miniature muffin tins. Mix bacon, blue cheese, walnuts, green onions, and mayonnaise; stir well. Fill each biscuit cup with mixture. Bake at 350° for 10–12 minutes. Makes 30 tartlets.

Editor's Extra: Can sub crumbled feta for blue cheese, and about ⅓ cup real bacon bits for bacon slices. This combination of the last 5 ingredients is delicious to stuff cherry tomatoes, too.

Apple Upside-Down Biscuits

Good with peaches or pineapple slices, too.

½ stick butter, melted
1 cup dark brown sugar
2 Granny Smith apples, peeled, cored, sliced into rings
1 (10-count) package frozen buttermilk biscuits, thawed
¾ cup pineapple juice
¾ cup granulated sugar

Mix butter and sugar in a 9x9-inch dish and pat smoothly. Place apple rings on top. Place in a 350° oven for 10 minutes. Remove dish from oven. Dip thawed biscuits in pineapple juice; roll in granulated sugar. Place biscuits on apple rings. Return to oven; bake 25 minutes, or until biscuits are brown and bubbly. Serves 8–10.

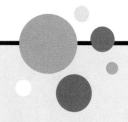

The origin of the word "biscuit" is from Latin via Middle French and means "cooked twice." Some of the original biscuits were British naval hard tack. That was passed down to American culture, and hard tack (biscuits) was made through the 19th century.

A biscuit in the UK is a hard baked sweet product like a small flat cake that in North America may be called a "cookie" or cracker."

In America, a "biscuit" is a small form of bread made with baking powder or baking soda as a leavening agent rather than yeast. They are soft and similar to scones. Biscuits are a common feature of southern U.S. cuisine.

No matter what you call them, they're *good.*

Easy Bisquiks

A classic. You'll make these again and again.

2 cups Bisquick mix
1 stick margarine, melted
1 (8-ounce) container sour cream

Mix all ingredients. Drop by spoonfuls into sprayed mini muffin tins. Bake at 400° till brown, 15–20 minutes. Makes 36.

Gorgonzola Biscuits

1 stick butter
1 (6-ounce) tub crumbled Gorgonzola cheese
1 (8-count) can flaky biscuits

Preheat oven to 350°. Melt butter in plate or casserole. Spread Gorgonzola cheese over butter. Cut or tear each biscuit into 4 pieces and place in butter/cheese. Bake 15–20 minutes. Makes 32.

Cookie Biscuits

Here's a favorite recipe for delicious biscuits (more like cookies) that come already buttered! Use shaped cookie cutters for specific party themes.

1 (3-ounce) package cream cheese, softened
1 stick butter, softened
1 cup flour

Preheat oven to 400°. Mix cream cheese and butter well, then add flour gradually. Make a ball and roll on floured surface to ¼-inch thickness. Cut with small cookie cutter. Place on ungreased baking sheet and bake for about 10 minutes. Makes about 40 small biscuits. Offer jam, but good without, too.

Cheesy Vidalia Fingers

1 cup shredded fresh Parmesan cheese
1 cup grated Swiss cheese
1 large purple or Vidalia onion, chopped
1⅓ cups mayonnaise
24 slices bread, crusts removed

Combine cheeses, onion, and mayonnaise in mixing bowl. Spread bread with mixture and bake in 400° oven 10–12 minutes. Remove and cut each into 3 finger slices before serving. Makes 72.

Crocked Cheese Fingers

12 slices white bread, crusts removed
2 cups shredded Cheddar cheese
4 egg yolks
½ cup beer

Place bread on 2 baking sheets. Broil 3–4 inches from heat about 1½ minutes, until bread begins to brown. Remove bread and reduce temperature to 375°.

Place cheese in a 8-cup glass measure. Microwave on HIGH about 1 minute (or more) to soften. Remove and vigorously stir in egg yolks and beer until mixture is fairly smooth. Spread a layer on each slice of bread, covering bread completely. Bake 8 minutes, or until cheese topping begins to puff. If desired, run under broiler 1 minute to brown top. Cut each slice into 3 fingers. Serve immediately. Makes 36.

Yummy Pockets

Good for breakfast, lunch, or light supper . . . great for parties.

½ (8-ounce) package cream cheese, softened
1 tablespoon Miracle Whip
2 teaspoons coarse mustard
5 slices deli ham or turkey, finely chopped
¼ cup shredded cheese of choice
1 (10-count) can refrigerated biscuits

Preheat oven to 400°. Process cream cheese, Miracle Whip, and mustard until well blended. Add deli meat and cheese; mix well; set aside. Press each biscuit to 3½-inch circle. Place 1 heaping teaspoon mixture onto each biscuit. Fold dough over filling and firmly press edges of dough together to seal. Place on greased baking sheet. Bake 10–12 minutes or till lightly browned. Makes 10.

Editor's Extra: This is also good spread on crackers, or as a sandwich filling.

It's Party Time!

Spread It On

Finger Sandwiches

Pita Pockets

Buns

Tortillas

Patés

Spreads

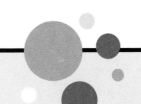

Easy Egg Salad Sandwiches

You may want to double this, as they disappear quickly.

½ cup mayonnaise
1 tablespoon minced sweet pickle
2 tablespoons minced celery
1 tablespoon minced sweet or green onion
2 teaspoons Dijon mustard
6 hard-boiled eggs, cooled, peeled, chopped
Salt and pepper to taste
12 slices bread, crusted (or not)

Mix mayonnaise, pickles, celery, onions, and mustard in a bowl. Stir in eggs and seasoning and stir gently. Spread on 6 slices of bread and top each with another slice of bread. Cut each into 4 squares or triangles. Refrigerate till time to serve. Makes 24.

Good-To-Go Cheese Sandwiches

Great sandwiches. Or as a spread with crackers.

2 cups grated Cheddar cheese
¼ cup chili sauce
¾ cup mayonnaise
½ cup chopped pecans
½ cup chopped stuffed olives
1 teaspoon Worcestershire
12 slices bread, crusted

Blend all ingredients well; cover and chill. Sandwich into bread slices and cut into 3 finger sandwiches. Refrigerate till ready to serve. Makes 18.

It's Party Time!

Simply Superb Chicken Salad Sandwiches

4 cups chopped cooked chicken
1 cup mayonnaise
¾ cup chopped celery
1 cup sliced seedless grapes
Salt and pepper to taste
½ teaspoon curry powder (optional)
1 long loaf bread, crusted

Mix all together except bread. Spread on half the bread slices; cover and quarter. Also nice to serve on lettuce, or in tomatoes or avocados. Makes 40.

Editor's Extra: If desired, spread a thin layer of mayo on bread slices before adding chicken salad.

Rotisserie chicken from the supermarket deli is well seasoned and makes tasty chicken salad.

Burst-Of-Flavor Chicken Sandwiches

Simply the best! Always the first to go.

1¼ cups mayonnaise, divided
1 loaf white bread, crusted
3 cups shredded cooked chicken
1 stalk celery, finely chopped
⅓ cup dried cranberries (optional)
Salt and pepper to taste
1 (3.75-ounce) package Honey-Roasted Almond Accents

Spread ½ cup mayonnaise on all slices of bread. Spread mixture of chicken, celery, cranberries, if desired, ¾ cup mayonnaise, and seasoning on half the bread slices; sprinkle almonds on each chicken sandwich; top with remaining bread slices. Cut into fourths. Makes 40.

195

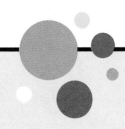

Have a picnic party by meeting several families at a nearby park. Make a picnic list and keep it handy for next time, adding the "forgots" when you get home. Keep a file for different kinds of parties. Computers make easy work of organizing.

Open & Closed Cucumber Sandwiches

Spread thick to close; thinner to leave open.

1 (8-ounce) package cream cheese, softened
1 tablespoon grated onion and juice
1 tablespoon minced parsley
1 cucumber, peeled, grated, drained
1 tablespoon lemon juice
1 teaspoon dry ranch-style salad dressing
Salt and red pepper to taste
1 loaf white or wheat bread, crusted

Combine ingredients except bread. Refrigerate several hours to blend flavors before spreading on bread slices; cover each with another bread slice, if desired; cut into squares. These keep for several days covered and refrigerated, or can be frozen. Makes 40 closed or 80 open.

Editor's Extra: You may add a drop of green food coloring, if desired. A sprinkle of paprika on open faces is pretty as well as tasty.

Pimento on Rye Snackwiches

1 (2-ounce) jar diced pimentos, drained
¼ cup mayonnaise
½ cup shredded Cheddar cheese
½ cup shredded Muenster cheese
⅛ teaspoon onion powder
16 slices cocktail rye bread

Combine all ingredients except bread; mix well. Spread on 8 bread slices; top with remaining bread slices. Serves 4–6.

Pocket Sandwiches with Heart

1 (14-ounce) can artichoke hearts, drained, chopped
1 (8-ounce) can pineapple chunks, drained
2 (6-ounce) packages cooked chicken strips, chopped
6 pita pockets
1 (12-ounce) package Swiss cheese slices, divided

Mix artichoke hearts, pineapple, and chicken together. Line pita pockets with ¾ of the cheese slices. Fill pockets with chicken mixture. Top with remaining cheese. Bake at 350° for 10 minutes till cheese melts. Serve warm, or cold with Cucumber Sauce. Makes 6.

CUCUMBER SAUCE:
6 ounces cucumber salad dressing
¼ cup sour cream
¼ cup plain yogurt

Mix all together well.

Deli Ham Salad Finger Sandwiches

½ pound deli ham, finely chopped or ground
¼ cup minced celery
2 tablespoons minced onion
⅓ cup mayonnaise
¼ cup sweet pickle relish
¼ teaspoon Old Bay seasoning
12 slices bread of choice

Combine all ingredients except bread in bowl; mix well. Sandwich between 2 slices crusted bread; cut in triangle quarters or strips. Makes 18–24.

Note: This is good as well with other deli meats, or a combo of shredded Cheddar and ham.

Instead of frying the grease into the meat, try adding a little water to the pan when browning ground meat. This way, more of the grease can be poured out when draining.

Sloppy Joe Bunners

Teenage party? Perfect! Fix plenty!

2 pounds ground meat
1 cup chopped onion
2 tablespoons Worcestershire
⅓ cup brown sugar
½ cup chili sauce
1 tablespoon mustard
1 (10¾-ounce) can cream of mushroom soup
12 hamburger buns

Brown meat and drain. Sauté onion a few minutes with meat; add remaining ingredients except buns. Heat, then simmer until thick. Serve on buns with napkins handy. Yum! Makes 12.

Speedy Sloppy Joes

This is a fast, fulfilling, popular dish for hungry guests.

1½ pounds ground beef
1 onion, chopped
1 envelope chili seasoning
½ cup ketchup
½ cup milk
2 tablespoons vinegar
12 hamburger buns

Brown beef and onion; drain. Stir in remaining ingredients, except buns. Simmer 5–10 minutes. Serve on toasted buns. Makes 12.

It's Party Time!

198

Reindeer Sandwiches

1 (7-ounce) jar marshmallow crème
1 (18-ounce) jar grape jelly and peanut butter
½ cup chopped honey roasted peanuts
1 loaf whole-wheat bread
80 Christmas tree pretzels (or pretzel sticks, broken)
20 maraschino cherries, halved
80 mini-chocolate chips

Mix marshmallow crème, peanut butter jelly, and peanuts. Trim crusts from bread; spread mixture on ½ the bread slices; cover with remaining slices. Cut twice diagonally to make 4 triangles. Stick 2 tree pretzels (or broken sticks) on flat edge of triangle (antlers), cherry on tip of triangle (nose), and 2 chips above nose for eyes. Makes 40.

Quick and Tasty Shrimp Wedges

8 small flour tortillas
¼ cup pesto
1 pound frozen, cooked salad shrimp
8 ounces shredded Colby Jack cheese
1 (4-ounce) can chopped black olives

Lay tortillas on Pam-sprayed foil on baking sheets. Spread pesto over each. Layer shrimp, cheese, and olives on top of pesto on each tortilla. Top each with another tortilla and spray lightly with Pam. Bake at 350° for about 20 minutes or until lightly browned. After about 5 minutes, cut each tortilla into 4–6 wedges and serve. Yields 32–48 slices.

Easy Shrimp Quesadillas

¼ cup tahini
4 (10-inch) flour tortillas
4 green onions, sliced
½ cup cooked salad shrimp, chopped
Salt to taste
1 cup vegetable oil

Spread tahini evenly over each tortilla, covering almost completely. Sprinkle green onions and shrimp over 2 tortillas. Season with salt. Top with other 2 tortillas, tahini side down, and press firmly together.

Fry in hot oil, pressing down with a spatula, until bottom is golden brown. Turn and brown other side; drain. Repeat with remaining quesadilla. Cut into wedges and serve warm. Serves 6–10.

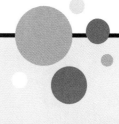

Super Salmon Paté

1 (7¾-ounce) can red salmon, drained
1 (8-ounce) package cream cheese, softened
2 tablespoons finely chopped onion
1 tablespoon lemon juice
1 teaspoon Worcestershire
⅛ teaspoon Tabasco
¼ teaspoon garlic powder

For easy cleanup of prepped ingredients, use flat-bottomed coffee filters, muffin cup liners, or paper cups to hold and separate chopped ingredients.

Mix all together well. Mold into wax paper-lined container. Chill several hours. Unmold onto plate, and garnish with parsley and cherry tomatoes Serve with crackers. Serves 8–10.

Red Pepper Crab Spread

1 (8-ounce) package cream cheese, softened
1 teaspoon garlic powder
1 teaspoon Old Bay seasoning
1 medium red or orange bell pepper, chopped
1 cup finely chopped onion
1 (6-ounce) can crabmeat, drained
1½ cups shredded mozzarella cheese, divided

Mix all but ½ cup mozzarella cheese. Spread into 9-inch pie plate. Bake at 375° for 20 minutes till top is lightly browned. Sprinkle with reserved ½ cup mozzarella cheese. Garnish with chopped parsley, if desired. Serve warm with assorted crackers. Serves 8–10.

Let's Celebrate!

Tasty Crab Spread

1 (8-ounce) package cream cheese, softened
2 tablespoons lemon juice
2 green onions, finely chopped
¼ teaspoon paprika
¼ teaspoon salt
⅛ teaspoon cayenne pepper
12 ounces crabmeat

Process or blend cream cheese, lemon juice, onions, paprika, salt, and pepper till smooth. Transfer to a serving bowl and stir in crabmeat. Refrigerate until ready to serve. Serve with crusty bread rounds or Melba toast. Makes about 2 cups.

Bayou Crawfish Spread

3 tablespoons butter
1½ cups frozen seasoning blend
1 cup finely chopped crawfish tails
½ teaspoon garlic salt
½ teaspoon cayenne pepper
1 (8-ounce) package cream cheese, softened

Melt butter in skillet over medium-high heat. Add seasoning blend and crawfish; sauté 2–3 minutes while stirring. Add garlic salt and pepper. Turn off heat and add cream cheese, stirring till mixed. Serve warm or chilled with dry toasted bread squares or hearty crackers.

Editor's Extra: Crawfish tails are available frozen in most supermarkets.

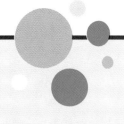

BLT Spread

You'll want to make a sandwich with this spread! But delicious on Wheat Thins or Ritz or scoops . . . or a spoon!

3 Roma tomatoes, halved
1 tablespoon prepared mustard
1 (8-ounce) package cream cheese, quartered
¼ teaspoon Cajun seasoning
1 cup sliced almonds
1 green onion, chopped
⅓ cup Real Bacon Bits

Place tomatoes, mustard, cream cheese, and Cajun seasoning in a food processor; mix till smooth. Add almonds, green onion, and bacon bits; pulse about 4 times. Refrigerate up to 2 days. Makes about 1½ cups.

Editor's Extra: If you're so inclined, to sub for the bacon bits, fry about 8 slices of real bacon crisp, then drain.

Frozen seasoning blend is a mixture of chopped onions, celery, and bell pepper. It is very convenient to have handy without having to chop fresh. Cajuns call this mixture the Holy Trinity, as few of their dishes start without these three vegetables sautéed, sometimes in a roux.

Swiss Reuben Spread

1 (8-ounce) package cream cheese, cubed
2 cups shredded Swiss cheese
1 (16-ounce) jar sauerkraut, rinsed, drained
1 (3-ounce) package deli corned beef, chopped
¼ cup prepared Thousand Island salad dressing
1 loaf party rye bread or crackers

In heavy saucepan, combine first 5 ingredients. Cook on medium heat, stirring often till cheese melts. Serve warm with rye bread or crackers. Yields 3½ cups.

Be sure to have some party food available in more that one room, particularly your kitchen—that's where guests usually gravitate.

Offer napkins in several places, too, and be sure to have trash receptacles where guests can easily find them.

Buttery Boursin Spread

1 (8-ounce) package cream cheese, softened
1 stick butter, softened
¼ teaspoon each: basil, oregano, thyme, dill weed, garlic powder, and pepper
Assorted crackers

Combine all ingredients until well blended. Best chilled at least 2 hours, but good right now. Serve with crackers. Makes 1½ cups.

Awesome Chocolate Peanut Butter Spread

Awesome on ice cream, too.

1 stick butter
3 tablespoons cocoa
½ cup honey
1¼ cups peanut butter
¼ teaspoon vanilla

Melt butter; add cocoa and honey, stirring till smooth. Take off heat and stir in peanut butter and vanilla. Jar and refrigerate. Spread on bread or crackers. Makes about a pint.

Savory Pastries

Won Tons

Squares

Pies

Phyllos

Foldovers

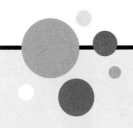

It's Party Time!

Don't hesitate to buy won tons. Unlike some difficult-to-deal-with pastry things, these are pull-off-the-stack easy. "Stars" require only that you push sheets into mini muffin pans and bake a few minutes . . . appealing as well as tasty.

Olé Chicken Stars

A tasty crisp treat in minutes.

12 won ton wrappers (about 3 inches square)
1½ tablespoons olive oil
1 large skinless, boneless chicken breast, diced
½ cup thick and chunky red salsa
12 sprigs cilantro

Preheat oven to 400°. Press won ton wrappers in miniature muffin cups. Bake 5 minutes till golden brown and crisp. Heat oil in a large frying pan; cook chicken 5–7 minutes. Stir in salsa and cook another minute till heated. When pastry cups are done, remove from oven and fill with chicken mixture. Garnish each cup with a sprig of cilantro.

Ranchero Sausage Stars

1 pound bulk sausage
3 cups grated Monterey Jack cheese
1 cup prepared Hidden Valley Ranch Original Salad
   Dressing Mix
1 (2¼-ounce) can sliced ripe olives
½ cup chopped red bell pepper
1 package fresh or frozen won ton wrappers

Preheat oven to 350°. Brown and drain sausage dry on paper towels; combine with cheese, salad dressing, olives, and red pepper. Lightly grease mini muffin pans and press 1 wrapper in each cup. Brush with oil. Bake 5 minutes until golden. Remove from tins, and place on baking sheet. Fill with sausage mixture. Bake 5 minutes until bubbly. Makes 4–5 dozen.

Editor's Extra: Easy to sub bottled salad dressing.

Sweet Little Chic Won Tons

½ pound ground chicken or turkey
¼ cup chopped celery
¼ cup chopped onion
1 tablespoon dry sherry (optional)
1 teaspoon grated fresh ginger
1 tablespoon soy sauce
2 teaspoons cornstarch
⅓ cup sweet and sour sauce
24 square won ton wrappers

Sauté chicken with celery and onion in a nonstick skillet over medium-high heat. Stir in sherry, ginger, soy sauce, cornstarch, and sweet and sour sauce. Cool. Place teaspoonfuls in center of each wrapper. Fold to opposite corners and pinch edges together to seal. Place filled won tons on Pam-sprayed cookie sheet; spray won tons lightly with cooking spray. Bake at 375° about 10 minutes till brown. Serve warm. Makes 24.

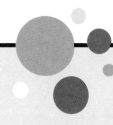

It's Party Time!

Can you freeze cheese? Yes, but if properly wrapped and stored, it keeps a good while in the refrigerator—just keep an eye on the expiration date. When close to that date, you can freeze it with some sacrifice of flavor and texture . . . it is usually just fine for cooking.

Chicken Salad in Biscuit Cups

2 cups chopped cooked chicken
1/3 cup chopped celery
1/3 cup mayonnaise
2 tablespoons chopped toasted sliced almonds
1 green onion, diced
Salt and pepper to taste
1 (5-count) can flaky biscuits
1/3 cup shredded Cheddar cheese

Grease 10 muffin cups. Fold together chicken, celery, mayonnaise, almonds, onion, salt and pepper until blended. Divide biscuits in half horizontally, then press each biscuit in bottom and up sides of muffin cups. Spoon chicken mixture into cups. Bake 13–15 minutes at 375° till edges are soft brown. Sprinkle with cheese. Makes 10.

Caesar City Chicken Squares

2 (8-ounce) cans crescent rolls
2 (3-ounce) packages cream cheese, softened
1/2 cup Caesar or ranch dressing, divided
1/2 cup chopped cooked chicken
1 1/2 cups shredded lettuce
3/4 cup chopped broccoli
1/2 cup shredded carrot
2 tablespoons chopped cooked bacon
3 tablespoons shredded Parmesan cheese

Unroll crescent rolls, place in ungreased 10x15-inch baking pan, and press in bottom and up sides to form crust. Seal perforations. Bake about 15 minutes or till golden brown. Cool 30 minutes.

Blend cream cheese with 1/4 cup dressing; add chicken. Spread over cooled crust. Top with remaining ingredients. Gently press into cream cheese. Drizzle remaining 1/4 cup dressing over top. Cut into squares. Serves 10–12.

Asparo-Squares

Pretty little asparagus spears all in a row.

½ pound fresh thin asparagus spears
1 (8-ounce) can refrigerated crescent dinner rolls
1½ cups finely shredded Swiss cheese, divided
1½ ounces thinly sliced deli ham, cut into 1-inch strips
2 teaspoons olive oil
¼ teaspoon crushed red pepper flakes

Heat oven to 375°. Drop asparagus in ½ inch of boiling water in a 10-inch skillet. Simmer, covered, for 3 minutes. Drain and immediately plunge asparagus into bowl of ice water to cool; drain on paper towels.

Unroll dough on ungreased cookie sheet and press into 8x11-inch rectangle, sealing perforations. Prick with fork. Bake 6–9 minutes until light golden brown. Sprinkle with ½ the cheese; top with ham strips. Sprinkle with remaining cheese. Place asparagus spears in rows over cheese, alternating tips. Brush asparagus with oil; sprinkle with pepper flakes.

Bake 5–7 minutes more until crust edges are golden brown and cheese is melted. Cool 5 minutes. Cut into squares. Serve warm. Makes 24 squares.

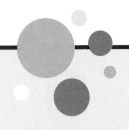

For a large buffet, it's a good idea to put out a few hot pads on your buffet table, reserving space for last minute hot dishes. Colorful tile blocks and footed trivets look nice empty . . . then save your table!

Mini Spini Crabmeat Pies

You can use refrigerated pie crust to make it quicker, but this pastry is worth the effort.

PASTRY:

2 cups all-purpose flour
¼ teaspoon salt
1 teaspoon chopped fresh thyme
1 stick firm butter, cut into pieces
½ cup sour cream
3–4 tablespoons cold water
1 egg, beaten
Fresh or dried thyme leaves

Combine flour, salt, and thyme. Cut in butter until mixture resembles coarse crumbs. Blend in sour cream. Gradually add water, 1 tablespoon at a time, until mixture forms a ball.

FILLING:

1 (10-ounce) package frozen cut leaf spinach, thawed, squeezed dry
6-ounces crabmeat
1 cup shredded Swiss cheese
¼ cup finely chopped red onion
¼ cup sour cream
¼ teaspoon salt

Mix all ingredients until well blended. Roll pastry on lightly floured surface till thin, about ¹⁄₁₆ inch thick. Cut into 2½- to 3-inch circles. Spoon about 1 teaspoon Filling in center of each circle. Brush edge of circle with water. Fold in half and press edges to seal. Place on ungreased, 10x15-inch, baking pan. Brush with egg, then sprinkle with thyme. Bake at 400° for 20 minutes or till golden brown. Makes 32 pies.

It's Party Time!

Crispy Crab Phyllo Roll-Ups

When you want to pull out all the stops . . .

4 shallots, minced
½ stick butter
2 garlic cloves, minced
½ cup chopped fresh parsley
1 teaspoon dill weed
2 tablespoons horseradish
12 ounces crabmeat
1 (1-pound) package phyllo dough, thawed
Melted butter

Sauté shallots in butter until limp. Remove from heat and stir in garlic, parsley, dill, horseradish, and crabmeat. Place 1 sheet of phyllo on a work surface and brush with butter. Cut lengthwise into 3 strips. Place 1 tablespoon crabmeat mixture in center on one end of each strip. Fold sides in over filling and roll up tightly. Brush outside with butter and place on a baking pan. Repeat with remaining ingredients. Bake in 350° oven 15 minutes or until golden brown. Makes about 72 roll-ups.

Note: To keep phyllo sheets from drying out while you are working, cover them with a slightly damp cloth.

Flaky Ham Pick Ups

Easily doubled or tripled and that's a good thing, 'cause these are always a hit.

1 sheet puff pastry
1 egg
1 tablespoon water
1 pound sliced cooked ham or turkey
1 cup shredded Cheddar cheese

Thaw pastry sheet about 30 minutes. Preheat oven to 400°. Mix egg with water; set aside. Unfold pastry on lightly floured surface. Roll into 12x16-inch rectangle. Layer ham on bottom half of pastry to within 1 inch of edges. Sprinkle with cheese. Starting at short side, roll up like a jellyroll. Place seam side down on baking sheet. Tuck ends under to seal. Brush with egg mixture. Bake 25 minutes or until golden. Slice and serve warm. Serves 6.

Flaky Pepperoni Pastries

1 (2-ounce) package pepperoni, diced
¼ teaspoon Tabasco (optional)
1 (15-ounce) jar pizza sauce, divided
Pastry for 2-crust pie
1 egg, beaten

Put pepperoni pieces in a bowl; stir in Tabasco, if desired, and ¼ cup pizza sauce.

Cut (3-inch) rounds from each crust. Spoon about 1 teaspoon pepperoni mixture onto each round; fold each in half; seal edges with fork. Cut slit in top of each with a sharp knife. Brush each foldover with beaten egg and place on ungreased cookie sheets. Bake at 425° for 9–11 minutes or until golden brown. Serve warm appetizers with remaining warmed pizza sauce for dipping. Makes about 22 appetizers.

It's Party Time!

Sweet Pick-Ups

Cookies

Bars

Candies

Clusters

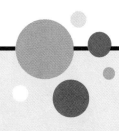

Try using a potato masher to imprint the top of the cookies instead of a fork—but don't mash too hard. Dip masher in water from time to time to keep from sticking.

Extra Special Chocolate Chip Cookies

The peanut brittle makes these chocolate chip cookies extra special.

1 stick butter, softened
⅓ cup Crisco shortening
1 cup packed brown sugar
½ cup sugar
1 teaspoon baking soda
½ teaspoon salt
2 eggs
2 teaspoons vanilla
2¼ cups all-purpose flour
1 (12-ounce) package semisweet chocolate
¾ cup chopped peanuts
½ cup crushed brickle bits

Blend butter and shortening with mixer for 30 seconds, then add sugars, baking soda, and salt. Mix until combined, scraping side of bowl occasionally. Mix in eggs and vanilla. Stir in flour by hand until combined, then stir in chocolate pieces and peanuts. Drop dough by rounded teaspoons 2 inches apart onto ungreased cookie sheet. Flatten slightly with fork, making criss-cross patterns. Sprinkle ½ teaspoon brickle bits over each cookie. Bake at 350° for about 10 minutes or until centers appear set. Makes about 4 dozen.

It's Party Time!

Hoppy Chocolate Frogs

Kids love to make and eat these.

3 squares semisweet chocolate
3 tablespoons butter
12 Oreo cookies
¼ cup peanut butter
24 mini pretzel twists
24 M&M's

Melt chocolate in butter in microwave 2 minutes on HIGH stirring halfway and again at end. Spread one side of each cookie with peanut butter; dip entire cookie into melted chocolate. Immediately press 2 pretzels under cookie, wide "feet" outward, and attach M&M's stuck on with a dab of chocolate for eyes. Makes 12 delicious frogs.

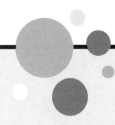

For easy removal of lace cookies, place entire cookie sheet in frig a few minutes right after baking to cool. Cookies come off foil or parchment easily and the cookie sheet can be re-used for the next batch.

Want to make lace cookie ice cream cups? Cut paper under each cookie; when baked, put paper with cookie on a cold plate to harden a bit, then mold over bottom of a custard cup by pressing with paper square. Bring on the mousse or custard or ice cream! Serve immediately.

Frilly Lace Cookies

This thin, crispy cookie is pretty and popular.

1 stick butter
1 cup quick oats
1 cup sugar
3 tablespoons all-purpose flour
¼ teaspoon baking powder
1 teaspoon salt
1 teaspoon vanilla
1 egg, beaten

Micro-melt butter in glass bowl. Stir in remaining ingredients. Refrigerate a few hours to firm. On foil or parchment-covered cookie sheets, place small teaspoon-size balls about 4 inches apart. Bake at 325° for 8–11 minutes.

Chipper Cookies

2 cups butter, softened
1 cup sugar
3¼ cups all-purpose flour
1 teaspoon vanilla
1 cup crushed potato chips
¼ cup confectioners' sugar

Cream butter and sugar in mixer bowl until light. Add flour and vanilla; mix well. Add crushed potato chips gradually, mixing well after each addition. Drop by teaspoonfuls onto ungreased cookie sheet. Bake at 350° for 15 minutes or until golden brown. Cool on wire rack. Sprinkle with confectioners' sugar. Makes about 36 cookies.

Peanut Butter Quickie Cookies

These have no flour. The kids will help you make . . . and eat these.

1 cup sugar
1 egg
1 teaspoon baking soda
1 cup creamy or chunky peanut butter

Cream sugar and egg; add baking soda; fold in peanut butter. Roll into balls, and place on cookie sheet. Push down balls with fork dipped in water. Bake 10 minutes at 350°. Makes 16–24.

Chocolate Coffee Iced Shortbread Cookies

1 package shortbread cookies

Spread each cookie with Chocolate Icing, then Coffee Icing. Let dry on rack. Makes about 28.

CHOCOLATE ICING:
1¾ cups confectioners' sugar, sifted
2 tablespoons hot water
2 tablespoons light corn syrup
½ cup bittersweet or semisweet chocolate chips or chunks, melted

Stir together hot water, confectioners' sugar, and corn syrup, stirring until smooth. Stir in melted chocolate and mix well.

COFFEE ICING:
2¼ cups confectioners' sugar
2 tablespoons light corn syrup
2 tablespoons hot water
1 tablespoon coffee powder

Combine first 3 ingredients, then add coffee powder and stir well.

Let's Celebrate!

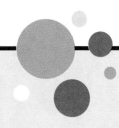

Teacakes in Great Britain and Ireland are light, sweet, yeast-based buns containing dried fruits. In the USA, the name generally refers to a sweet cookie or small cake you would serve with tea or coffee.

Granny's Old-Fashioned Teacakes

1 stick butter, softened
1 cup sugar
2 eggs, beaten
1 teaspoon vanilla or lemon flavoring
1 teaspoon milk
2¼ cups self-rising flour

Mix ingredients well. Roll out dough on a lightly floured board ½ inch thick, sprinkling with additional flour, as necessary. Cut with cookie cutter. Bake on cookie sheet at 350° for 12–15 minutes. Makes 36.

In-A-Hurry Cake Cookies

A so-simple recipe for a great in-a-hurry cookie.

1 (18¼-ounce) box cake mix (any flavor)
2 eggs
1 (8-ounce) carton Cool Whip, thawed
Powdered sugar

Mix cake mix, eggs, and Cool Whip. Drop teaspoonfuls into powdered sugar and form into small balls. Place on greased cookie sheet. Bake 10–12 minutes at 350°. Makes 24–30.

Cornflake Creatures

1 cup light corn syrup
1 cup creamy peanut butter
1 cup sugar
1 teaspoon vanilla extract
6–7 cups cornflake cereal

Heat and stir all ingredients except cereal on medium in heavy saucepan. Stir in cereal; drop by teaspoonfuls onto wax paper shaping into "creature" shapes. Let stand until set. Makes about 24.

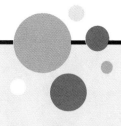

Fast and Fabulous Sugar Cookies

1 cup sugar
½ cup butter, softened
1 egg
2 tablespoons lemon juice
2 cups all-purpose flour
½ teaspoon baking soda
½ teaspoon salt

Preheat oven to 375°. Mix all ingredients. Roll into small balls. Flatten on greased cookie sheet with bottom of a glass dipped in sugar. Bake for 10 minutes. Makes 24–30.

Editor's Extra: Fun to add colorful sprinkles before baking.

Pecan Momoons

Call them sand tarts, call them cocoons, but whatever you call these crescent moon cookies, they are always incredibly delicious and popular.

2 sticks butter, softened
2 cups all-purpose flour
⅓ cup powdered sugar (plus more for coating)
1 tablespoon vanilla
1¼ cups finely chopped pecans

Mix all together with hands. Break into walnut-size and shape into crescents on ungreased cookie sheet. Bake at 300° until slightly brown, 30–35 minutes. Remove; roll in additional powdered sugar while still hot. When cool, roll in powdered sugar again. Makes 3–4 dozen.

Not enough cookie sheets? Use parchment paper. While one batch is baking, spoon next batch on another sheet. Slide baked cookie paper onto baking rack to cool, and slide raw cookie paper onto same cookie sheet to bake. Parchment paper cuts down on sticking and cleanup, too.

Let's Celebrate!

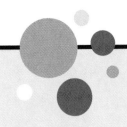

When making cookies, if you have over-softened your butter so that it has melted, save it for something else. Butter's physical properties are changed when melted, preventing it from being properly mixed with the flour—it coats flour differently from softened butter. Bite the bullet and soften another stick.

Toasted Butter Pecan Cookies

1¾ cups chopped pecans
1 tablespoon plus 1 cup butter, softened, divided
1 cup packed brown sugar
1 egg, separated
1 teaspoon vanilla
2 cups self-rising flour
1 cup pecan halves

Toast chopped pecans and 1 tablespoon butter in a baking pan in 325° oven for 5–7 minutes until browned, stirring frequently. Set aside.

Cream brown sugar, remaining butter, egg yolk, and vanilla. Gradually add flour. Mix well. Cover and refrigerate for 1 hour.

Roll into 1-inch balls, then roll in toasted pecans. Place 2 inches apart on ungreased cookie sheets. Dip pecan halves in beaten egg white, then gently press one into each ball. Bake at 375° for 10–12 minutes or until golden brown. Cool for 2 minutes before removing to wire racks. Makes about 4 dozen.

It's Party Time!

Gnome Hats

2 egg whites, room temperature
½ teaspoon vanilla
Pinch of cream of tartar
3 drops green or red food coloring
⅔ cup sugar
6 ounces semisweet chocolate
⅔ cup finely chopped pecans
Colored decorator icing

Preheat oven to 300°. To egg whites, add vanilla, cream of tartar, and 3 drops food coloring. Beat with an electric mixer until soft peaks form. Gradually add sugar, beating on high speed until stiff.

Spoon or pipe egg white mixture into small 1-inch-high mounds with angled tips on greased cookie sheets. Place in preheated oven. After 1 minute, turn oven off; let cookies dry in oven about 1 hour. Let cool, then carefully remove to parchment or wax paper.

Melt chocolate over low heat in small heavy pan, stirring frequently. Dip bottoms of cooled cookies into melted chocolate, then into chopped pecans. Top each meringue with a colored icing dot. Makes about 50 cookies.

You can chop pecans with a chopper or food processor or just a knife. Or try closing them in a zipper bag and crushing with a rolling pin. No clean-up is always nice.

Chocolate Drizzled Caramel Yummies

2 cups all-purpose flour
½ cup confectioners' sugar
2 sticks cold butter
1 (14-ounce) can sweetened condensed milk
½ cup whipping cream
1 teaspoon vanilla
1½ cups chopped pecans or walnuts (optional)
¾ cup semisweet chocolate chips, melted

Preheat oven to 350°. In medium bowl, combine flour and confectioners' sugar; cut in butter until crumbly. Press firmly on bottom of 9x13-inch baking pan. Bake 15 minutes or until lightly browned around edges.

In heavy saucepan, combine condensed milk, whipping cream, and vanilla. Over medium-high heat, cook and stir until mixture comes to a boil. Reduce heat to medium; cook and stir until mixture thickens, 8–10 minutes. Stir in nuts, if desired.

Spread over crust. Bake 20 minutes or until golden brown; cool. Drizzle with chocolate. Chill. Cut into triangles. Serves 10–12.

Editor's Extra: Chocolate spreads easier with 1 teaspoon shortening added when melting chocolate.

Margarita Cookie Bars

CRUST:

1¾ cups all-purpose flour
½ cup powdered sugar
1 cup butter, softened

Heat oven to 350°. Mix ingredients with electric mixer on low speed until crumbly. With floured fingers, press mixture firmly in bottom of ungreased 9x13-inch pan. Bake 20–25 minutes or until light golden brown.

FILLING:

4 eggs
1¾ cups sugar
¼ cup all-purpose flour
¾ teaspoon baking powder
⅓ cup frozen margarita mix concentrate, thawed
2 teaspoons grated lime peel
2 tablespoons confectioners' sugar

Beat eggs slightly in large bowl. Mix in granulated sugar, flour, and baking powder until well blended. Stir in margarita mix and lime peel. Remove pan from oven. Pour Filling over warm crust. Bake 18–22 minutes longer or until top is golden brown and Filling is set. Cool completely, at least an hour. Just before serving, cut into bars, and sprinkle with confectioners' sugar. Makes about 30.

Editor's Extra: For easy lemon squares, make the same crust and substitute lemon juice for margarita mix in Filling; just leave out the lime peel. Or use lemon peel. Yum!

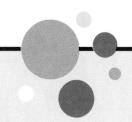

Brownie Popsicles

1 (1-pound, 6-ounce) package brownie mix
1 cup semisweet and/or white chocolate chips
2 teaspoons shortening
Decorative sprinkles

Make brownie mix as directed on box. Pour batter into Pam-sprayed totally foil-lined 9x13-inch baking pan. Bake at 350° for 24–28 minutes; cool completely. Freeze for 30 minutes. Pull foil from sides of brownies; cut into 24 rectangular bars. Carefully insert wooden craft stick into end of each bar, peeling away foil. Freeze another 30 minutes on baking sheet.

Microwave chips and shortening in 2- or 4-cup glass measure on HIGH 1½ minutes; stir until smooth. Dip top ½ of each brownie into chocolate; sprinkle with decorative candies. Lay flat on foil or wax paper to dry. Makes 24.

It's Party Time!

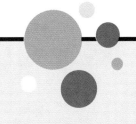

Chocolate Peanut Butter Bars

1 (18¼-ounce) yellow cake mix
1½ cups peanut butter, divided
⅓ cup water
1 egg
1 (15-ounce) can chocolate frosting

Mix cake mix, 1 cup peanut butter, water, and egg. Pour into a greased 11x17-inch pan. Bake at 350° for 13–16 minutes till springy to touch. Mix chocolate frosting and remaining ½ cup peanut butter together; frost when cake is cool. Decorate with M&M's, nuts, chips, or anything seasonal, edible, and fun. Makes about 36.

Simply Divine Chess Pie Bars

Not just good . . . really good.

1 (18¼-ounce) box butter cake mix
4 eggs, divided
½ cup butter, melted
1 (8-ounce) package cream cheese, softened
1 (1-pound) box powdered sugar
2 teaspoons vanilla

Mix cake mix, 1 egg, and butter well; spread with a small spatula into a buttered 9x13-inch baking dish. Blend remaining 3 eggs with rest of ingredients and spread evenly over cake mixture. Bake at 350° for 30–40 minutes. Cool and cut into squares. Makes about 36.

Swirl different color squeeze gel icings on top of plain fudge, brownies, cakes, and cookies for easy party theme match-ups. Use red, green and white for Christmas; purple, green and yellow for Mardi Gras, etc.

Let's Celebrate!

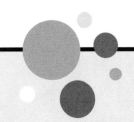

Black-Bottom Toffee-Top Cheesecake Bars

Yum—O!

1 cup confectioners' sugar
1¼ cups all-purpose flour
½ cup unsweetened cocoa powder
¼ teaspoon baking soda
1½ sticks butter
1 (8-ounce) package cream cheese, softened
1 (14-ounce) can sweetened condensed milk
2 eggs
1 teaspoon almond extract
1 (10-ounce) package toffee bits, divided

Mix confectioners' sugar, flour, cocoa, and baking soda; cut in butter till crumbly. Press into bottom of ungreased 9x13-inch baking pan. Bake at 350° for 15 minutes.

Meanwhile beat cream cheese in a large bowl until fluffy. Beat in condensed milk, eggs, and almond extract till smooth. Add 1 cup toffee bits. Pour over hot crust. Bake 25 minutes till edges slightly brown. Cool 10 minutes. Sprinkle remaining ¾ cup toffee bits evenly over top. Cool. Refrigerate covered. Makes 3 dozen bars.

Editor's Extra: Pretty to leave ½ of the cheesecake batter white; add ¼ cup cocoa to remaining, and layer chocolate layer over white.

It's Party Time!

Stir-And-Bake Chocolate Bars

1¼ sleeves graham crackers, crumbled
1 (14-ounce) can sweetened condensed milk
1½ cups chocolate chips

Stir all in bowl till well mixed. Pour into buttered 9x9-inch pan and bake for 30 minutes at 350°. Makes 12.

Streaked-With-Strawberries Cheesecake Bars

Truly a taste sensation . . . not just for cheesecake lovers.

1 (10-ounce) package frozen strawberries, thawed
1 tablespoon cornstarch
1¾ cups finely crushed graham cracker crumbs
½ stick butter, melted
2 (8-ounce) packages cream cheese, softened
1 (14-ounce) can sweetened condensed milk
2 eggs
⅓ cup lemon juice
1 teaspoon vanilla

Blend or process strawberries until smooth. Pour into saucepan with cornstarch; cook over medium heat and stir until thickened. Cool.

In a bowl, combine graham cracker crumbs and butter; press firmly on bottom of greased 9x13-inch baking pan. Preheat oven to 350°.

In mixing bowl, beat cream cheese until fluffy; beat in condensed milk. Add eggs, lemon juice, and vanilla; mix well. Pour over crust. Drop strawberry mixture by spoonfuls over batter. Gently swirl with knife. Bake 25–30 minutes till center is set. Cool, then chill. Makes 2–3 dozen bars.

To make a strawberry fan, hold by the stem on its side and slice five or six slices vertically all the way through, leaving a ¼-inch cap of strawberry uncut under the stem. Then fan gently and place on dessert or plate.

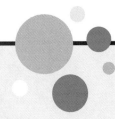

Cookie Almond Joys

Even more of a good thing.

1 (16-ounce) package refrigerated brownie dough
1 (7-ounce) can shredded coconut
1 (14-ounce) can sweetened condensed milk
1 (4-ounce) package whole almonds
1 (12-ounce) package semisweet chocolate chips

Press brownie dough into a lightly greased 9x13-inch baking dish. Bake at 350° for 15 minutes or until lightly browned. Remove from oven and cool completely. Mix coconut and condensed milk. Spread on cooled cookie crust. Sprinkle almonds over top and press in slightly. Melt chocolate chips in microwave 2 minutes on HIGH. Stir and spread gently over almonds. Refrigerate. Cut into squares with a sharp knife. Makes 24 squares.

Peanut Butter S'mores Bars

1 (16½-ounce) roll refrigerated peanut butter cookie dough
3½ cups miniature marshmallows
1 cup milk chocolate chips
2 teaspoons shortening
1½ cups M&M's

Allow dough to sit on counter 5–10 minutes to soften. Cut into 24 slices. Place on ungreased baking pan, and pinch edges together to form solid bottom. Bake at 350° for 18–20 minutes or until lightly browned. Sprinkle with marshmallows; bake 2–3 minutes longer to let marshmallows get puffy.

Melt chocolate chips and shortening in 2- or 4-cup glass measure; stir until smooth. Sprinkle M&M's over marshmallows; drizzle with melted chocolate. Chill before cutting.

Peachy Keen Bars

So tasty. Good with other kinds of preserves, too.

1 (16½-ounce) can refrigerated sugar cookie dough
1 (16-ounce) jar peach preserves
1½ cups sliced almonds, divided
4 egg whites
1½ cups sugar

Soften dough at room temperature 5–10 minutes. Press into ungreased 9x13-inch baking pan. Bake for 12–15 minutes at 350° till golden brown. Spread preserves over crust. Sprinkle with half the almonds. Beat egg whites till soft peaks form. Gradually beat in sugar until stiff peaks form. Spread meringue over almonds. Sprinkle with remaining almonds. Bake 20–25 minutes or until lightly browned. Cool. Refrigerate. Cut into 24 bars.

Dotted Swiss Cookie Bars

1 (16½-ounce) tube refrigerated sugar cookie dough
1 cup semisweet chocolate chips
⅓ cup chopped pecans
⅓ cup flaked coconut

Let dough soften at room temperature for 5–10 minutes. Press into ungreased 9x13-inch baking pan. Bake at 350° for 10–12 minutes. Sprinkle with chocolate chips, pecans, and coconut. Bake 12–15 minutes longer or until golden brown. Cool on wire rack. Yields 2 dozen.

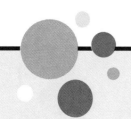

Cookie Pops

These are good with any kind of cookie dough.

1 (18-ounce) roll refrigerated chocolate chip cookie dough
1 cup finely chopped honey-roasted peanuts
12 pretzel rods or pirouette cookie sticks

Preheat oven to 375°. Lightly grease cookie sheets; set aside. Make 24 dough balls. Roll in peanuts, pressing to coat dough balls evenly. Insert cut end of a halved rod into each ball, pressing the rod to, but not through, end of dough ball. Place 3 inches apart on lightly greased cookie sheets.

Bake 8–10 minutes or until tops are lightly browned. Let cool 1 minute before removing to a wire rack to cool.

It's Party Time!

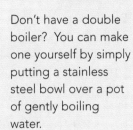

None Better Pecan Squares

½ cup butter
1 (16-ounce) box brown sugar
4 eggs, beaten
2 cups self-rising flour
2 cups chopped pecans

Melt butter with sugar in top of a double boiler; stir in eggs. Heat over boiling water 15–20 minutes, stirring occasionally. Stir in flour and pecans. Transfer to a greased 9x13-inch baking pan. Bake at 325° for 30 minutes. Cut into 24 bars.

Don't have a double boiler? You can make one yourself by simply putting a stainless steel bowl over a pot of gently boiling water.

Boogie Bars

1 (16½-ounce) tube refrigerated peanut butter cookie dough
½ cup peanut butter chips
1 (16-ounce) can buttercream frosting
¼ cup peanut butter
¼–½ cup jelly or seedless jam

Soften dough at room temperature for 5–10 minutes. Press into an ungreased 9x13-inch baking pan; sprinkle with peanut butter chips. Bake at 375° for 15 minutes or till lightly browned. Allow to cool 15–20 minutes.

Mix frosting and peanut butter until smooth. Spread over bars. Dollop spoonfuls of jelly (or jam) over frosting; swirl with a knife. Cut into small squares. Makes 36–40.

Dark brown sugar is 6.5% molasses; light brown sugar is 3.5% molasses. You can make your own by mixing one table-spoon molasses to one cup of white sugar for dark, less for light brown sugar. Generally when a recipe calls for brown sugar, it is referring to dark; use light only when specified.

Natural brown sugar is a name for raw sugar, which comes from the first crystallization of sugar cane.

Cheesecake-In-The-Middle Cookies

1 (8-ounce) package cream cheese, softened
¼ cup sugar
2 cups frozen whipped topping, thawed
40 pecan sandies cookies
2 squares chocolate almond bark, melted

Mix cream cheese and sugar with mixer; mix in whipped topping on lower speed. Spread mixture on half the cookie bottoms; top with bottoms of remaining cookies. Dip ⅔ of each cookie in choco-late. Freeze or refrigerate, covered, till chocolate is set. Thaw to serve. Makes 40.

Editor's Extra: To sub for chocolate, roll edges in colored sprinkles or chopped nuts.

Big Taste Trail Mix Bars

Wrap these winners for a bike party, hike party, or whatever-you-like party.

¼ cup butter
1 cup packed brown sugar
2 tablespoons all-purpose flour
½ cup light corn syrup
4 cups Cheerios
3 cups trail mix

In a Dutch oven, melt butter over medium-high heat; mix in brown sugar, flour, and corn syrup, stirring occasionally, until mixture comes to a full boil. Boil a full minute, stirring constantly. Mix cereal and trail mix in large bowl, then pour into Dutch oven mixture, tossing to coat all the way to bottom. Press into greased 9x13-inch pan; cool and cut into 30 bars.

Yummy-To-The-Tummy Brownies

1 (20-ounce) package fudge brownie mix
1 (16-ounce) jar marshmallow crème
1 cup peanut butter
1 (12-ounce) bag semisweet chocolate chips
3 cups crisp rice cereal

Bake brownie mix as directed; cool. Frost with marshmallow crème; refrigerate.

Melt peanut butter and chocolate chips in saucepan over medium heat, stirring constantly. Pour over cereal in bowl, stirring until evenly coated; spread over frosted brownies. Cool before cutting into bars. Makes 24.

Did you know there are half-circle perforations on both ends of tinfoil and clear wrap boxes for you to punch in so the roll won't come out when you're pulling it? I didn't, till my daughter pointed it out to me. I did know about the one in the middle of the wax paper box that comes all the way out so you can encourage the paper away from the box with your finger. Sure makes it easier.

Mardi Gras Microwave Pralines

2 cups sugar
1½ cups pecan halves
¾ cup buttermilk
3 tablespoons salted butter
1 teaspoon baking soda

Mix first 4 ingredients in a 2-quart glass bowl. Microwave on HIGH 12 minutes, stirring every 4 minutes. Add soda, stirring well while it foams. Microwave on HIGH 1 minute longer. Beat mixture until it thickens and loses its gloss. Drop by teaspoonfuls onto buttered wax paper; let stand until firm.

Hidden Kiss Meringues

2 egg whites
¼ teaspoon cream of tartar
½ cup sugar
¼ teaspoon almond extract
1 (1-ounce) square semisweet chocolate, grated
42 milk chocolate Hershey's Kisses
Baking cocoa

Beat egg whites until foamy. Add cream of tartar and continue beating until soft peaks form, about 5 minutes. Gradually add sugar, beating another 5 minutes until stiff peaks form. Beat in extract; fold in grated chocolate.

With a star tip in a pastry or plastic bag filled with meringue, pipe 42 (1-inch) disks on lightly greased baking sheets. Press a Hershey's Kiss into center of each. Pipe meringue around each Hershey's Kiss in continuous circles from the base to the top until kiss is completely covered. Dust with cocoa.

Bake at 325° for 20–28 minutes or until edges are lightly browned. Immediately remove to wire racks to cool. Makes 3½ dozen.

Voted-Most-Popular Pink Meringues

3 egg whites
1½ ounces raspberry Jell-O
¾ cup sugar
⅛ teaspoon salt
1 teaspoon white vinegar
1 (6-ounce) package semisweet chocolate chips
½ cup finely chopped pecans or walnuts

Beat egg whites until barely stiff. Add gelatin gradually, then sugar a little at a time. Beat in salt and vinegar until stiff peaks form. Fold in chips and nuts. Drop small teaspoonfuls on foil-lined baking sheets. Bake 20 minutes at 250°. Turn off heat and leave in oven 2 hours. Makes about 80.

Deep-Fried Chocolate Kisses

24 milk chocolate Hershey's Kisses
24 won ton wrappers
Confectioners' sugar

Place Hershey's Kiss in center of each won ton wrapper. Moisten edges with water; bring edges together over kiss to completely enclose.

Deep-fry won tons in hot oil for 2–3 minutes, until golden brown. Drain, then dust with confectioners' sugar. Makes 24 kisses.

Editor's Extra: Fill won ton wrappers a few at a time, keeping others covered with a damp paper towel until ready to use.

To get a head start on Christmas cookie baking, prepare two different cookie recipes every day for a week; freeze cookies. Then a week or two before Christmas, defrost them, arrange on pretty holiday paper plate, and cover with colorful plastic wrap and a bow for taking to neighbors and friends.

It's Party Time!

Over-The-Top Candy Bars

1 (16½-ounce) roll refrigerated chocolate chip cookie
  dough, softened
4 nutty s'mores trail mix bars, chopped
1 (12-ounce) package butterscotch chips
2½ cups mini marshmallows
1 cup chopped walnuts
1½ cups mini pretzels
1 (12-ounce) package peanut butter chips
¾ cup light Karo syrup
½ stick butter, cubed
1 (12-ounce) package milk chocolate chips, melted

With hands, combine dough and trail mix bars. Press into an ungreased 11x17-inch baking pan. Bake at 350° about 10 minutes, or until golden. Sprinkle with butterscotch chips and marshmallows. Bake 3–4 minutes more or until marshmallows turn golden. Sprinkle with walnuts and pretzels. Melt peanut butter chips, Karo, and butter; brush over bars. Drizzle melted chocolate over bars. Chill until firm before cutting. Makes 36 bars.

Cranberry Candy Crunch

2 (12-ounce) bags white chocolate chips
1 (14-ounce) can sweetened condensed milk
½ (15-ounce) bag pretzel sticks or twists
1 cup dried cranberries or craisins

In a large saucepan, melt chips with condensed milk over medium heat until smooth. Add pretzels, stirring to coat.

Immediately spread mixture into foil-lined 10x15-inch pan. Sprinkle with dried cranberries; press down lightly with back of big spoon. Chill until set. Break into chunks.

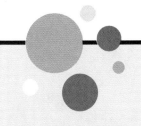

Heavenly Almond Candy

1 (24-ounce) package almond bark
1 (14-ounce) can sweetened condensed milk
⅛ teaspoon salt
1 teaspoon almond extract
3 cups whole almonds, toasted

Melt candy coating with condensed milk and salt in heavy saucepan over low heat. Remove from heat; stir in almond extract, then almonds. Spread evenly into wax-paper-lined jellyroll pan. Chill 2 hours or until firm. Turn onto cutting board; peel off paper; cut into triangles or squares. Store tightly covered at room temperature. Makes about 3 dozen.

Editor's Extra: If your frig won't accommodate a jellyroll pan, use 2 (8- or 9-inch) square pans.

Zebra Pecan Clusters

Or call them Bear Pecan Clusters if you don't make zebra stripes.

2 cups pecan halves
2 tablespoons butter, melted
8 ounces chocolate almond bark
1 ounce white almond bark (optional)

Coat pecans with butter and spread in one layer in a 10x15-inch baking pan. Bake at 300° for 20 minutes, stirring after 10 minutes. Melt chocolate almond bark in a heavy saucepan over low heat. Cool 2 minutes. Stir in toasted pecans, coating well. Drop by rounded teaspoons onto wax paper. If desired, melt white bark and drizzle over. Let stand until cool. Makes about 18–20 "zebras" or "bears."

Almond bark is an artificial chocolate made with vegetable fats instead of cocoa butter, and with coloring and flavors added. Also known as vanilla-flavored candy coating, it is sold in 24-ounce packages—vanilla or chocolate—in the baking aisle, and sort of resembles an ice cube tray with easy-to-cut-apart 2-ounce cubes. You can also find it in round discs where candy supplies are sold.

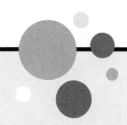

Don't forget to have your camera handy and charged. Memories of these fun parties are good, but photos that capture the happy times are priceless.

It's Party Time!

Chocolate Pretzels

½ cup butter, softened
1 cup peanut butter
3 cups confectioners' sugar
60 miniature pretzels
1½ cups milk chocolate chips
1 tablespoon shortening

In a small mixing bowl, beat butter and peanut butter until smooth. Beat in confectioners' sugar. Shape into 1-inch balls; press one on each pretzel. Place on wax-paper-lined baking sheets. Refrigerate about 1 hour or until set.

Melt chocolate chips and shortening. Dip pretzels into chocolate. Return to baking sheet, pretzel side down. Chill 30 minutes before serving. Store in an airtight container in the refrigerator. Makes 5 dozen.

Crunchy Almond Candy

A delicious take-along gift when you're invited for dinner or potluck.

1 cup slivered almonds
1 stick butter
½ cup sugar
1 tablespoon light corn syrup

Line bottom and sides of an 8- or 9-inch cake pan with aluminum foil. Set aside. Boil all ingredients in a 10-inch skillet over medium heat, stirring constantly, till it turns golden brown, about 6 minutes. Quickly spread in foil-lined pan. Cool about 15 minutes, then break into bite-size pieces. Makes about 25.

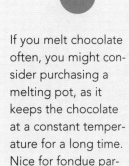

World's Best Turtles

Anybody can make these; everybody wants to eat them!

1½ pounds chocolate Hershey's Kisses
1 (7-ounce) jar marshmallow crème
1 stick butter
5 cups sugar
1 (13-ounce) can evaporated milk
6 cups pecans

Peel Hershey's Kisses and put in a large bowl; add marshmallow crème; set aside. In a saucepan, put butter, sugar, and milk. Boil, and bring to soft-ball stage (about 8 minutes). Pour immediately over Kisses and crème; blend well; add pecans and mix. Drop by teaspoonful on wax paper. Makes about 130 turtles.

Chocolate Peanut Butter Bubbles

1 stick butter, softened
1 pound confectioners' sugar
1¼ cups peanut butter
1 teaspoon vanilla
¼ stick paraffin
1 (12-ounce) package chocolate chips

Mix butter, sugar, peanut butter, and vanilla. Form into small balls; refrigerate 2 hours or longer. Melt paraffin in double boiler; when almost melted, add chocolate chips till all is smooth. Dip cold balls in chocolate with toothpicks. Place on wax paper to cool and harden. Makes 40–50 balls.

If you melt chocolate often, you might consider purchasing a melting pot, as it keeps the chocolate at a constant temperature for a long time. Nice for fondue parties, too.

Chocolate melts easier and quicker if it is in small pieces. And it likes to be stirred at intervals. Don't let any water get in with the chocolate or it will "seize up" and not melt properly.

It's Party Time!

Kicky Chocolate Bark

1 pound milk chocolate candy coating, chopped
½ cup chopped cashews, toasted
½ cup chopped pecans, toasted
¼ teaspoon cayenne pepper

In a glass bowl, melt candy coating 2 minutes on HIGH; stir; add 20 seconds if not melted. Stir in nuts and cayenne. Spread onto a wax-paper-lined baking sheet. Chill for 20 minutes. Break into small pieces. Store in airtight container in refrigerator. Serves 8–10.

Chipper Chocks

8 (1-ounce) squares chocolate or white baking chocolate
1¾ cups crushed potato chips
½ cup chopped pecans

Microwave chocolate in a large glass bowl for 2 minutes. Stir in chips and pecans. Drop by tablespoonfuls onto wax-paper-lined baking sheets. Refrigerate until set. Makes 36–40.

Nutty Peanut Butter Balls

No-bake honeys.

1 cup finely chopped roasted peanuts
½ cup peanut butter
½ cup honey
1 cup dry milk

Pour peanuts in a pie plate. Mix peanut butter and honey together, then stir in dry milk. Form this mixture into small balls; roll in peanuts.

Orange Pecan Balls

Make-ahead, pretty, delicious!

1 (12-ounce) package vanilla wafers, crushed
1½ cups confectioners' sugar, divided
½ stick butter, softened
1 (6-ounce) can frozen orange juice concentrate, thawed
1 teaspoon vanilla
1¼ cups chopped pecans

Combine crumbs and 1 cup sugar; mix with butter and orange juice concentrate; add vanilla and nuts. Shape into small balls; shake in bag with remaining ½ cup confectioners' sugar. Arrange orange balls in single layer on tray; store uncovered overnight in refrigerator. Make 40–50 balls.

Yummy Chocolate Bourbon Balls

1 cup semisweet chocolate chips
¼ cup sugar
3 tablespoons light corn syrup
⅓ cup bourbon
2½ cups finely crushed vanilla wafers
½ cup finely chopped pecans
Powdered sugar, and/or unsweetened cocoa powder

In a heavy medium saucepan, heat chocolate over low heat until melted. Remove from heat. Stir in sugar and corn syrup; stir in bourbon. Add vanilla wafer crumbs and pecans to chocolate mixture; stir well. Let stand 30 minutes.

Shape mixture into 1-inch balls. Roll in powdered sugar and/or cocoa powder to coat. If desired, drizzle with additional melted chocolate. Makes about 50 balls.

Editor's Extra: Also nice to roll in coarse sugar.

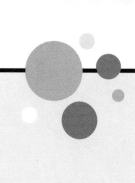

It's Party Time!

Cheesecake Bonbons

1 small store-bought cheesecake
1 (12-ounce) package milk chocolate chips, melted
1 cup semisweet chocolate chips, melted
1 cup white chocolate chips, melted

Cut cheesecake into 24–36 small squares. Place on parchment-paper-lined baking sheet; freeze 1–2 hours.

Remove frozen bonbons from freezer and dip into melted milk chocolate. Place back on parchment paper till set. Drizzle with another chocolate, white or semisweet; set aside to set. May be placed in zip-top freezer bag at this point. Will keep frozen up to 2 months.

Fudge in Minutes

3¾ cups powdered sugar
½ cup cocoa
1 stick margarine, cut in 8 pieces
¼ cup milk
1 teaspoon vanilla
½ cup chopped nuts

Place sugar and cocoa in a 2-quart bowl. Put margarine pats on top; pour milk over; do not stir! Microwave on HIGH 3 minutes. Now stir and add vanilla and nuts. Pour into a greased 8x8-inch pan. Cool; cut into 64 squares.

Have Your Cake and Eat It, Too!

Cakes

Cupcakes

Cheesecakes

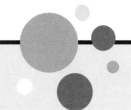

Peachy Spice Upside-Down Bundt Cake

¼ cup butter, melted
½ cup brown sugar
1–2 (15-ounce) cans sliced peaches, drained
1 (18¼-ounce) box spice cake mix
1 (8-ounce) can crushed pineapple
Whipped cream and more peaches for garnish

Brush a fluted Bundt pan with a little melted shortening to grease. Mix butter and brown sugar; spoon into bottom of pan. Put peaches with their outside nestling through sugar into every other flute. Prepare cake mix per directions, subbing the undrained can of pineapple for 1 cup of the water called for, and carefully pour over fruit. Bake at 350° for 35–45 minutes till toothpick comes out clean. Garnish slices with whipped cream. Serves 10–12.

Editor's Extra: Try other cake flavors . . . butter, pineapple, gingerbread, or lemon.

Rave Pineapple Pound Cake

This serves lots of people . . . and they will love it!

1 pound butter, softened
3 cups sugar
1 teaspoon salt
8 eggs
1 (8-ounce) can crushed pineapple, drained
3 cups all-purpose flour

Preheat oven to 325°. In mixer, cream butter; add sugar gradually till creamy. Add salt, then eggs, pineapple, and flour alternately to ensure good mixing throughout the process. Bake in greased and floured tube pan 60–70 minutes. Serves 12–16.

Editor's Extra: Pretty and delicious to garnish with pineapple slices with cherry halves in center.

Honeycomb Cake

Great to take . . . an easy winner.

1 (3-ounce) box vanilla pudding (not instant)
2 cups milk
1 (18¼-ounce) box yellow cake mix
1 (12-ounce) package butterscotch morsels

In a saucepan, mix pudding with milk and bring to a boil. Stir in cake mix. Spread into a greased and floured 9x13-inch pan. Sprinkle on butterscotch morsels. Bake in 350° oven for 30 minutes. Cool and serve. Serves 10–12.

Pineapple Paradise

½ cup butter, softened
1 cup granulated sugar
2 eggs
1 (18¼-ounce) box yellow cake mix
1 (20-ounce) can crushed pineapple, drained, reserve juice
¾ cup packed brown sugar
¾ cup chopped pecans
¾ cup coconut (optional)

Beat butter and sugar till creamy; add eggs. Alternately add cake mix and reserved pineapple juice; fold in pineapple. Spread into a greased 9x13-inch baking pan. Combine brown sugar, nuts, and coconut, if desired; sprinkle over batter. Bake in 350° oven 30–35 minutes or till toothpick inserted in center comes out clean. Best served warm. Serves 10–12.

Instead of flouring the baking pan, use a bit of the dry cake mix—there won't be any white on the outside of the cake.

Let's Celebrate!

245

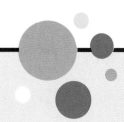

Big Easy Praline Cake

Moist . . . and oh my, such a delicious praline taste!

1 (18¼-ounce) box yellow cake mix
1 (3-ounce) box vanilla instant pudding
¾ cup chopped pecans
4 eggs
½ cup vegetable oil
½ cup praline liqueur*
½ cup water

Beat all cake ingredients in mixer about 5 minutes on medium speed. Pour into greased Bundt pan and bake at 350° for 50–60 minutes. Remove cake from oven; let sit about 3 minutes. Loosen edges with knife, then remove to cake plate with lip. After it cools slightly, carefully fork holes all over cake; spoon Glaze slowly over (it may puddle at bottom; spoon it back over; it will eventually get absorbed by cake). Serve with a dollop of whipped cream, if desired. Serves 12–15.

GLAZE:
½ stick butter
½ cup sugar
¼ cup praline liqueur

Melt butter in small pot; dissolve sugar in it; stir in praline liqueur.

Editor's Extra: Praline liqueur is also good drizzled on a slice of bought pound cake, over ice cream, or over cracked ice with some cream as an after-dinner sipper. *You can substitute ⅓ cup dark brown sugar boiled in ¾ cup water for the praline liqueur.

It's Party Time!

Big Taste Banana Cake

1 (14-ounce) box banana muffin mix
⅓ cup vegetable oil
¾ cup water
½ cup cream of coconut
3 eggs
⅓ cup creamy peanut butter

Mix all together well; pour into greased 9x13-inch baking pan. Bake at 350° on top rack for 27 minutes.

COCONUT CREAM PEANUT BUTTER FROSTING:
½ cup cream of coconut
⅓ cup creamy peanut butter
1 (1-pound) box confectioners' sugar
Maraschino cherry halves for garnish
Banana slices and sugar sprinkles for garnish

Mix all together except cherries, bananas, and sprinkles. Add more powdered sugar or coconut milk for right consistency. Frost cake, then decorate with cherry halves, preferably one in each of 24 squares. (If frosting is too thick to spread, add a tablespoon of regular milk.) Place cherry halves, banana slices, and sprinkles arranged on 24 squares of cake.

Editor's Extra: Sprinkle a little lemon or pineapple juice on banana slices to keep from darkening. Remove bananas if cake is not all eaten. Fat chance.

Greasing a pan can be as easy as spraying with baking spray. Melted butter or shortening spreads nicely and effectively with a brush, especially to get in crevices for the likes of a Bundt pan.

But if you need to use shortening or cold butter, put your hand in a sandwich bag to pinch off a bit, then spread away. Now you don't have to spend scrub time at the sink trying to get it off your fingers. Just throw away your "glove."

Apple Pie Coffee Cake

1 (18¼-ounce) package yellow cake mix
1 (21-ounce) can apple pie filling
3 eggs
3 tablespoons sugar
1 teaspoon cinnamon
Whipped topping

Mix cake mix, pie filling, and eggs well by hand till all cake mix lumps are smooth. Spread in a 9x13-inch Pam-sprayed pan. Mix sugar and cinnamon; sprinkle over cake batter. Bake, uncovered, at 350° for 30 minutes. Test with a toothpick. Serve warm with whipped topping on top. Serves 8–12.

Pineapple Orange Squares

Cool and refreshing . . . a nice summertime treat.

1 (20-ounce) can crushed pineapple, drained, save juice
1 (18¼-ounce) package orange cake mix
⅓ stick butter, softened
3 cups confectioners' sugar
1 teaspoon vanilla
Cherry halves for decoration (optional)

Measure saved pineapple juice in a 2-cup measure, adding enough water to equal 1⅓ cups. Make cake per package directions using juice/water mixture instead of all water. Bake in greased 11x15-inch baking pan about 18–22 minutes till springy. While baking, mix butter, sugar, vanilla, and pineapple, adding more sugar for consistency, if needed. Spread over cooled cake. Decorate with cherry halves, if desired.

It's Party Time!

Lazy Days Lemon Cake

Little effort . . . big taste.

1 (1-pound) frozen pound cake, thawed
⅔ cup jarred lemon curd, or canned lemon pie filling, divided
⅔ cup seedless blueberry jam, divided
1 (8-ounce) tub frozen whipped topping, thawed

Carefully slice cake into 5 horizontal layers. Spread lemon curd on first layer, blueberry jam on second, lemon on third, blueberry on fourth. Frost with whipped topping. Serves 12–15.

Editor's Extra: Fun to decorate with lemon slices and real blueberries and mint leaves. May sub any white frosting for Cool Whip. Blackberry jam is good as a sub, but be sure it's seedless. Use more or less jam, curd, or topping, as desired.

Need some fresh lemon juice? Twist a fork in the cut half of a lemon, lime, or orange to get a small amount . . . squeeze for more.

Let's Celebrate!

Halloween Spider-Web Cake

1 (18¼-ounce) box white cake mix
1 (3-ounce) box orange flavor gelatin
1 cup boiling water
½ cup cold water
1 (8-ounce) tub frozen whipped topping, thawed
1 tablespoon Kahlúa
½ teaspoon yellow food coloring
¼ teaspoon red food coloring
Smucker's Magic Shell Chocolate Topping

Prepare cake as directed for 9x13-inch baking pan. Cool 15 minutes. Pierce with large fork all over.
Stir dry gelatin into boiling water until completely dissolved; stir in cold water. Carefully pour over cake. Refrigerate 3 hours.

Tint whipped topping orange with food coloring; spread on top of cake. Refrigerate at least 1 hour. Draw spider web with chocolate glaze. Serves 10–12.

It's Party Time!

Absolutely Superb Chocolate Kahlúa Cake

1 (18¼-ounce) package chocolate cake mix
1 pint sour cream
1 (3-ounce) box vanilla instant pudding
4 eggs
⅔ cup vegetable oil
¼ cup Kahlúa
1 (12-ounce) package semisweet chocolate chips,
** divided**

Combine all but ½ the chocolate chips and pour into a well-greased, floured Bundt pan. Bake at 350° for 45–60 minutes or till cake springs back at touch. Melt remaining chocolate chips and drizzle over turned-out cooled cake. Serves 8–12.

Editor's Extra: You can substitute strong coffee for the Kahlúa . . . the mocha flavor makes it nice.

Super Easy Dump Cake

1 (15-ounce) can crushed pineapple
1 (21-ounce) can cherry pie filling
1 (18¼-ounce) package yellow or white cake mix
1 stick butter, melted

Layer pineapple and cherries into a 9x13-inch pan. Sprinkle cake mix over top, then pour melted butter over mix. Bake at 350° for 45 minutes or until brown and bubbling. Serve warm or cold.

Editor's Extra: You can sub most any kind of pie filling for variety. Sprinkle any kind of nuts on top of cake during last 10 minutes of baking for a fruit-and-nut lovers' supreme dessert.

Melting chocolate can be done several ways:
- In a double boiler over simmering water
- In a microwave (usually for 2 minutes on HIGH in a glass measure, then stir)
- On the warming plate of a coffee pot in a Pyrex dish or cup
- In an electric melting pot

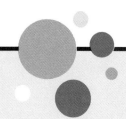

Touchdown Football Cake

It scores!

1 devil's food cake mix
1 (15-ounce) can chocolate frosting
1 (.68-ounce) tube glossy white icing

Grease a 10-inch round cake pan. Prepare cake mix as directed. Bake 45–50 minutes at 350°. Cut a 2-inch slice from center of cake. (Let the kids eat this middle slice.) Push 2 outer sides together to shape like a football. Ice with chocolate frosting. Make laces with white icing. Serves 10–12.

Editor's Extra: You can bake in 2 (8-inch) pans about 25 minutes, making 2 layers, if you want to have frosting in the middle.

Magnificent Marbled Mocha

Creamy, tasty, cool, and pretty, this dessert is easy to prepare ahead of time and freeze.

2 cups finely crushed Oreos
3 tablespoons butter, melted
1 (8-ounce) package cream cheese, softened
1 (14-ounce) can sweetened condensed milk
1 teaspoon vanilla extract
2 cups heavy cream, whipped
2 tablespoons instant coffee granules
1 tablespoon hot water
½ cup chocolate syrup

In a bowl, combine crumbs and butter. Press firmly onto bottom and 1½ inches up sides of foil-lined 5x9-inch loaf pan.

Beat cream cheese in large mixing bowl until light and fluffy. Add milk and vanilla; mix well. Fold in whipped cream. Spoon half into another bowl and set aside. Dissolve coffee in hot water; fold into remaining cream cheese mixture, then fold in chocolate syrup.

Spoon half chocolate mixture over crust, then half reserved cream cheese mixture. Repeat layers. Cut through layers with a knife to swirl chocolate (pan will be full). Cover and freeze 5–6 hours or overnight.

To serve, lift out of pan, remove foil, and cut into slices. Makes about 12 servings.

Crush cookies or crackers in a food processor, not too many at a time, for evenly fine crumbs. Rather have no clean-up? Put cookies or crackers in a zipper bag, seal air out, and roll with a rolling pin.

253

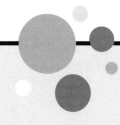

Need to pack regular frosted cupcakes in lunch boxes? Cut the cupcake in half horizontally and turn frosted half upside down onto bottom half, putting the icing in the middle. Now it's easy to wrap the "cupcake sandwich." Tastes just as good!

When serving ice cream in pointy-bottomed cones, drop a mini-marshmallow in the bottom before scooping in ice cream. This keeps the soft ice cream from dripping out.

Frosted Cone Cakes

Kids and teachers love these, as they are fun and less messy than cakes or cupcakes.

1 (18¼-ounce) cake mix of choice
24 flat-bottomed ice cream cones
1 (15-ounce) can frosting of choice

Mix cake mix as directed on package. Fill cones ⅔ full and place close together in a 9x13-inch baking pan to keep them upright. Bake according to package directions for cupcakes. Cool and frost, mounding tops to look like ice cream. Makes 24.

Editor's Extra: These invite theme decorations, as well as chocolate or sugar sprinkles, candy corn, chocolate chips, M&M's, Gummy Bears, etc.

Raspberry Chocolate Swirl Cheesecake

CRUST:
1½ cups vanilla wafers or graham cracker crumbs
½ cup powdered sugar
¼ cup cocoa
⅓ cup butter, melted

Mix all together well and press into bottom and an inch up sides of 9-inch springform pan; chill.

CHEESECAKE:
1 (10-ounce) package swirled dark chocolate and raspberry morsels, divided
3 (8-ounce) packages cream cheese, softened
1 (14-ounce) can sweetened condensed milk
3 eggs
2 teaspoons vanilla

Micro-melt half the chocolate chips for 90 seconds on HIGH in glass measure; stir and set aside. Beat cream cheese in mixer bowl till fluffy; gradually beat in milk, eggs, and vanilla, then melted chips till smooth. Pour into chilled crust. Bake in 300° oven 65 minutes. Let sit for 10 minutes; run knife around pan to loosen; sprinkle remainder of morsels over top. Refrigerate, covered loosely with wax paper. When thoroughly chilled, remove rim and cut into small wedges. Serves 12.

Editor's Extra: Be even more decadent by serving on a ribbon of chocolate sauce with a dollop of whipped cream. If you can't find chocolate and raspberry morsels, use any kind . . . it'll work!

It's usually a good idea to put tin foil around a springform pan. Or put a pizza pan on the rack beneath it . . . just in case.

Let's Celebrate!

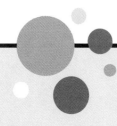

Want your cake to look extra shiny? A hair dryer will make your iced cake have a professional lustrous look. Also use it to warm a block of chocolate before shaving to make chocolate curls.

Cherry Chocolate Cake

1 (18¼-ounce) package devil's food cake mix
2 cups frozen whipped topping, thawed
½ cup chopped maraschino cherries
1 (15-ounce) can chocolate frosting

Prepare batter as directed on package. Divide batter evenly between 2 greased and floured (8-inch) cake pans. Bake in 350° oven as directed on package. Slice each baked cake layer horizontally to make 4 layers.

Fold cherries into whipped topping. Spread between cooled cake layers. Frost with chocolate frosting. Store in refrigerator. Serves 8–10.

It's Party Time!

Always Fun Dirt Cake Trifle

Lots of people are aware of this fun dessert, but you always catch a few by surprise. And it is soooo delicious!

2 (8-ounce) packages cream cheese, softened
2 cups confectioners' sugar
3 cups milk
2 (3-ounce) boxes vanilla instant pudding
1 teaspoon vanilla
1 (16-ounce) carton Cool Whip
2 (16-ounce) packages Oreo cookies, crushed finely

Mix cream cheese and sugar in large bowl until smooth. Beat milk and pudding until thick; blend into cream cheese. Combine vanilla and Cool Whip, and blend into main mixture. Put wax paper circles in bottom of 2 new 8-inch plastic flowerpots or 3 (6-inch) or 10 tiny pots to cover holes. Layer pudding and cookie crumbs into flowerpots, ending with Oreo crumbs on top. Decorate with plastic flowers or gummy worms. Serves 12–15.

Editor's Extra: Use a food processor for easiest cookie crushing. Eating "dirt" has never been so delicious!

Halloween Pumpkin Muffins

Don't wait for the ghoulies to come out to make these . . . great anytime.

1 (18¼-ounce) box spice cake mix
1 (15-ounce) can pumpkin
¼ cup water
1 (15-ounce) can cream cheese frosting
Halloween candies for decorations

Mix cake mix, pumpkin, and water well (no oil or eggs necessary). Line 24 muffin pans with cupcake liners and fill each ⅔ full. Bake in 350° oven 18–22 minutes. Remove and let cool. Frost with cream cheese frosting, and decorate with Halloween candies, if desired.

Editor's Extra: Put a few drops of yellow and red food coloring in frosting to make orange frosting.

It's Party Time!

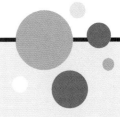

Brownie Cheesecake

You can exercise your braggin' rights with this one.

1 (family-size) package brownie mix
4 (8-ounce) packages cream cheese, softened
1 cup sugar
1 teaspoon vanilla
½ cup sour cream
3 eggs
2 squares semisweet baking chocolate, melted

Line a 9x13-inch baking pan with foil, allowing foil to extend over sides; Pam-spray foil. Prepare brownie mix per package; pour into prepared pan. Bake 18–20 minutes till top of brownie is shiny and center is almost set.

Beat cream cheese, sugar, and vanilla till well blended; add sour cream; mix well. Add eggs, mixing on low speed after each addition just until blended. Spoon over partially baked brownie bottom.

Bake about 40 minutes till center is almost set. Run knife or spatula around rim of pan; cool completely. Refrigerate at least 4 hours. Let stand at room temperature 30 minutes before serving. Using foil, lift cheesecake from pan. Drizzle with slightly cooled melted chocolate; let stand till chocolate is firm. Cut into bars to serve. Refrigerate leftovers. Serves 10–12.

Egg freshness is easy to determine. Ever heard of a Julian date? It's the three-number code on the small side of an egg carton that tells you the day the eggs were packed. The number 001 is January 1 and 365 is December 31. The eggs will keep in your refrigerator at least 4–5 weeks after this date without significant quality loss. Properly handled and stored, eggs rarely "spoil."

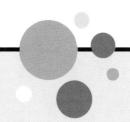

Dy-No-Mite Chocolate Cheesecake

1 (18-ounce) package refrigerated triple-chocolate cookie dough
1 (8-ounce) package chocolate toffee bits, divided
½ (12-ounce) package semisweet chocolate chips
3 (8-ounce) packages cream cheese, softened
1 (14-ounce) can sweetened condensed milk
1 (6-ounce) carton vanilla yogurt
4 eggs, lightly beaten
1 teaspoon almond extract
Whipped cream

Let dough soften 5–10 minutes. Press ¾ of the dough into an ungreased 9x13-inch baking pan (save remaining dough for another time). Sprinkle all but 2 tablespoons toffee bits over dough.

Microwave chocolate chips 2 minutes; stir. Beat cream cheese, milk, and yogurt until smooth; add eggs; beat until combined; fold in almond extract and melted chocolate. Pour over crust.

Bake at 350° for 40–45 minutes till center is almost set. Cool. Refrigerate at least 4 hours. Garnish with whipped cream and remaining 2 tablespoons toffee bits. Serves 12–15.

It's Party Time!

Delightful Desserts

Pies

Trifles

Pizzas

Mousses

Parfaits

Margarita Pie in a Glass

PRETZEL CRUST:
1½ cups crushed pretzel sticks
¼ cup sugar
1 stick butter, melted

Mix pretzels, sugar, and butter. Carefully press into 4–6 margarita glasses and chill.

FILLING:
1 (14-ounce) can sweetened condensed milk
⅓ cup fresh lime juice
2 tablespoons tequila
2 tablespoons Triple Sec
2 drops green food coloring
1 cup whipping cream, whipped

Mix milk, lime juice, tequila, Triple Sec, and food coloring, if desired. Fold whipped cream into mixture. Pour into crusted glasses and freeze until firm (several days is okay). To serve, garnish each glass with lime slice and/or course-salted rim. Serves 4–6.

It's Party Time!

Baklava Diamonds

1 (1-pound) box phyllo pastry
1 cup sugar
¾ teaspoon cinnamon
1 cup chopped nuts
¾ cup butter, melted

Cut phyllo dough in half and trim to fit into a 9x13-inch pan. Lay half on bottom. Mix sugar, cinnamon, and nuts; spread over phyllo; put remaining half of pastry over top. Cut into diamonds. Pour butter over top. Bake at 325° about 50 minutes.

GLAZE:
¾ cup sugar
½ cup water
1 teaspoon lemon juice

Combine all in saucepan; bring to a boil. Simmer to consistency of thick syrup; cool. Drizzle over hot baklava diamonds. Makes 18–24.

Know how to be a "diamond cutter"? For a 9x13-inch pan, cut six equal strips lengthwise. Then cut 1½-inch strips diagonally.

Tiny Pecan Pies

These are always a hit.

2 eggs, beaten
1 cup brown sugar
½ stick butter, melted
½ cup light corn syrup
½ teaspoon vanilla
Dash of salt
¾ cup chopped pecans
16 frozen individual pie tarts

Mix by hand the eggs, brown sugar, butter, corn syrup, vanilla, and salt. Divide pecans evenly in pastry shells. Pour filling on top, filling each ⅔ full. Bake at 350° for 20–25 minutes. Makes 16.

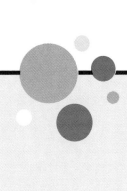

Caramel Pecan Chocolate Mousse Pie

1 (12-ounce) jar caramel ice cream topping, divided
1 chocolate pie crust
1 cup chopped pecans
2 cups heavy cream
1 (3-ounce) package chocolate instant pudding
2 cups frozen whipped topping, thawed

Pour ½ the caramel topping in chocolate pie crust. Sprinkle pecans over caramel topping. Beat heavy cream and pudding mix at high speed until stiff peaks form. Spoon over caramel and pecans. Freeze. Before serving, allow pie to soften about 15 minutes at room temperature. Add mound of whipped topping to top of individual servings. Serves 8–10.

Bing-Bing-Bing Cherry Pie

Fast, fast, fast and good, good, good!!!

1 (14-ounce) can sweetened condensed milk
1 (16-ounce) can dark sweet cherries, drained
½ cup lemon juice
¾ teaspoon red food coloring
1 (12-ounce) carton frozen whipped topping, thawed
1 (9-inch) graham cracker crust

Mix milk, cherries, lemon juice, and food coloring. Fold whipped topping into mixture and put in crust. Chill before serving.

Editor's Extra: Decorate with maraschino cherries and mint leaves, if desired. Also nice to add ½ cup or so of chopped pecans, walnuts, or almonds.

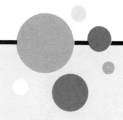

Fat-Free Key Lime Pie

1 (3-ounce) box sugar-free lime Jell-O
1 cup hot water
2 (6-ounce) cartons vanilla yogurt
1 (8-ounce) carton Cool Whip, thawed
1 (9-inch) low-fat graham cracker crust

Mix Jell-O with water till dissolved. Fold in yogurt and Cool Whip. Pour into pie crust and refrigerate till serving time. Serves 6–8.

Think about guests who may be diabetic or vegetarian by offering labeled dishes saying that they are sugar-free or vegan. Also be sure to always have nonalcoholic and low-calorie beverages on hand.

Impressive Peanut Butter Cream Cheese Chocolate Swirl Pie

Oh my, this is good! And beautiful!

⅓ cup semisweet or milk chocolate chips
1 (8-ounce) package low-fat cream cheese
1 cup powdered sugar
3 tablespoons peanut butter
1 teaspoon almond extract
2 large eggs
1 (8-ounce) carton frozen whipped topping, thawed
1 chocolate pie crust

Microwave chocolate chips in glass measure 1 minute on HIGH; stir. Mix cream cheese, powdered sugar, peanut butter, and almond extract till smooth. Add eggs and beat till smooth. Add whipped topping and mix on lowest speed till incorporated. Pour into crust. Put 4 dollops of chocolate in a cross atop pie; swirl gently with a table knife only a few times around till pretty. Freeze. Take out 15 minutes before serving. Will keep in refrigerator for a softer pie that's ready without waiting. Serves 8–10.

S'more Trifle, Please

This takes a little assembly time, but it is soooo worth it!

1 (7-ounce) jar marshmallow crème
1 (8-ounce) tub creamy Cool Whip
1 (3-ounce) box white chocolate instant pudding
2 cups cold milk
1 cup heavy whipping cream
½ (3-ounce) box chocolate fudge instant pudding
Dark chocolate syrup
½ (16-ounce) package graham crackers, crumbled, divided
Milk chocolate ice cream topping

Mix marshmallow crème and Cool Whip until creamy; refrigerate. Mix white chocolate pudding mix and milk according to package directions; refrigerate. Mix heavy cream with ½ box chocolate fudge pudding mix until cream starts to thicken. (Add a little chocolate syrup for a darker color.)

In a glass trifle bowl, layer ¼-inch of graham cracker crumbs, then all of white chocolate mixture. Drizzle chocolate syrup and milk chocolate topping over. Add another layer of graham crackers, then drizzle again with chocolate syrup and milk chocolate topping. Add all of chocolate fudge mousse, then more graham crackers. Top with marshmallow crème mixture. Refrigerate until ready to serve. Drizzle with more syrups before serving. Serves 12–16.

Variation: This can also be fixed in individual stemmed glasses.

Classic Chocolate Trifle

1 (6-ounce) package instant chocolate pudding mix
1 baked or bought chocolate cake
½ cup coffee liqueur or strong coffee
1 (16-ounce) carton frozen whipped topping, thawed
6 (1.4-ounce) chocolate-covered toffee bars, crushed

Prepare pudding according to package directions and set aside. Crumble cake and place half in bottom of a large trifle bowl. Layer with half the liqueur, half the pudding, half the whipped topping, and half the crushed candy bars. Repeat layers. Refrigerate several hours before serving. Serves 12–16.

Cherry Chocolate Caramel Cookie Trifle

Taste that impresses.

1 (8-ounce) package cream cheese, softened
1 (3-ounce) package vanilla instant pudding
1⅓ cups milk
1 (8-ounce) carton whipped topping, thawed
2 (7-ounce) boxes Hershey's Milk Chocolate Dipped
   Cookies with Caramels
1 (21-ounce) can cherry pie filling
Maraschino cherries for garnish

Combine cream cheese, pudding mix, and milk; mix till smooth and thickened. Fold in whipped topping on lowest speed. Crush cookies 1 box at a time in food processor.

In a trifle bowl, layer ⅓ creamed mixture, half the cookie crumbs, ⅓ the creamed mixture, all the cherry pie filling, remaining ⅓ creamed mixture, and top with remaining ½ cookie crumbs. Serves 12–15.

Let's Celebrate!

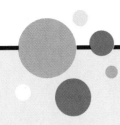

Presenting food attractively adds to the enjoyment of the party. Eye appeal is so important.

Consider the food colors and try to have a complimentary serving dish, one that does not distract from the food. Generally, solid colors work well. Remember baskets and vases can be used to hold napkins and silverware. And a cake on a pedestal "makes a statement"!

Fruit Bowl Trifle

A punch bowl or large glass bowl is essential to show off this very pretty dessert.

1 baked or bought yellow cake
16 ounces vanilla ready-made pudding
2 (8-ounce) cans crushed pineapple, with juice
1 (21-ounce) can cherry pie filling, divided
1 (7-ounce) packages flaked coconut (optional)
2 (8-ounce) containers Cool Whip
Maraschino cherries for garnish (optional)

Break cake into 1-inch pieces. Layer ½ of cake pieces in bottom of large glass bowl. Spoon ½ pudding evenly over cake pieces; top with 1 can pineapple with juice, ½ cherry pie filling, and ½ package coconut, if desired. Spread 1 container of Cool Whip evenly over top. Repeat layer, ending with Cool Whip and coconut on top. Garnish with maraschino cherries. Serves 12–16.

Chocolate Cherry Wine Glass Trifles

1 pint whipping cream
2 tablespoons sugar
18 Oreos, crumbled small (not fine)
Chocolate syrup
⅓ cup chopped pecans, toasted
18 maraschino cherries (12 cut; 6 whole)

Whip cream with sugar till firm. Layer twice: cream, cookie crumbles, syrup drizzles, pecans, and cut cherries into 6 wine glasses. Finish with whipped cream and whole cherries on top. Yum.

Cherries Jubilee

½ stick butter
1 tablespoon cornstarch
¼ cup sugar
¼ cup brandy
1 (16-ounce) can pitted cherries, drained

Heat butter in skillet. Stir in cornstarch-sugar mixture. Add brandy; ignite. Add cherries. Serve warm over ice cream. Serves 4–6.

Chocolate Chunk Brownie Dessert

1 (19-ounce) package fudge brownie mix
1 (12-ounce) package peanut butter (or vanilla or butterscotch) chips, divided
1 cup dark chocolate chips
1¼ cups pecan pieces, divided
Ice cream (optional)

Mix brownies according to package directions. Stir in half peanut butter chips, all chocolate chips, and ½ cup pecans. Spread in greased 9x13-inch baking pan and bake in 350° oven 30 minutes or until set. Sprinkle remaining peanut butter chips on top and bake another minute. Cool.

FROSTING:
¼ cup butter, softened
2 cups powdered sugar
¼ cup cocoa
1 teaspoon vanilla
2 tablespoons water

Mix butter, powdered sugar, cocoa, vanilla, and water till smooth; spread on cooled cake. Sprinkle with remaining ¾ cup pecans. Serve with a scoop of ice cream, and/or onto a plate drizzled with chocolate syrup. A stemmed cherry on top would be nice.

Strawberry Brownie Pizza

Chocolate brownie pizza with strawberries . . . what's not to love?

BROWNIE PIZZA:
1 (family-size) package fudge brownie mix
⅓ cup boiling water
¼ cup vegetable oil
1 egg

Mix ingredients well. Spread batter into a buttered and floured 12-inch pizza pan. Bake at 350° for 25 minutes.

FRUIT TOPPING:
1 (8-ounce) package cream cheese, softened
1 egg
¼ cup sugar
1 teaspoon vanilla extract
2 cups sliced fresh strawberries
1 (1-ounce) square semisweet chocolate, melted
Whipped topping (optional)

Mix cream cheese, egg, sugar, and vanilla until smooth. Spread over Brownie Pizza. Bake 15 minutes, until topping is set. Allow to cool on a wire rack. Before serving, place strawberries over top. Drizzle with chocolate, and decorate with whipped topping, if desired. Serves 10–14.

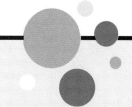

Chocolate Dessert Pancakes

½ cup biscuit mix
2 tablespoons cocoa
1 tablespoon sugar
½ cup milk
1 egg
1 tablespoon vegetable oil
15–20 mini marshmallows
¼ cup pecan pieces

Mix first 6 ingredients, stirring till smooth. Mix in marshmallows and pecans. Pour tablespoonfuls onto greased hot griddle. Flip when bubbles burst. Serve stacks on plates and top with ice cream or whipped topping and chocolate syrup, if desired. Serves 4.

Chocolate Cappuccino Mousse

¾ cup cold strong coffee
1 cup milk
1 (3-ounce) box chocolate instant pudding mix
3 tablespoons sugar plus ¼ cup sugar, divided
1 pint whipping cream

Whisk coffee, milk, pudding mix, and 3 tablespoons sugar in large bowl with until slightly thickened. In mixer bowl, beat whipping cream and ¼ cup sugar until stiff; fold into coffee mixture. Spoon into stemware or dessert dishes. Refrigerate till set, about 15 minutes. Serves 6.

For smaller conversation-piece desserts, layer crumbs, mousse, and whipped cream in small wine glasses, champagne flutes, or shooters. It looks, feels, and *tastes* fancy . . . and is.

Out of whipped cream for garnish? If you have ice cream, you can soften and beat it just like you would whipping cream. Be aware it won't last as long since it will melt.

Very cold evaporated milk beaten in a cold bowl with cold beaters whips as well. Though these are both "temps," they are great for on-the-spot single-serving toppers.

Heavenly Homemade Chocolate Mousse

1 (12-ounce) package chocolate chips
4 eggs, pasteurized
4 tablespoons strong hot coffee
6 tablespoons rum
1½ cups boiling milk
Whipped cream for garnish

In blender, combine first 5 ingredients and blend for 2–3 minutes. Place in individual dishes. Chill overnight. Top with whipped cream just before serving. Serves 8.

Mousse-On-The-Loose Brownie Dessert

1 (family-size) package brownie mix, with syrup
⅓ cup vegetable oil
⅓ cup water
5 eggs, divided
¾ cup whipping cream
1 (6-ounce) package semisweet chocolate chips
⅓ cup sugar

Prepare brownie mix using oil, water, and 2 eggs. Spread batter in greased 9x13-inch pan.

Heat cream with chips over medium heat, stirring constantly till chocolate melts; cool slightly. Beat 3 eggs and sugar on medium speed until foamy; stir in chocolate mixture; pour over batter.

Bake at 350° about 45 minutes till topping is set; cool completely. Serve now or chilled; store tightly covered. Serves 10–16.

Editor's Extra: This can be done in a springform pan; bake about 1 hour.

Delicate Dessert Kabobs

Easy and impressive.

18 tiny frozen cream puffs, thawed
12 fresh medium-size strawberries
3 tablespoons semisweet chocolate chips
1 tablespoon butter

On 6 bamboo skewers, thread 3 cream puffs and 2 strawberries alternately. Put chocolate chips and butter in zipper freezer bag and seal. Microwave on HIGH 30 seconds or till melted. Mix by squeezing bag. Cut tiny corner tip and drizzle chocolate over kabobs. Place on wax-paper-lined cookie sheet. Refrigerate at least 10 minutes or until set. Keep in the frig till ready to serve. Makes 6, but they're sharable.

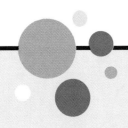

A nice finishing touch to an evening cocktail party is a dessert buffet and a selection of coffees and teas. Fun to have after-the-theatre cocktail party in which coffee drinks, such as Irish coffee, are served along with a selection of desserts.

Elegant After-Dinner Parfait

Simple, simple to prepare, the perfect ending . . . .

2 tablespoons dark brown sugar
½ cup amaretto liqueur
6 cups vanilla ice cream
1 cup whipped cream
6–8 maraschino cherries

Dissolve brown sugar in amaretto. Blend with ice cream in blender till smooth.

Fill wine or parfait glasses ¾ full; freeze. Serve with a dollop of whipped cream and a cherry. Makes 6–8 depending on size of glass.

Cheery Cherry Parfait

You can't find a more refreshing or prettier dessert. It's all last-minute, and if you have fun guests, they are usually happy to help you get them ready. Or make and freeze them ahead of time.

½ gallon cherry vanilla ice cream
¾ cup dark brown sugar
½ cup sour cream
1 (7-ounce) can whipped cream
8 cherries for garnish

Place one generous scoop ice cream into 8 parfait glasses (or any stemware). Sprinkle with a teaspoon or so of brown sugar. Then put in another scoop ice cream, and this time put a generous teaspoon of sour cream. Sprinkle with more brown sugar. Squirt a hat of whipped cream on top and pop a cherry into the cream. You may need a third layer depending on size of glass. Put another ice cream scoop on top, if needed to come slightly over the top. Makes 8. Or you can make 16 one-scoopers in small wine glasses, using just the second layer.

It's Party Time!

Index

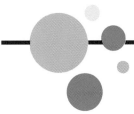

Absolutely Superb Chocolate Kahlúa Cake 251
Almonds:
  Almond Chip Cheese Ball 95
  Cookie Almond Joys 228
  Crazy Craisin Party Mix 50
  Crunchy Almond Candy 238
  Heavenly Almond Candy 237
  Peachy Keen Bars 229
  Pineapple Almond Cheddar Spread 104
  Pine Cone Made of Cheese, A 102
  Toasted Almond Chicken Nuggets 131
Always Fun Dirt Cake Trifle 257
Amigo Cheese Squares 86
Amigos Bean Dip 72
Apples:
  Apple Pie Coffee Cake 248
  Apple Upside-Down Biscuits 189
  Pearly Whites 128
Artichokes:
  Awesome Artichoke Dip 69
  Famous Crab & Artichoke Dip, The 69
  Glorious Green Dip 80
  Greener Pastures Dip 54
  Heart-Melting Dip, A 81
  Pocket Sandwiches with Heart 197
  Popeye Popovers 108
Asparo-Squares 209
Aunt Mamie's Mint Tea 29
Avocados:
  Avocado Cheese Crisps 88
  Avocado Salsa 61
  Cloud Nine 'Cado Dip 60
  Guacamole Dunk 60
  Kicky Layered Dip 62
Awesome Artichoke Dip 69
Awesome Chocolate Peanut Butter Spread 204

Bacon:
  Bacon and Tamale Bites 141
  Bacon and Tomato Layer Dip 57
  Bacon Blue Tartlets 189

BLT Bites 134
BLT Bruschetta 182
Bundles of Sweet Beans 109
Buttery Bacon and Cheese Bread 178
Dog Bites Everybody Likes 141
Favorite Scallops Appetizer 144
Miracle Red Grape Broccoli Salad 124
Sweet Bacon-y Brie 90
Sweety Meat Bites 141
Pepper Canoes 121
Pick-Apart Bacon-Ranch Bread Ring 180
Baked Parmesan Chicken Nuggets 133
Baklava Diamonds 263
Banana Pepper-Ronies 120
Bananas:
  Big Taste Banana Cake 247
  Deep-Fried Banana Logs 128
Bang-Bang Buffalo Chicken Dip 74
Bars:
  Big Taste Trail Mix Bars 232
  Black Bottom Toffee Top Cheesecake Bars 226
  Boogie Bars 231
  Brownie Popsicles 224
  Chocolate Peanut Butter Bars 225
  Cookie Almond Joys 228
  Dotted Swiss Cookie Bars 229
  Margarita Cookie Bars 223
  None Better Pecan Squares 231
  Over-The-Top Candy Bars 236
  Peachy Keen Bars 229
  Peanut Butter S'mores Bars 228
  Simply Divine Chess Pie Bars 225
  Stir-And-Bake Chocolate Bars 227
  Streaked-With-Strawberries Cheesecake Bars 227
  Yummy-To-The-Tummy Brownies 233
Bayou Crawfish Spread 202
Bayside Mini Crab Cakes 173
Beans:
  Amigos Bean Dip 72
  Bundles of Sweet Beans 109
  Can-Can Taco Soup 162

Corny Bean Salsa 63
Mexican Bean Scoop 73
Mexican Mix-Up 121
Perfected Baked Beans 109
Quesadilla Bean Bites 140
Some-Like-It-Hot Crockpot Tailgate Chili 163
Beef:
  Beefy Cheese Ball 93
  'Bello Beef Bites 135
  Best Brisket Ever 161
  Can't Beat These Meatballs 150
  Can-Can Taco Soup 162
  Caramelized Sirloin Skewers 167
  Crockpot BBQ Balls 151
  Easy-Do Crocked Barbecue 160
  Good-To-The-Last Drop Cheeseburger Dip 82
  Gotta-Love-The-Juice Brisket 162
  Jalapeño Crockpot Meatballs 151
  Meatball Penguins 149
  Mexican Nacho Dip 73
  Moo-Cow in a Blanket 185
  Party in a Bag 172
  Queso Meatballs 153
  Quick Dinner Party Lasagna 164
  Roast Beef Roll-Ups 138
  Shape and Bake Meatballs 152
  Sloppy Joe Bunners 198
  Sombrero Dip 59
  Some-Like-It-Hot Crockpot Tailgate Chili 163
  Speedy Sloppy Joes 198
  Sweet-And-Sour Meatball Kabobs 168
  Swiss Reuben Spread 203
  While-You-Sleep Italian Beef 161
'Bello Beef Bites 135
Berry Mint Iced Tea 30
Best Brisket Ever 161
Betsy's Tomato Crackers 134
Better-With-Butter Veggie Platter 108
Beverages:
  Aunt Mamie's Mint Tea 29
  Berry Mint Iced Tea 30
  Blender Bloody Mary Mix 37
  Category 5 Hurricanes 35

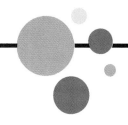

Circus Citrus Slush 28
Company Tea 30
Hello Punch 33
Holiday Party Punch 30
Holiday Wassail 39
Hot Buttered Rum 40
Iced Coffee Coolers 33
Island Splendor Punch 31
Jolly Good Bloody Mary, A 37
Kicky Lemon Tea Slush 28
Killer Margaritas 35
Luck-Of-The-Irish Cream 38
Mama's Spiced Tea 29
MJ's Flavored Water Cooler 34
Noggin of Good Cheer, A 40
Old-Fashioned Root Beer Float 26
Party Martinis 34
Pink Mimosas 34
Raymond's Milk Punch 32
Sangria Serenade 36
Sherri's Frosted Chocolate Shake 26
Simply Refreshing Punch 31
Summertime Peach Smoothie 27
Sweet Sippin' Limoncello 38
Warming Winter Wassail 39
Welcome Wine 36
Big Easy Praline Cake 246
Big Taste Banana Cake 247
Big Taste Trail Mix Bars 232
Bing-Bing-Bing Cherry Pie 264
Biscuits:
    Apple Upside-Down Biscuits 189
    Bacon Blue Tartlets 189
    Chicken Salad in Biscuit Cups 208
    Cookie Biscuits 190
    Easy Bisquiks 190
    Gorgonzola Biscuits 190
    Yummy Pockets 192
Black-Bottom Toffee-Top Cheesecake Bars 226
Blender Bloody Mary Mix 37
Bloody Mary Mix, Blender 37
Bloody Mary, A Jolly Good 37
BLT Bites 134
BLT Bruschetta 182
BLT Spread 203
Bodacious Salsa 63
Boogie Bars 231
Bread Boat Sausage Dip 78
Bread Bowl of Beef Dip 77

Breads:
    Apple Upside-Down Biscuits 189
    BLT Bruschetta 182
    Bacon Blue Tartlets 189
    Buttery Bacon and Cheese Bread 178
    Cheesy Italian Garlic Bread 177
    Cheesy Vidalia Fingers 191
    Chicken Salad in Biscuit Cups 208
    Colorful Crusty Bruschetta 182
    Cookie Biscuits 190
    Crocked Cheese Fingers 191
    Easy Bisquiks 190
    Easy Cheese Bowl 82
    Gorgonzola Biscuits 190
    Grilled Mozza-Roma Bites 181
    Hot 'n Bubbly Bread 179
    Lemony Garlic Bread 179
    Mexicali Shotgun Bread 180
    Moo-Cow in a Blanket 185
    N'Awlins Party Pull Bread 178
    Pesto Crostini 181
    Pick-Apart Bacon-Ranch Bread Ring 180
    Pita Christmas Trees 183
    Pizzazzy Fondue 84
    Quiche-y Crescent Cups 185
    Rum Roll Bites 177
    Simple Sausage Rolls 176
    Soft Sunrise Rolls 176
    Toasted Parmesan Triangles 45
    Wheel o' Brie Bread Bowl 78
    Yummy Pockets 192
Broccoli:
    Better-With-Butter Veggie Platter 108
    Broccoli Cornbread Mini Muffins 187
    Caesar City Chicken Squares 208
    Chicken Broccoli Pizza Spirals 186
    Cocktail Garden Platter 107
    Easy Breezy Broccoli Dip 80
    Miracle Red Grape Broccoli Salad 124
Brownies:
    Brownie Cheesecake 259
    Brownie Popsicles 224
    Chocolate Chunk Brownie Dessert 269
    Strawberry Brownie Pizza 270

    Yummy-To-The-Tummy Brownies 233
Bundles of Sweet Beans 109
Burst-Of-Flavor Chicken Sandwiches 195
Buttery Bacon and Cheese Bread 178
Buttery Boursin Spread 204
Buttery Chicken Nuggets 132
Buttery Sweet Toasted Pecans 47

C

Caesar City Chicken Squares 208
Cajun-Style Packet Potatoes 114
Cakes:
    Absolutely Superb Chocolate Kahlúa Cake 251
    Always Fun Dirt Cake Trifle 257
    Apple Pie Coffee Cake 248
    Big Easy Praline Cake 246
    Big Taste Banana Cake 247
    Brownie Cheesecake 259
    Cherry Chocolate Cake 256
    Dy-No-Mite Chocolate Cheesecake 260
    Frosted Cone Cakes 254
    Halloween Pumpkin Muffins 258
    Halloween Spider-Web Cake 250
    Honeycomb Cake 245
    Lazy Days Lemon Cake 249
    Magnificent Marbled Mocha 253
    Peachy Spice Upside-Down Bundt Cake 244
    Pineapple Orange Squares 248
    Pineapple Paradise 245
    Pound Cake, Rave Pineapple 244
    Raspberry Chocolate Swirl Cheesecake 255
    Rave Pineapple Pound Cake 244
    Super-Easy Dump Cake 251
    Touchdown Football Cake 252
Can't Beat These Meatballs 150
Can-Can Taco Soup 162
Candies:
    Cheesecake Bonbons 242

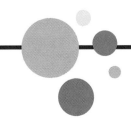

Chipper Chocks 240
Chocolate Peanut Butter Bubbles 239
Cranberry Candy Crunch 236
Crunchy Almond Candy 238
Deep-Fried Chocolate Kisses 235
Fudge in Minutes 242
Heavenly Almond Candy 237
Hidden Kiss Meringues 234
Kicky Chocolate Bark 240
Mardi Gras Microwave Pralines 234
Nutty Peanut Butter Balls 240
Orange Pecan Balls 241
Over-The-Top Candy Bars 236
Voted-Most-Popular Pink Meringues 235
World's Best Turtles 239
Yummy Chocolate Bourbon Balls 241
Zebra Pecan Clusters 237
Caramel Fruit Dip 64
Caramel Pecan Chocolate Mousse Pie 264
Caramelized Sirloin Skewers 167
Category 5 Hurricanes 35
Caviar Party Potatoes 114
Caviar, Nancy's Country 64
Celery Bites, Mango-Stuffed 128
Cheery Cherry Parfait 274
Cheese:
Almond Chip Cheese Ball 95
Amigo Cheese Squares 86
Amigos Bean Dip 72
Avocado Cheese Crisps 88
Baked Parmesan Chicken Nuggets 133
Beefy Cheese Ball 93
Bread Boat Sausage Dip 78
Buttery Bacon and Cheese Bread 178
Cheese 'n Chile Cubes 87
Cheese Sauce 83
Cheesy Chile Bites 87
Cheesy Chili con Queso Cups 99
Cheesy Hot Quesadillas 99
Cheesy Italian Garlic Bread
Cheesy Party Pastries 89
Cheesy Salsa Spinach Dip 79
Cheesy Vidalia Fingers 191
Chicken Enchilada Dip 75

Crescent-Wrapped Pepper Jelly Brie 90
Crispy Cheese Wafers 45
Crocked Cheese Fingers 191
Deep-Fried Cheese 'n Pepperoni Balls 86
Easy Cheese Bowl 82
5-Minute Boursin Cheese 101
Fried Cheese with Marinara Sauce 91
Game-Time Nachos 98
Good-To-Go Cheese Sandwiches 194
Good-To-The-Last-Drop Cheeseburger Dip 82
Good, Good Gouda Spread 101
Good-To-Go Cheese Sandwiches 194
Green Chile Cheese Dip 76
Grilled Mozza-Roma Bites 181
Gorgonzola Biscuits 190
Ham and Cheese Pinwheels 138
Heart-Melting Dip, A 81
Hot 'n Bubbly Bread 179
It's a Snowman Cheese Ball 92
Jack Cheese Tortilla Wedges 96
Jalapeño Cheese in a Jar 103
Mexican Nacho Dip 73
Mighty Meaty Mexican Dip 72
Mini Cheese Balls 93
Nutty Olive Cheese Ball 95
Olive-Cheese Balls 94
One-Ingredient Crispies 88
Pecan Cheese Wafers 46
Pepperoni Tortillas on the Grill 97
Peppered Peppers 110
Pigs in a Cheese Trough 83
Pineapple Almond Cheddar Spread 104
Pine Cone Made of Cheese, A 102
Queso Meatballs 153
Quick Mozzarella Tortillas 97
Ring Around the Berries 89
Savory Pepper Jelly Cheesecake 100
Smoky Bar Cheese 96
Super Nachos 98
Sweet Bacon-y Brie 90
Sweet Bite of Brie, A 91
Sweet Cha Cha Cheese Ball 94

Swiss Reuben Spread 203
Tiny Quiche Bites 135
Toasted Parmesan Triangles 44
Zesty Beefy Cheese Log 103
Wheel o' Brie Bread Bowl 78
Cheesecake:
Black-Bottom Toffee-Top Cheesecake Bars 226
Brownie Cheesecake 259
Cheesecake Bonbons 242
Cheesecake-In-The-Middle Cookies 232
Dy-No-Mite Chocolate Cheesecake 260
Pumpkin Cheesecake Dip 66
Raspberry Chocolate Swirl Cheesecake 255
Streaked-With-Strawberries Cheesecake Bars 227
Cherries:
Bing-Bing-Bing Cherry Pie 264
Cheery Cherry Parfait 274
Cherries Jubilee 269
Cherry Chocolate Cake 256
Cherry Chocolate Caramel Cookie Trifle 267
Chocolate Cherry Wine Glass Trifles 268
Elegant After-Dinner Parfait 274
Chicken:
Baked Parmesan Chicken Nuggets 133
Bang-Bang Buffalo Chicken Dip 74
Burst-Of-Flavor Chicken Sandwiches 195
Buttery Chicken Nuggets 132
Caesar City Chicken Squares 208
Chicken Broccoli Pizza Spirals 186
Chicken Enchilada Dip 75
Chicken Salad in Biscuit Cups 208
Coconut Chicken Bites 130
Cracker-Crusted Drummettes 156
Cranberry Barbecue Wings 155
Crispy Onion Chicken Nuggets 131
Crockpot Hot Wing Things 156

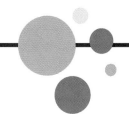

Crockpot Teriyaki Drumsticks 158
Dippy Drummettes with Sassy Sauce 157
Drummette Lollipops 159
Juicy Sauced Chicken Wings 154
Mexicali Shotgun Bread 180
Microwave Chicken Nuggets 133
9x13 Chicken Salad 126
Olé Chicken Stars 206
Pocket Sandwiches with Heart 197
Pop-In-Your-Mouth Chicken Nuggets 132
Pretzel-Crusted Chicken Nuggets 130
Ritzy Hot Wings 154
Simply Superb Chicken Salad Sandwiches 195
Smoky Red Wingers 155
Strawberry and Chicken Salad Trifle 126
Sweet Little Chic Won Tons 207
Taco Chicken Drummettes 158
Tangy Grilled Chicken Kabobs 167
Toasted Almond Chicken Nuggets 131
Chipper Chocks 240
Chipper Cookies 216
Chips, Full of Flavor Pita 43
Chips, Homemade Tortilla 43
Chocolate:
Absolutely Superb Chocolate Kahlúa Cake 251
Almond Chip Cheese Ball 95
Awesome Chocolate Peanut Butter Spread 204
Brownie Cheesecake 259
Brownie Popsicles 224
Caramel Pecan Chocolate Mousse Pie 264
Cheesecake Bonbons 242
Cherry Chocolate Cake 256
Cherry Chocolate Caramel Cookie Trifle 267
Chipper Chocks 240
Chocolate Cappuccino Mousse 271
Chocolate Cherry Wine Glass Trifles 268
Chocolate Chunk Brownie

Dessert 269
Chocolate Coffee Iced Shortbread Cookies 217
Chocolate Dessert Pancakes 271
Chocolate Drizzled Caramel Yummies 222
Chocolate Icing 217
Chocolate Peanut Butter Bars 225
Chocolate Peanut Butter Bubbles 239
Chocolate Peanut Butter Chow 52
Chocolate Pretzels 238
Classic Chocolate Trifle 267
Cookie Almond Joys 228
Cranberry Candy Crunch 236
Dotted Swiss Cookie Bars 229
Deep-Fried Chocolate Kisses 235
Dy-No-Mite Chocolate Cheesecake 260
Extra Special Chocolate Chip Cookies 214
Fudge in Minutes 242
Heavenly Homemade Chocolate Mousse 272
Hidden Kiss Meringues 234
Hoppy Chocolate Frogs 215
Impressive Peanut Butter Cream Cheese Chocolate Swirl Pie 265
Kicky Chocolate Bark 240
Mousse-On-The-Loose Brownie Dessert 272
Over-The-Top Candy Bars 236
Peanut Butter S'mores Bars 228
Raspberry Chocolate Swirl Cheesecake 255
Sherri's Frosted Chocolate Shake 26
Stir-And-Bake Chocolate Bars 227
Touchdown Football Cake 252
Voted-Most-Popular Pink Meringues 235
World's Best Turtles 239
Yummy Chocolate Bourbon Balls 241
Yummy-To-The-Tummy Brownies 233
Zebra Pecan Clusters 237
Circus Citrus Slush 28
Classic Chocolate Trifle 267

Classic Party Potatoes 111
Climb-A-Mountain Mix 50
Cloud Nine 'Cado Dip 60
Cocktail Garden Platter 107
Cocktail Weiners 160
Coconut:
Coconut Chicken Bites 130
Coconut Cream Peanut Butter Frosting 247
Coconut Shrimp Caribe 146
Cookie Almond Joys 228
Cold Dips:
Avocado Salsa 61
Bacon and Tomato Layer Dip 57
Caramel Fruit Dip 64
Cloud Nine 'Cado Dip 60
Corny Bean Salsa 63
Creamy Amaretto Dip 65
Easy Breezy Veggie Dip 57
Easy-As-Can-Be Salsa 62
Fiesta Dip 57
Goodness Gracious Good Veggie Dip 55
Greener Pastures Dip 54
Guacamole Dunk 60
Honey Mustard Dip 169
Irene's Shrimp Dip 55
Kicky Layered Dip 62
Mellow Mallow Fruit Dip 64
Mexican Mix-Up 121
Nancy's Country Caviar 64
Pretty Cranberry Cream Cheese Centerpiece 66
Pumpkin Cheesecake Dip 66
Quick Chick Blender Hummus 56
Quicker-Than-Quick Shrimp Dip 55
Rainbow Corn Dip 58
Sedona Sun-Dried Tomato Dip 58
Sombrero Dip 59
Taco Dip 118
Touch of Spice Fruit Dip 65
Tropical Fruit Dip 65
Waldorf Spinach Dip in a Bread Bowl 56
You-Won't-Believe-How-Good-It-Is Mustard Dip 54
Colorful Corn Salad 124
Colorful Crusty Bruschetta 182
Company Tea 30

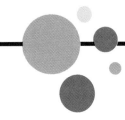

Cookie Almond Joys 228
Cookie Biscuits 190
Cookies:
Big Taste Trail Mix Bars 232
Black-Bottom Toffee-Top
Cheesecake Bars 226
Boogie Bars 231
Brownie Popsicles 224
Cheesecake-In-The-Middle
Cookies 232
Chipper Cookies 216
Chocolate Coffee Iced
Shortbread Cookies 217
Chocolate Drizzled Caramel
Yummies 222
Chocolate Peanut Butter Bars
225
Cookie Almond Joys 228
Cookie Pops 230
Cornflake Creatures 218
Dotted Swiss Cookie Bars 229
Extra Special Chocolate Chip
Cookies 214
Fast and Fabulous Sugar
Cookies 219
Frilly Lace Cookies 216
Gnome Hats 221
Granny's Old-Fashioned
Teacakes 218
Hoppy Chocolate Frogs 215
In-A-Hurry Cake Cookies 218
Margarita Cookie Bars 223
None Better Pecan Squares
231
Over-The-Top Candy Bars 236
Peachy Keen Bars 229
Peanut Butter Quickie
Cookies 217
Peanut Butter S'mores Bars
228
Pecan Momoons 219
Simply Divine Chess Pie Bars
225
Stir-And-Bake Chocolate Bars
227
Streaked-With-Strawberries
Cheesecake Bars 227
Toasted Butter Pecan Cookies
220
Yummy-To-The-Tummy
Brownies 233
Cool Garden Pizza Rounds 119

Corn:
Can-Can Taco Soup 162
Colorful Corn Salad 124
Corny Bean Salsa 63
Easy Corn and Tomato Salad
123
Easy Spicy Corn Dip 71
Rainbow Corn Dip 58
Spicy Grilled Corn Cobbies
106
Mexican Mix-Up 121
Cornbread Mini Muffins, Broccoli
187
Cornflake Creatures 218
Cowboy Popcorn 49
Crab:
Bayside Mini Crab Cakes 173
Crab English Muffin Bites 143
Crispy Crab Phyllo Roll-Ups
211
Delectable Crabmeat Dip 70
Elegant Crabmeat Imperial
165
Famous Crab & Artichoke
Dip, The 69
French Fried Onion Crab Dip
71
Fried Crab Puffs 143
King Crab Louie 125
Mad About Crab Puffs 173
Mini Spini Crabmeat Pies 210
Quick Hot Crab Dip 70
Red Pepper Crab Spread 201
Tasty Crab Spread 202
Cracker-Crusted Drummettes 156
Crackers:
Betsy's Tomato Crackers 134
Fun-To Munch Oyster
Crackers 42
Roll-Out-The-Barrel Crackers
42
Cranberries:
Cranberry Barbecue Wings
155
Cranberry Candy Crunch 236
Pretty Cranberry Cream
Cheese Centerpiece 66
Crawfish Spread, Bayou 202
Crazy Craisin Party Mix 50
Creamy Amaretto Dip 65
Crescent Roll Veggie Tree 184
Crescent-Wrapped Pepper Jelly
Brie 90
Crispy Cheese Wafers 45
Crispy Crab Phyllo Roll-Ups 211

Crispy Onion Chicken Nuggets
131
Crispy Pita Wedges 44
Crispy Pizza Dip Sticks 186
Crocked Cheese Fingers 191
Crockpot:
Crockpot BBQ Balls 151
Crockpot Hot Wing Things
156
Crockpot Teriyaki Drumsticks
158
Easy-Do-Crocked Barbecue
160
Jalapeño Crockpot Meatballs
151
Some-Like-It-Hot Crockpot
Tailgate Chili 163
Crunchy Almond Candy 238
Cucumbers:
Cucumber Sauce 197
Cuke and Cream Canapés 122
Open & Closed Cucumber
Sandwiches 196

Dare Deviled Eggs 146
Deep-Fried Cheese 'n Pepperoni
Balls 86
Deep-Fried Banana Logs 128
Deep-Fried Chocolate Kisses 235
Delectable Crabmeat Mornay 70
Deli Ham Salad Finger
Sandwiches 197
Deli-Licious Party Wheels 137
Delicate Dessert Kabobs 273
Delicious Deli Roll-Ups 122
Desserts:
Baklava Diamonds 263
Cheery Cherry Parfait 274
Cherries Jubilee 269
Chocolate Cappuccino
Mousse 271
Chocolate Chunk Brownie
Dessert 269
Chocolate Dessert Pancakes
271
Chocolate Pretzels 238
Delicate Dessert Kabobs 273
Elegant After-Dinner Parfait
274
Heavenly Homemade
Chocolate Mousse 272
Mousse-On-The-Loose
Brownie Dessert 272
Strawberry Brownie Pizza 270

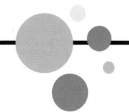

Dippy Drummettes with Sassy Sauce 157

Dips:
Amigos Bean Dip 72
Avocado Salsa 61
Awesome Artichoke Dip 69
Bacon and Tomato Layer Dip 57
Bang-Bang Buffalo Chicken Dip 74
Bread Boat Sausage Dip 78
Bread Bowl of Beef Dip 77
Caramel Fruit Dip 64
Cheesy Salsa Spinach Dip 79
Chicken Enchilada Dip 75
Cloud Nine 'Cado Dip 60
Corny Bean Salsa 63
Creamy Amaretto Dip 65
Delectable Crabmeat Mornay 70
Easy Breezy Broccoli Dip 80
Easy Breezy Veggie Dip 57
Easy Cheese Bowl 82
Easy Cheesy Chili Dip 76
Easy Spicy Corn Dip 71
Easy-As-Can-Be Salsa 62
Famous Crab & Artichoke Dip, The 69
Fiesta Dip 57
French Fried Onion Crab Dip 71
Glorious Green Dip 80
Good-To-The-Last-Drop Cheeseburger Dip 82
Goodness Gracious Good Veggie Dip 55
Green Chile Cheese Dip 76
Greener Pastures Dip 54
Guacamole Dunk 60
Heart-Melting Dip, A 81
Honey Mustard Dip 169
Hot Tamale Dip 77
Irene's Shrimp Dip 55
Kicky Layered Dip 62
Mellow Mallow Fruit Dip 64
Mexican Bean Scoop 73
Mexican Mix-Up 121
Mexican Nacho Dip 73
Mighty Meaty Mexican Dip 72
Nancy's Country Caviar 64
Pigs in a Cheese Trough 83
Pizzazzy Fondue 84
Pretty Cranberry Cream Cheese Centerpiece 66
Pumpkin Cheesecake Dip 66

Quick Chick Blender Hummus 56
Quick Hot Crab Dip 70
Quicker-Than-Quick Shrimp Dip 55
Rainbow Corn Dip 58
Reuben, Reuben Dip 68
Sedona Sun-Dried Tomato Dip 58
Sombrero Dip 59
Speedy Gonzales Chili Dip 76
Sweet Georgia Onion Dip 68
Taco Dip 118
Touch of Spice Fruit Dip 65
Tropical Fruit Dip 65
Waldorf Spinach Dip in a Bread Bowl 56
Wheel o' Brie Bread Bowl 78
You-Won't-Believe-How-Good-It-Is Mustard Dip 54
Zippy Spinach Dip 79
Dog Bites Everybody Likes 141
Dogs in Coats 142
Dotted Swiss Cookie Bars 229
Dressing, King Louie 125
Drummette Lollipops 159
Dy-No-Mite Chocolate Cheesecake 260

Easter Surprise Ham 171
Easy Bisquiks 190
Easy Breezy Broccoli Dip 80
Easy Breezy Veggie Dip 57
Easy Cheese Bowl 82
Easy Cheesy Chili Dip 76
Easy Corn and Tomato Salad 123
Easy Egg Salad Sandwiches 194
Easy Overnight Turkey Bake 165
Easy Shrimp Quesadillas 200
Easy Spicy Corn Dip 71
Easy-As-Can-Be Salsa 62
Easy-Do Crocked Barbecue 160
Eggs:
Dare Deviled Eggs 146
Easy Egg Salad Sandwiches 194
Noggin of Good Cheer, A 40
Tiny Quiche Bites 135
Elegant After-Dinner Parfait 274
Elegant Crabmeat Imperial 165
Extra Special Chocolate Chip Cookies 214

Famous Crab & Artichoke Dip, The 69
Fast and Fabulous Sugar Cookies 219
Fat-Free Key Lime Pie 265
Favorite Scallops Appetizer 144
Fiesta Dip 57
Fish: (see specific fish)
5-Minute Boursin Cheese 101
Flaky Ham Pick Ups 212
Flaky Pepperoni Pastries 212
French Fried Onion Crab Dip 71
French Fried Onion Potato Bites 113
Fried Cheese with Marinara Sauce 91
Fried Crab Puffs 143
Fried Pasta Bites 136
Frilly Lace Cookies 216
Frosted Cone Cakes 254
Fruit Dips:
Caramel Fruit Dip 64
Creamy Amaretto Dip 65
Mellow Mallow Fruit Dip 64
Touch of Spice Fruit Dip 65
Tropical Fruit Dip 65
Fruits: (see also specific fruits)
Fruit Bowl Trifle 268
Miracle Red Grape Broccoli Salad 124
Ring Around the Berries 89
Fudge In Minutes 242
Full-Of-Flavor Pita Chips 43
Fun-To-Munch Oyster Crackers 42
Funny Face Muffins 188

G
Game-Time Nachos 98
Garden Pizza Wedges 119
Gingered Shrimp Kabobs 170
Glorious Green Dip 80
Gnome Hats 221
Good, Good Gouda Spread 101
Good-To-Go Cheese Sandwiches 194
Good-To-The-Last-Drop Cheeseburger Dip 82
Goodness Gracious Good Veggie Dip 55

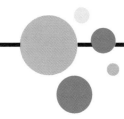

Gorgonzola Biscuits 190
Gotta-Love-The-Juice Brisket 162
Granny's Old-Fashioned
    Teacakes 218
Green Chile Cheese Dip 76
Greener Pastures Dip 54
Grilled Mozza-Roma Bites 181
Guacamole Dunk 60
Gwen's Baked Sausage Meatballs
    148

H

Halloween Pumpkin Muffins 258
Halloween Spider-Web Cake 250
Ham:
    Asparo-Squares 209
    Deli Ham Salad Finger
        Sandwiches 197
    Deli-Licious Party Wheels 137
    Easter Surprise Ham 171
    Flaky Ham Pick Ups 212
    Ham and Cheese Pinwheels
        138
    Heavenly Sweet Party Ham
        171
    Pigs in a Cheese Trough 83
    Yummy Pockets 192
Haystack of Onion Rings 118
Heart-Melting Dip, A 81
Heavenly Almond Candy 237
Heavenly Homemade Chocolate
    Mousse 272
Heavenly Sweet Party Ham 171
Hello Punch 33
Hidden Kiss Meringues 234
Holiday Party Punch 30
Holiday Wassail 39
Homemade Tortilla Chips 43
Honeycomb Cake 245
Hoppy Chocolate Frogs 215
Hot Dips:
    Amigos Bean Dip 72
    Awesome Artichoke Dip 69
    Bang-Bang Buffalo Chicken
        Dip 74
    Bread Boat Sausage Dip 78
    Bread Bowl of Beef Dip 77
    Cheesy Salsa Spinach Dip 79
    Chicken Enchilada Dip 75
    Delectable Crabmeat Mornay
        70
    Easy Breezy Broccoli Dip 80

Easy Cheese Bowl 82
Easy Cheesy Chili Dip 76
Easy Spicy Corn Dip 71
Famous Crab & Artichoke
    Dip, The 69
French Fried Onion Crab Dip
    71
Glorious Green Dip 80
Good-To-The-Last-Drop
    Cheeseburger Dip 82
Green Chile Cheese Dip 76
Heart-Melting Dip, A 81
Hot Tamale Dip 77
Mexican Bean Scoop 73
Mexican Nacho Dip 73
Mighty Meaty Mexican Dip 72
Pigs in a Cheese Trough 83
Pizzazzy Fondue 84
Quick Hot Crab Dip 70
Reuben, Reuben Dip 68
Speedy Gonzales Chili Dip 76
Sweet Georgia Onion Dip 68
Wheel o' Brie Bread Bowl 78
Zippy Spinach Dip 79
Hot 'n Bubbly Bread 179
Hot Buttered Rum 40
Hot Tamale Dip 77
Hummus, Quick Chick Blender 56
Hurricanes, Category 5 35

I

Iced Coffee Coolers 33
Impressive Peanut Butter Cream
    Cheese Chocolate Swirl Pie
    265
In-A-Hurry Cake Cookies 218
Irene's Shrimp Dip 55
Island Splendor Punch 31
It's a Snowman Cheese Ball 92

J

Jack Cheese Tortilla Wedges 96
Jalapeño Cheese in a Jar 103
Jalapeño Crockpot Meatballs 151
Jellyroll Reubens 142
Jolly Good Bloody Mary, A 37
Juicy Sauced Chicken Wings 154

K

Kabobs:
    Caramelized Sirloin Skewers
        167
    Delicate Dessert Kabobs 273
    Gingered Shrimp Kabobs 170
    Sensational Salad Skewers 166

Sweet-And-Sour Meatball
    Kabobs 168
Tangy Grilled Chicken Kabobs
    167
Turkey Lurkey Skewers 166
Veggie Kabobs with Honey
    Mustard Dip 169
Key Lime Pie, Fat-Free 265
Kicked-Up-A-Notch Peanuts 49
Kicky Chocolate Bark 240
Kicky Layered Dip 62
Kicky Lemon Tea Slush 28
Kicky Sausage Balls 148
Killer Margaritas 35
King Crab Louie 125

L

Lasagna, Quick Dinner Party 164
Lazy Days Lemon Cake 249
Lemony Garlic Bread 179
Lite 'n Crunchy Party Mix 51
Luck-Of-The-Irish Cream 38

M

Mad About Crab Puffs 173
Magnificent Marbled Mocha 253
Mama Mia Mushrooms 117
Mama's Spiced Tea 29
'Maters in Shells 111
Mango-Stuffed Celery Bites 128
Mardi Gras Microwave Pralines
    234
Margarita Cookie Bars 223
Margarita Pie in a Glass 262
Margaritas, Killer 35
Marinade, Mitch's Marvelous 174
Martinis, Party 34
Meatballs:
    Can't Beat These Meatballs
        150
    Crockpot BBQ Balls 151
    Gwen's Baked Sausage
        Meatballs 148
    Jalapeño Crockpot Meatballs
        151
    Kicky Sausage Balls 148
    Meatball Penguins 149
    Queso Meatballs 153
    Shape and Bake Meatballs
        152
    Sweet-And-Sour Meatball
        Kabobs 168
Meringues, Hidden Kiss 234
Meringues, Voted-Most-Popular
    Pink 235

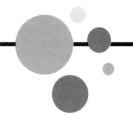

Mellow Mallow Fruit Dip 64
Mexicali Shotgun Bread 180
Mexican Bean Scoop 73
Mexican Mix-Up 121
Mexican Nacho Dip 73
Microwave Chicken Nuggets 133
Mighty Meaty Mexican Dip 72
Mimosas, Pink 34
Mini Cheese Balls 93
Mini Spini Crabmeat Pies 210
Miracle Red Grape Broccoli Salad 124
Mitch's Marvelous Marinade 174
MJ's Flavored Water Cooler 34
Moo-Cow in a Blanket 185
Mother's Dry Roasted Pecans 47
Mother's Toasted Pecans 48

Mousse:
Chocolate Cappuccino Mousse 271
Heavenly Homemade Chocolate Mousse 272
Mousse-On-The-Loose Brownie Dessert 272

Muffins:
Broccoli Cornbread Mini Muffins 187
Funny Face Muffins 188
Halloween Pumpkin Muffins 258
Pecan Muffinettes188
Quick Muffin Pizzas 187

Mushrooms:
'Bello Beef Bites 135
Cocktail Garden Platter 107
Mama Mia Mushrooms 117
Porto Mushroom Fries 116
Savory Stuffed 'Shrooms 115
Savory Stuffing Bites 139
Stuffed MMMMMushrooms 116
Stuffed Portobellos Supreme 115
Veggie Kabobs with Honey Mustard Dip 169

Nachos:
Game-Time Nachos 98
Mexican Nacho Dip 73
Super Nachos 98
Nancy's Country Caviar 64
N'Awlins Party Pull Bread 178
9x13 Chicken Salad 126
Noggin of Good Cheer, A 40

None Better Pecan Squares 231
Nutty Olive Cheese Ball 95
Nutty Peanut Butter Balls 240

Old-Fashioned Root Beer Float 26
Olé Chicken Stars 206
Olive Cheese Ball, Nutty 95
Olive-Cheese Balls 94
One-Ingredient Crispies 88
Onion Dip, Sweet Georgia 68
Onion Rings, Haystack of 118
Open & Closed Cucumber Sandwiches 196
Orange Pecan Balls 241
Over-The-Top Candy Bars 236

P

Parfait, Cheery Cherry 274
Parfait, Elegant After-Dinner 274
Party in a Bag 172
Party Martinis 34
Party Mixes:
Chocolate Peanut Butter Chow 52
Climb-A-Mountain Mix 50
Crazy Craisin Party Mix 50
Lite 'n Crunchy Party Mix 51
Super-Duper Snack Mix 51
Wonderful White Trash 52
Pasta Bites, Fried 136
Paté, Super Salmon 201
Peach Smoothie, Summertime 27
Peachy Keen Bars 229
Peachy Spice Upside-Down Bundt Cake 244
Peanut Butter:
Awesome Chocolate Peanut Butter Spread 204
Chocolate Peanut Butter Bars 225
Chocolate Peanut Butter Bubbles 239
Impressive Peanut Butter Cream Cheese Chocolate Swirl Pie 265
Nutty Peanut Butter Balls 240
Peanut Butter Quickie Cookies 217
Peanut Butter S'mores Bars 228
Reindeer Sandwiches 199
Peanuts, Kicked-Up-A-Notch 49
Peanuts, Persnickety Pesto 48

Pearly Whites 128
Pecans:
Big Easy Praline Cake 246
Buttery Sweet Toasted Pecans 47
Caramel Pecan Chocolate Mousse Pie 264
Chipper Chocks 240
Mardi Gras Microwave Pralines 234
Mini Cheese Balls 93
Mother's Dry Roasted Pecans 47
Mother's Toasted Pecans 48
None Better Pecans Squares 231
Orange Pecan Balls 241
Pecan Cheese Wafers 46
Pecan Momoons 219
Pecan Muffinettes 188
Pretty Cranberry Cream Cheese Centerpiece 66
Pecan Momoons 219
Strawberry and Chicken Salad Trifle 126
Sweet Toasted Pecans 48
Tiny Pecan Pies 263
Toasted Butter Pecan Cookies 220
Zebra Pecan Clusters 237
Pepper Canoes 121
Pepper Jelly:
Crescent-Wrapped Pepper Jelly Brie 90
Savory Pepper Jelly Cheesecake 100
Sweet Bite of Brie, A 91
Peppered Peppers 110
Pepperoni:
Deep-Fried Cheese 'n Pepperoni Balls 86
Flaky Pepperoni Pastries 212
Pepperoni Party Pinwheels 139
Pepperoni Tomato Pops 121
Pepperoni Tortillas on the Grill 97
Quick Muffin Pizzas 187
Sensational Salad Skewers 166
Peppers:
Banana Pepper-Ronies 120
Pepper Canoes 121

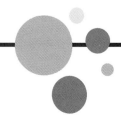

Peppered Peppers 110
Perfected Baked Beans 109
Perky Pea Pods 123
Persnickety Pesto Peanuts 48
Pesto Crostini 181
Pesto Pizza Wedges 120
Pick-Apart Bacon-Ranch Bread Ring 180

Pies:
Bing-Bing-Bing Cherry Pie 264
Caramel Pecan Chocolate Mousse Pie 264
Fat-Free Key Lime Pie 265
Impressive Peanut Butter Cream Cheese Chocolate Swirl Pie 265
Margarita Pie in a Glass 262
Tiny Pecan Pies 263
Pigs in a Cheese Trough 83
Pimento on Rye Snackwiches 196

Pineapple:
Pineapple Almond Cheddar Spread 104
Pineapple Orange Squares 248
Pineapple Paradise 245
Rare Pineapple Pound Cake 244
Pine Cone Made of Cheese, A 102
Pink Mimosas 34

Pita:
Crispy Pita Wedges 44
Full-Of-Flavor Pita Chips 43
Pita Christmas Trees 183

Pizzas:
Chicken Broccoli Pizza Spirals 186
Cool Garden Pizza Rounds 119
Crispy Pizza Dip Sticks 186
Garden Pizza Wedges 119
Pesto Pizza Wedges 120
Quick Muffin Pizzas 187
Strawberry Brownie Pizza 270
Pizzazzy Fondue 84
Pocket Sandwiches with Heart 197
Pop-In-Your-Mouth Chicken Nuggets 132
Popcorn, Cowboy 49
Popeye Popovers 108
Porto Mushroom Fries 116

Potatoes:
Cajun-Style Packet Potatoes 114
Caviar Party Potatoes 114
Classic Party Potatoes 111
French Fried Onion Potato Bites 113
Potato Salad Boats 112
Potluck Potato Salad 112
Pralines, Mardi Gras Microwave 234
Pretty Cranberry Cream Cheese Centerpiece 66
Pretzel-Crusted Chicken Nuggets 130
Pumpkin Cheesecake Dip 66
Pumpkin Muffins, Halloween 258

Punches:
Hello Punch 33
Holiday Party Punch 30
Island Splendor Punch 31
Raymond's Milk Punch 32
Simply Refreshing Punch 31

Quesadillas:
Cheesy Hot Quesadillas 99
Easy Shrimp Quesadillas 200
Quesadilla Bean Bites 140
Queso Meatballs 153
Quiche Bites, Tiny 135
Quiche-y Crescent Cups 185
Quick and Tasty Shrimp Wedges 200
Quick Chick Blender Hummus 56
Quick Dinner Party Lasagna 164
Quick Hot Crab Dip 70
Quick Mozzarella Tortillas 97
Quick Muffin Pizzas 187
Quicker-Than-Quick Shrimp Dip 55

Rainbow Corn Dip 58
Ranchero Sausage Stars 206
Raspberry Chocolate Swirl Cheesecake 255
Rave Pineapple Pound Cake 244
Raymond's Milk Punch 32
Red Pepper Crab Spread 201
Red Pepper Shrimp 145
Reindeer Sandwiches 199

Reuben:
Jellyroll Ruebens 142
Reuben, Reuben Dip 68

Swiss Reuben Spread 203
Ring Around the Berries 89
Ritzy Hot Wings 154
Roast Beef Roll-Ups 138
Roll-Out-The-Barrel Crackers 42

Rolls:
Rum Roll Bites 177
Simple Sausage Rolls 176
Soft Sunrise Rolls 176
Root Beer Float, Old-Fashioned 26
Rum Roll Bites 177

Salads:
Chicken Salad in Biscuit Cups 208
Colorful Corn Salad 124
Deli Ham Salad Finger Sandwiches 197
Easy Corn and Tomato Salad 123
Easy Egg Salad Sandwiches 194
King Crab Louie 125
Miracle Red Grape Broccoli Salad 124
9x13 Chicken Salad 126
Potato Salad Boats 112
Potluck Potato Salad 112
Simply Superb Chicken Salad Sandwiches 195
Strawberry and Chicken Salad Trifle 126
Watermelon Cube Salad 127
Salmon Paté, Super 201
Salmon, Wasabi 144

Salsas:
Avocado Salsa 61
Bodacious Salsa 63
Cheesy Salsa Spinach Dip 79
Corny Bean Salsa 63
Easy-As-Can-Be Salsa 62

Sandwiches:
Burst-Of-Flavor Chicken Sandwiches 195
Deli Ham Salad Finger Sandwiches 197
Easy Egg Salad Sandwiches 194
Good-To-Go Cheese Sandwiches 194
Open & Closed Cucumber Sandwiches 196
Pimento on Rye Snackwiches 196

Pocket Sandwiches with Heart 197
Reindeer Sandwiches 199
Simply Superb Chicken Salad Sandwiches 195
Sangria Serenade 36
Sauces:
Cheese Sauce 83
Cucumber Sauce 197
Sassy Sauce 157
Sausage:
Bread Boat Sausage Dip 78
Flaky Pepperoni Pastries 212
Gwen's Baked Sausage Meatballs 148
Kicky Sausage Balls 148
Mighty Meaty Mexican Dip 72
Pepperoni Party Pinwheels 139
Pizzazzy Fondue 84
Ranchero Sausage Stars 206
Simple Sausage Rolls 176
Some-Like-It-Hot Crockpot Tailgate Chili 163
Tiny Quiche Bites 135
Savory Pepper Jelly Cheesecake 100
Savory Stuffed 'Shrooms 115
Savory Stuffing Bites 139
Scallops Appetizer, Favorite 144
Seafood: (see specific seafood)
Sedona Sun-Dried Tomato Dip 58
Sensational Salad Skewers 166
Shape and Bake Meatballs 152
Sherri's Frosted Chocolate Shake 26
Shrimp:
Coconut Shrimp Caribe 146
Easy Shrimp Quesadillas 200
Gingered Shrimp Kabobs 170
Irene's Shrimp Dip 55
Perky Pea Pods 123
Quick and Tasty Shrimp Wedges 200
Quicker-Than-Quick Shrimp Dip 55
Red Pepper Shrimp 145
Shrimp in Circles 145
Simple Sausage Rolls 176
Simply Divine Chess Pie Bars 225
Simply Refreshing Punch 31
Simply Superb Chicken Salad Sandwiches 195
Sloppy Joe Bunners 198
Sloppy Joes, Speedy 149

Slush, Circus Citrus 28
Slush, Kicky Lemon Tea 28
Smoky Bar Cheese 96
Smoky Red Wingers 155
Soft Sunrise Rolls 176
Sombrero Dip 59
Some-Like-It-Hot Crockpot Tailgate Chili 163
S'more Trifle, Please 266
Speedy Gonzales Chili Dip 76
Speedy Sloppy Joes 198
Spicy Grilled Corn Cobbies 106
Spinach:
Cheesy Salsa Spinach Dip 79
Glorious Green Dip 80
Ham and Cheese Pinwheels 138
Mini Spini Crabmeat Pies 210
Popeye Popovers 108
Waldorf Spinach Dip in a Bread Bowl 56
Zippy Spinach Dip 79
Spreads:
Awesome Chocolate Peanut Butter Spread 204
Bayou Crawfish Spread 202
BLT Spread 203
Buttery Boursin Spread 204
Red Pepper Crab Spread 201
Super Salmon Paté 201
Swiss Reuben Spread 203
Tasty Crab Spread 202
Stir-And-Bake Chocolate Bars 227
Strawberries:
Delicate Dessert Kabobs 273
Strawberry and Chicken Salad Trifle 126
Strawberry Brownie Pizza 270
Streaked-With-Strawberries Cheesecake Bars 227
Sunshine Stuffed Strawberries 127
Streaked-With-Strawberries Cheesecake Bars 227
Stuffed MMMMMushrooms 116
Stuffed Portobellos Supreme 115
Summertime Peach Smoothie 27
Sunshine Stuffed Strawberries 127
Super Easy Dump Cake 251
Super Nachos 98
Super Salmon Paté 201
Super-Duper Snack Mix 51
Sweet Bacon-y Brie 90
Sweet Bite of Brie, A 91

Sweet Cha Cha Cheese Ball 94
Sweet Georgia Onion Dip 68
Sweet Little Chic Won Tons 207
Sweet Sippin' Limoncello 38
Sweet Tater Won Ton Stars 117
Sweet Toasted Pecans 48
Sweet-And-Sour Meatball Kabobs 168
Sweetie Meat Bites 141
Swiss Reuben Spread 203

Taco Chicken Drummettes 158
Tangy Grilled Chicken Kabobs 167
Tasty Crab Spread 202
Tasty Parmesan Tomato Bites 134
Tasty Tortilla Bites 140
Tea:
Aunt Mamie's Mint Tea 29
Berry Mint Iced Tea 30
Company Tea 30
Kicky Lemon Tea Slush 28
Mama's Spiced Tea 29
Terrific Tomato Tarts 110
Tiny Pecan Pies 263
Tiny Quiche Bites 135
Toasted Almond Chicken Nuggets 131
Toasted Butter Pecan Cookies 220
Toasted Parmesan Triangles 44
Toasties 45
Tomatoes:
Betsy's Tomato Crackers 134
BLT Bites 134
BLT Bruschetta 182
Bodacious Salsa 63
Can-Can Taco Soup 162
Easy Corn and Tomato Salad 123
Easy-As-Can-Be Salsa 62
Grilled Mozza-Roma Bites 181
'Maters in Shells 111
Pepperoni Tomato Pops 121
Sedona Sun-Dried Tomato Dip 58
Some Like It Hot Crockpot Tailgate Chili 163
Tasty Parmesan Tomato Bites 134
Terrific Tomato Tarts 110

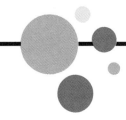

Touch of Spice Fruit Dip 65
Touchdown Football Cake 252
Trifles:
    Cherry Chocolate Caramel
        Cookie Trifle 267
    Chocolate Cherry Wine Glass
        Trifles 268
    Classic Chocolate Trifle 267
    Fruit Bowl Trifle 268
    S'more Trifle, Please 266
Tropical Fruit Dip 65
Turkey Bake, Easy Overnight 165
Turkey Lurkey Skewers 166

**Vegetables: (see also specific
vegetable)**
    Banana Pepper-Ronies 120
    Better-With-Butter Veggie
        Platter 108
    Cocktail Garden Platter 107
    Colorful Corn Salad 124

Cool Garden Pizza Rounds
    119
Crescent Roll Veggie Tree 184
Cuke and Cream Canapés 122
Delicious Deli Roll-Ups 122
Garden Pizza Wedges 119
Haystack of Onion Rings 118
Mexican Mix-Up 121
Open & Closed Cucumber
    Sandwiches 196
Pepper Canoes 121
Peppered Peppers 110
Perky Pea Pods 123
Popeye Popovers 108
Sweet Tater Won Ton Stars
    117
Veggie Kabobs with Honey
    Mustard Dip 169
Veggie Ponies 120
Veggie Ranch Pinwheels 136
Voted-Most-Popular Pink
    Meringues 235

Waldorf Spinach Dip in a Bread
    Bowl 56

Warming Winter Wassail 39
Wasabi Salmon 144
Wassail, Holiday 39
Wassail, Warming Winter 39
Watermelon Cube Salad 127
Welcome Wine 36
Wheel o' Brie Bread Bowl 78
While-You-Sleep Italian Beef 161
Wonderful White Trash 52
World's Best Turtles 239

You-Won't-Believe-How-Good-It-
    Is Mustard Dip 54
Yummy Chocolate Bourbon Balls
    241
Yummy Pockets 192
Yummy-To-The-Tummy Brownies
    233

Zebra Pecan Clusters 237
Zesty Beefy Cheese Log 103
Zippy Spinach Dip 79
Zucchini Stix Dippers 106